BESTSELLING BOOK SERIES

YouTube For Dummies

W9-AIE-363

Cheat Sheet

YouTube Video Terms

Term	Definition
Title	The title you enter for a video upon upload. The title is displayed above the YouTube player and is used as a parameter when a YouTube user searches for videos.
Category	The category in which you decide to place a video upon upload. A video can be placed only in one category. You can, however, change the category by editing video information.
Description	Information you enter about a video upon upload. The description is displayed to the right of the YouTube player and is used as a parameter when a YouTube user searches for videos. You can modify the description by editing your video.
Tags	Tags are single words used to describe a video. Each tag is separated by a space. You can use as many tags as you want when uploading a video. Tags are used as a parameter when a YouTube user searches for videos. You can modify tags by editing your video.

YouTube Video Parameters

Parameter	Guideline
Acceptable file formats	AVI, MP4, MOV, MPG, WMV
Recommended frame size	320 × 240 pixels
Recommended frame rate for full-motion video	30 fps
Recommended frame rate for video capture of a computer application	5 fps or greater
Maximum file size and duration for a YouTube account	File size can't exceed 10MB; video duration can't exceed 10 minutes
Maximum file size and duration for a Comedians, Directors, Gurus, or Musicians account	Unlimited

Video-Editing Applications

Application	Description
Windows Movie Maker	Windows-only video-editing application that's included with Windows XP and Windows Vista operating systems.
Apple iMovie	Macintosh-only video-editing application that's included with the iLife suite.
Apple QuickTime Pro	An upgrade from the Apple QuickTime video player.
Sony Vegas Movie Studio and DVD	Windows-only application that supports multiple tracks. The application can also be used to create DVDs from edited videos.
Apple Final Cut Express HD	Macintosh-only application that supports multiple video layers. This application also edits HD (High Definition) video.

YouTube For Dummies®

Sections in Your My Account Page

Section	Description
Videos	In this section, you find links to pages that enable you to manage your videos and playlists. You also find a link to upload videos to YouTube.
Subscriptions and Subscribers	In this section, you find links to manage your subscriptions and subscribers to your channel.
Groups	In this section, you find links to create new groups as well as manage the groups to which you belong and groups you own.
Channel Settings	In this section, you find links to manage your channel info, channel design, personal info, location info, and channel URL.
Inbox	In this section, you find links to view messages, manage friend invites, view received videos, view comments on your videos, view video responses, and view sent messages. There's also a button to compose new messages.
Friends and Contacts	In this section, you find links to manage your Contact list, Friends list, and Family list. You also find a button to invite more friends.
Account Settings	In this section, you find links to change your password, modify e-mail options, change personal info, as well as video posting and mobile settings. There's also a link to set up a Developer profile and close your account.

Tips for Creating Quality Video

- Pan and zoom slowly.
- Don't use digital zoom.
- Use a tripod when recording an interview.
- Use manual exposure when recording backlit subjects or subjects in heavy shade.
- Manually focus the camcorder when shooting a night scene.
- Don't break the time code when recording a tape.
- Use a Pop filter when recording yourself or interviewing someone.
- Use your camcorder wind filter when recording in windy conditions.
- Shoot a few extra seconds at the start and end of each scene.

Copyright © 2007 Wiley Publishing, Inc. All rights reserved. Item 4925-6.

For more information about Wiley Publishing, call 1-800-762-2974.

For Dummies: Bestselling Book Series for Beginners

by Doug Sahlin and Chris Botello

Wiley Publishing, Inc.

YouTube™ For Dummies®

Published by
Wiley Publishing, Inc.
111 River Street
Hoboken, NJ 07030-5774

www.wiley.com

For general information on our other products and services, please contact our Customer Care Department within the U.S. at 800-762-2974, outside the U.S. at 317-572-3993, or fax 317-572-4002.

For technical support, please visit www.wiley.com/techsupport.

Wiley also publishes its books in a variety of electronic formats. Some content that appears in print may not be available in electronic books.

Library of Congress Control Number: 2007926394

ISBN: 978-0-470-14925-6

10 9 8 7 6 5 4 3 2 1

WILEY

About the Authors

Doug Sahlin is an author, photographer, and videographer living in Lakeland, Florida. He is also the president of Superb Images, Inc., which is a wedding and event photography and videography company. He has written or co-authored 20 books on graphic, Web design, and video-editing and image-editing applications, including *50 Fast Digital Video Techniques* and *Photoshop CS2 for Digital Photographers Only*. While working on his books, Doug has produced commercial photographs and video of actors, authors, architecture, automobile races, fashion models, food, landscapes, and products for his clients. His work has taken him from coast to coast and north to south, and has been seen in print and on the Web.

Chris Botello is a Photoshop artist and graphic designer living in Los Angeles, where he works as a retoucher and finisher on movie posters and marketing campaigns for the motion-picture industry.

Chris began his career in the graphic arts as print production manager for *Premiere* magazine. He designed movie posters for Miramax Films and was the art director for Microsoft's launch of sidewalk.com/boston.

Chris is the author of a successful series of books on Adobe Photoshop, Illustrator, and InDesign for Thomson Course Technology. When not working, Chris loves to travel and gets the opportunity to do so as a guest instructor for Crystal Cruise Lines.

Dedication

Doug Sahlin: This book is dedicated to my best friend and mentor: my mother, Inez. I miss you, kiddo. **Chris Botello:** This book is dedicated to my friend Bill Miltenberger, who for years told me to "Get an agent, and in jig-time, you'll be writing books in the big time." Finally, I listened.

Authors' Acknowledgments

Doug Sahlin: This is the section of the book where the authors have a chance to acknowledge, berate, condescend to, or mention people, places, or things that were helpful, instrumental, or played a major or minor part in the writing of the book. First and foremost, I would like to acknowledge my co-author: live and in living color from the Left Coast, the effervescent, holistic and synergistic Chris Botello. Many thanks to the fine folks at Wiley for publishing this really fine book. Thanks to Acquisitions Editor Steve Hayes for making this project possible and for reminding us when a deadline was about to go whooshing past. Thanks to our Project Editor, the ebullient, enthusiastic, and ecologically friendly Christopher Morris for providing copious comments and moral support while keeping us on track. Thanks to Margot Maley Hutchison for tidying up contractual details and tending to all the fine print. As always, thanks to my friends, mentors, and family. Special thanks to Karen, Ted, Colin, and Niki the Cat, also known as "Queen of the Universe."

Chris Botello: With so many thank-you's to go around, my first is to Doug Sahlin, co-author and Floridian mentor, who guided me through my first *For Dummies* book with wit and good humor. Thank you to Acquisitions Editor Steve Hayes and Project Editor Christopher Morris for shepherding the project and keeping us on track. Thanks to Carole McClendon for putting me in the right place at the right time. And thank you as always to my friends, my family, and Rex Rosen.

Publisher's Acknowledgments

We're proud of this book; please send us your comments through our online registration form located at `www.dummies.com/register/`.

Some of the people who helped bring this book to market include the following:

Acquisitions, Editorial, and Media Development

Senior Project Editor: Christopher Morris

Senior Acquisitions Editor: Steven Hayes

Copy Editors: Teresa Artman, Jennifer Riggs

Technical Editor: Douglas Spotted Eagle

Editorial Manager: Kevin Kirschner

Media Development and Quality Assurance: Angela Denny, Kate Jenkins, Steven Kudirka, Kit Malone

Media Development Coordinator: Jenny Swisher

Media Project Supervisor: Laura Moss-Hollister

Editorial Assistant: Amanda Foxworth

Senior Editorial Assistant: Cherie Case

Cartoons: Rich Tennant (`www.the5thwave.com`)

Composition Services

Project Coordinator: Jennifer Theriot

Layout and Graphics: Carl Byers, Stephanie D. Jumper, Laura Pence, Heather Ryan, Alicia B. South, Christine Williams

Proofreaders: Aptara, John Greenough

Indexer: Aptara

Anniversary Logo Design: Richard Pacifico

Publishing and Editorial for Technology Dummies

    Richard Swadley, Vice President and Executive Group Publisher

    Andy Cummings, Vice President and Publisher

  Mary Bednarek, Executive Acquisitions Director

    Mary C. Corder, Editorial Director

Publishing for Consumer Dummies

    Diane Graves Steele, Vice President and Publisher

    Joyce Pepple, Acquisitions Director

Composition Services

    Gerry Fahey, Vice President of Production Services

    Debbie Stailey, Director of Composition Services

Contents at a Glance

Table of Contents

Introduction

• •

Do you have a video you want to share with a few friends, or perhaps, the world? Or perhaps, you're the eclectic type who likes weird, wonderful, and obscure videos, the videos you can't find at your local rental store. Either way, you can get what you want at YouTube.

YouTube is one of the most popular hangouts on the Internet. At YouTube, you find videos from actor wannabes, businessmen, and even political candidates. It's a wild and wooly place, and like the New World when Columbus set foot on it in 1492, almost completely uncharted.

If you think of YouTube as a place where young adolescents spend their time watching questionable video clips, it's time for you to experience the true marvels of YouTube and its wide and diverse community. It doesn't matter what type of video trips your trigger, you'll find it on the Tube. Oh yeah, you might as well get used to it; the *Tube* is how we refer to YouTube. And we call the people who use YouTube *Tubers*.

About This Book

The Tube has evolved during the past year. The Tube has so many new features and so many things you can do that assimilating them all is nearly impossible without a road map. The YouTube Web site has no road map, so we provide the next best thing: *YouTube For Dummies* (Wiley).

With this book, you have a handy reference to all features of the Tube and then some. When you need to find quick, concise information on how to do something, like find your type of video, all you need to do is let your fingers do the walking to the index or table of contents. That's right, you don't need to read this book from cover to cover; although we prefer that you do. Read the section that contains the information you need to know right now and then get back to the serious fun of surfing the Tube.

How to Use This Book

Park this book right next to your computer monitor, but please keep it out of the trajectory of any potential harm, such as coffee spills. Or if you're in need of some exercise, put the book on a convenient bookshelf. But do remember where you put it. We guarantee that after you start surfing the Tube, you'll refer to our book often.

The table of contents and the index can point you toward the information you need. But this isn't just a reference book. Plenty of sections show you how to do things. For example, we devote entire chapters to showing you how to search for videos, how to shoot and upload videos, and how to get noticed on the Tube.

Foolish Assumptions

We assume that you have a computer with an Internet connection. We also assume that you have a connection that's robust enough to play streaming video without interruption. That's right, YouTube isn't for those with dialup connections. We also assume that you have a video card capable of displaying millions of colors. Oh yeah, a sound card is a must too — that is, unless you like silent movies.

If you want to upload videos to the Tube, a camcorder or digital camera with a movie mode is a huge help. Otherwise, you'll need a slew of videos to which you own the rights. That's right, we assume you don't want to break any copyright laws or fall afoul of the YouTube police. We also assume that you have a YouTube account. But if you don't, there's no need for concern. We show you how to set up a YouTube account in Chapter 2.

Conventions Used in This Book

Wiley designed the *For Dummies* series for busy people who don't have time to read an entire book when they want to master a computer application or an interactive Web site, such as YouTube. The nice thing about a *For Dummies* book is that you don't need an instruction manual to decipher the book. Each *For Dummies* book is neatly mapped out and easy to understand, with little or no technical lingo, and no bitter aftertaste. This book keeps with the tradition of a very user-friendly book.

When we show you how to do something, it's all neatly broken down into steps. When instructions include something, like choose File⇨New, all you have to do is click the word File and then choose the word New from the drop-down list. (If you're using Windows Vista for your operating system, File has been replaced with the Office Button, at the top-left of the window.)

How This Book Is Organized

This book is divided into five parts. Each part is comprised of chapters that contain related material. Each chapter is further subdivided into orderly segments that cover activities you'll want to do at YouTube and techniques on how to create stellar videos for the Tube. Here's the lowdown on each part.

Part I: Curtain Up on Streaming Video

Part I introduces you to the wonderful word of shared video that is YouTube. In Chapter 1, we give you a brief overview to what you can expect to find in the following chapters. After that, we give you a guided tour of the Tube and show you how to create your very own YouTube account.

Part II: So Many Videos, So Little Time

This part shows you how to find the type of videos you like to watch, how to customize your experience on YouTube, and how to become part of the YouTube community. In this part, we also show you how to subscribe to a YouTube channel, create playlists, and much more.

Part III: Broadcasting Your Video to the World

In Part III, we show you how to record videos with your camcorder, capture them to your computer, and then edit them. We also show you how to add pizzazz to your videos with video transitions, effects, titles, and more. We show you these techniques in Windows Movie Maker and iMovie. We also show you how to upload your videos to the Tube and then get them noticed.

Part IV: Famous Final Scene: YouTube for Fun and Profit

YouTube offers something for everyone. In this part, we show you how to embed YouTube videos in your Web site, blog, or MySpace page. We also show you how to utilize the Tube if you have a product to sell or want to direct traffic from the Tube to your Web site. Oh yeah, we also show you how to add a YouTube video to your eBay auction. How cool is that?

Part V: The Part of Tens

Part V tosses in 40 extra, little items designed to optimize your YouTube experience. In this section, you find tips for video and video bloggers, as well as a rundown of the ten best features you want to start using today, and a useful list of ten things to *not* include in your videos.

Icons Used in This Book

This book uses several icons, which you find in the page margins. Each icon represents a tidbit of wisdom we've discovered while surfing the Tube, creating video for the Tube, and so on.

When you see this icon, you find a little nugget of wisdom that shows you the best way to approach a task.

These are red flags to things you shouldn't do. Trust us, when you see this icon, heed our advice because we've already found out the hard way.

These sections are for *geeks,* or people who tape their broken glasses back together and wear pocket pals. You know who you are.

These are little memory joggers; information pertinent to the task at hand that's been covered already.

Where to Go from Here

Skim through the table of contents or the index and then read a section that piques your curiosity. We also suggest that you fire up your computer, launch your favorite Web browser, and log in to the Tube to put your newly found wisdom to immediate use.

Part I
Curtain Up on Streaming Video

The 5th Wave   By Rich Tennant

"Honey — remember that pool party last summer where you showed everyone how to do the limbo in just a sombrero and a dish towel? Well, look at what I just found on YouTube."

In this part . . .

Chapter 1 gives you a general overview of YouTube and what you find in the rest of this book. Chapter 2 shows you how to set up and manage a YouTube account. Chapter 3 is a whirlwind tour of the Tube and a great introduction to all the cool and practical features you can start using today.

Chapter 1

Everything You Wanted to Know about YouTube

*Y*ouTube is: A: an appliance; B: an ergonomic chair; C: the coolest video site on the Internet? If you answered A or B, you really need this book. But the fact that you own this book or are skimming through these pages at your favorite bookseller means you probably answered correctly, but need to know more about YouTube, which is great because these pages are written by a couple of card-carrying geeks who love video and think YouTube is the coolest thing since one-terabyte hard drives.

We cover a lot of ground in this book. In this chapter, we give you an overview of *what* we cover and *how* we cover it.

Charting YouTube

YouTube popped out of the woodwork when three PayPal employees brainstormed to start a video sharing service. They were at a party, and people were shooting digital photos and capturing videos. After the party, they tried to share the videos via e-mail but ran into difficulties due to differences in file formats and codecs. That's when the lads came up with the idea to start an online video sharing service. Their idea was probably one of those blinding flashes of inspiration, like the kind that wakes you from a sound sleep; the modern day equivalent to getting hit on the head with an apple and deciding that gravity is a really cool concept. However, getting a great idea without acting on it is like inspiration with no perspiration. Most people never make it past the inspiration phase. Then, a few months after you dismiss the idea, you find someone else is marketing it, and you kick yourself squarely on whatever part of your body you can comfortably reach for not acting on your idea. Fortunately for Chad Hurley, Steve Chen, and Jawed Karim (the founders of YouTube) and those of us who like posting videos that can be shared with a worldwide audience, they acted on their inspiration. Their first brainstorming sessions took place in Chad Hurley's garage, where they mapped out a strategy to simplify the process of sharing video with friends, family, and the world. The initial site design incubated from a tiny germ of an idea, and an Internet giant was born.

Free video, how cool a concept is that? Well, that's exactly what Chad and Steve (Jawed left the company to further his education) supplied from their office in San Mateo, California. Development of the YouTube site commenced in February 2005, and the beta was launched in May 2005. YouTube was officially launched in December 2005. The goal was simple: Get as much traffic as possible and build a loyal following. You know, the old build-it-and-they-will-come mentality. After a short period of time, the YouTube site had more traffic than some of the most popular existing video and short film Web sites, including Atom Films (www.atomfilms.com). In the final days of their beta phase, *Tubers* (this book's official term for people who use the YouTube site) viewed a staggering three million video clips a day and uploaded close to eight million clips a day. Can you imagine the bandwidth YouTube consumed? And the founders weren't getting paid for their efforts, but they were getting a lot of press. A solid influx of cash had to be on their timeline in the very near future.

YouTube gained momentum and then they got cash — $3.5 million greenbacks of venture capital to be exact. And then YouTube gained more momentum, and Google bought them for $1.65 Billion; however, YouTube is still a private entity calling its own shots. The history of YouTube is still being written and might change considerably while we're writing this book. Lots of interesting tidbits about the history of YouTube haven't even been mentioned yet. Figure 1-1 shows the YouTube Web site, playing a video of the staff's last day in their San Mateo office.

There are no free lunches. You have to give to get. You can surf the *Tube* (our slang for the YouTube Web site — a new entry in our unabashed dictionary of YouTube terms) as often as you like in perfect anonymity. However, when you want to do something interesting, like interact with other Tubers, create playlists, subscribe to channels, and upload your own videos, you have to create an account. But rest easy, the account is free, and YouTube doesn't pester you for a lot of information, like a credit card number, the title to your '57 Chevy, or anything like that. All you have to do is agree to their terms of service and supply some simple information. We show you all the subtle intricacies involved in creating a YouTube account in Chapter 2.

Figure 1-1:
The YouTube staff celebrating their last day in their original office.

You can maintain multiple personalities on YouTube. It's as easy as creating multiple accounts. You use one username when you want to upload your Dr. Jekyll videos, and log in under another username when you want to upload your Mr. Hyde videos.

Touring the Tube

When you visit YouTube for the first time, you might be wondering what all the hubbub is about. YouTube isn't a particularly cool-looking site, which in a way is a good thing. After all, the coolness is in the *content,* not the *interface.* Nevertheless, you have to be able to find what you want quickly, which is the hallmark of any good Web design. The YouTube Web site looks inviting enough. Figure 1-2 shows the site as it appears to someone who hasn't set up an account. You're greeted with little icons that have a plus sign in the lower-left corner. We won't tell you what that icon's used for — at least not now.

Viewing videos on YouTube is easy. Just click an icon and then the page changes, the video is served up — *danger Will Robinson, video is loading* — and begins playing in a little window. Viewing a video is just that simple. Each video comes complete with a controller that lets you pause the video when you have to take care of some annoying task, like answering the phone or responding to your boss's e-mail. You can also control the volume of the video. When the video finishes playing, you can replay the video, share it with a friend, look for another video, or do something really boring — like your day job.

Figure 1-2:
YouTube
welcomes
you with
featured
videos.

Plus signs

After you view a couple videos, you can get adventurous and click one of the blue buttons (actually the buttons are a gradient from white to a lovely shade of blue) and gain access to all the videos in the YouTube vault. You can browse the Videos section of the site, check out videos in the Categories section of the site, reach for your remote in the Channels section of the site, or smile on your brother in the Community section of the site. No matter where you go in the vast YouTube universe, you get to watch an animated ad on the right side of the site. After all, someone's got to pay for the terabytes of bandwidth that YouTube consumes every month. Here's a question to ponder: If YouTube removed half the videos and advertisements from their vast Web site, would it be half-vast?

YouTube invites you to upload videos on every page of the site. If you're a registered user and click the Upload Video button, you can upload a video — a task that we simplify in Chapter 7. However, if you don't have a YouTube account and click the button, you're presented with a simple form to fill out, which makes you an official Tuber. After you're an official Tuber, you get to enjoy all the benefits of the YouTube Web site and become a part of the YouTube community. After you sign in, the site welcomes you with your username and statistics, as shown in Figure 1-3.

Tubers get to upload videos as often as they want, and the price is zip, zilch, nada. Tubers who like videos provided by a specific user can subscribe to that user's channel. Subscribing to a channel is as simple as clicking a button. When you subscribe to a channel, an icon of the channel appears on your Subscriptions list, which is part of your Channel. Click the *Channel icon* — the

Tuber's equivalent of a remote control — and you're transported to that channel. Another benefit of subscribing to a channel is that you see a thumbnail of the most recent uploaded video from each of the channels you subscribe to when you log in to the Tube (see Figure 1-4).

Figure 1-3:
Hello, hello.
I don't know
why you say
goodbye,
YouTube
says hello.

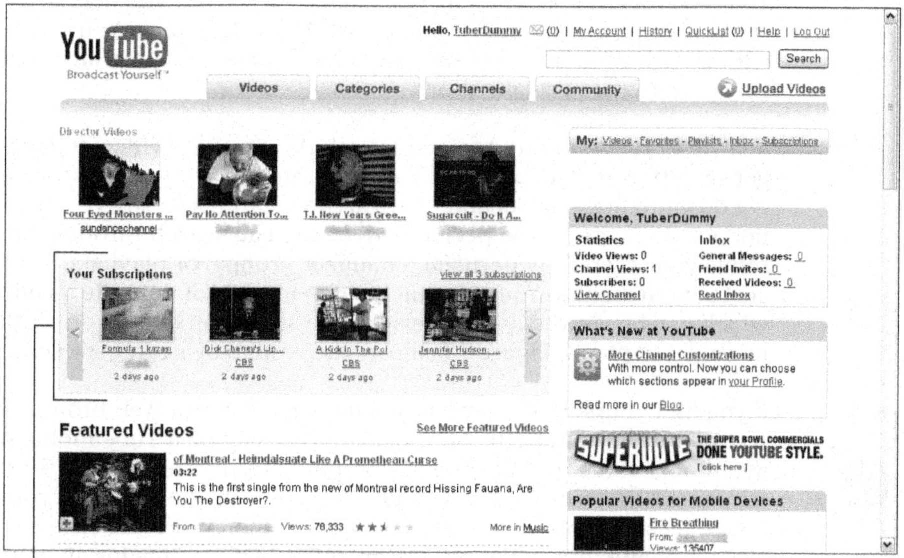

Figure 1-4:
Get free sub-
scriptions
with no
strings
attached.

Subscriptions

When you start uploading your own videos and other Tubers take notice, you'll probably get some subscribers to your channel. You may also get requests to be added to other Tuber's Friends list. If you're really lucky, you may get some Tuber groupies. Just don't let your significant other know.

But if you want to do some really cool stuff, like look for some videos you actually want to view, you need to know how to get from Point A to Point B to Point C. The YouTube designers have made that task relatively simple. You get reminders when new stuff is available or when new features are added. You can take the point-and-click approach to finding out what YouTube has to offer or follow our road map in Chapter 3.

If you're watching a YouTube video at work and you hear the unmistakable stiletto click of your supervisor's high heels rushing toward your cubicle, mute the sound and dim your monitor so that the video isn't visible. When your supervisor arrives, slap the side of the monitor and frown. If you're lucky, your supervisor will think you're experiencing a technical malfunction, not watching a YouTube video.

The previous tip doesn't work if you're employed by the IT department of your company.

Finding the Perfect Video

YouTube has videos. Lots of videos. Finding a video you actually want to view is like looking for the proverbial needle in the haystack. You can randomly sift through each portal of the YouTube Empire until you find what you want. However, that could take years.

Instead of randomly tip-toeing through the YouTube video collection, you can get scientific and search YouTube. You can do a wild-guess search, or really get down to brass tacks and use YouTube features to search the vault and find what you deem the perfect video. You can search through all videos or refine your search by perusing channels, groups, or playlists. You can also sort search results. You view each video in turn, or compile a Quicklist, which can be viewed at your leisure. We show you how to do all this and more in Chapter 4. Figure 1-5 shows the results of a category search.

If you find yourself frequently opening your favorite Web browser and typing **www.youtube.com** in the address bar, you may be a Tubeaholic. Advanced symptoms of the disease include keeping the YouTube Web site open in a minimized browser so that you can maximize it when none of your fellow employees or supervisors are nearby. Fortunately, the disease isn't harmful to your health, but it can pose problems when it's time for an employee review. Unfortunately, little help is available for this problem. Tubeaholics Anonymous hasn't been invented yet.

Figure 1-5:
Searching
the Tube for
a way-cool
video is
easy.

Changing Your YouTube Preferences

When you first set up a YouTube account, you have a giant clean slate. But that can change quickly if you use even just a fraction of what YouTube offers. When you create a YouTube account, you get a channel with your username, as shown in Figure 1-6. As you can see, a new account has a squeaky clean channel. Think of a channel as a place for your stuff, such as favorite videos, subscribers, uploaded videos, and so on. The channel has placeholders for all these things (see Figure 1-6). Your mission as a virgin Tuber is to get some stuff to fill in the blanks. You can put in the stuff that matters to you in your channel. You can save videos in your channel, create playlists, look at comments posted by other viewers, and so on.

The *channel* is your home base on the Tube. That's where you and other Tubers go to find your videos, view your playlists, and so on. You can change the way your channel looks by changing the channel design. Your channel features an *icon,* which by default is a frame from the last video you uploaded, or you can choose an icon from your favorite video. Figure 1-7 shows a user channel that's tricked out 27 ways to Sunday. We show you how to customize your channel and fine-tune your YouTube experience in Chapter 5.

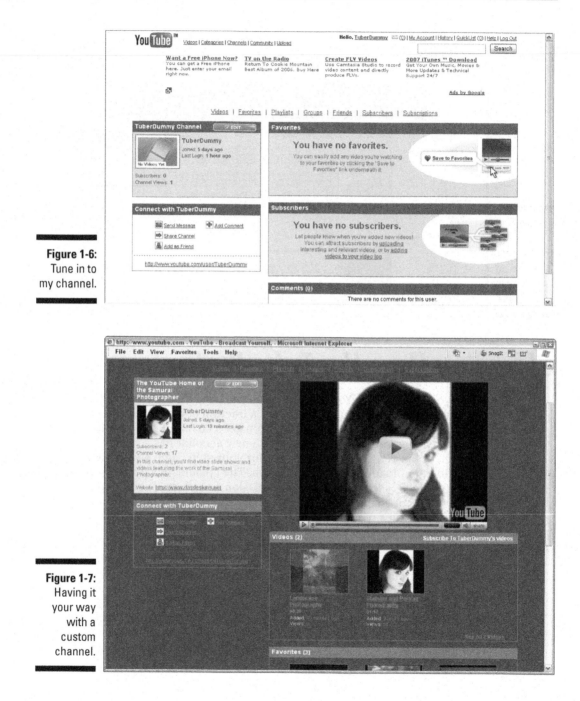

Figure 1-6:
Tune in to
my channel.

Figure 1-7:
Having it
your way
with a
custom
channel.

Getting to Know Other Tubers

YouTube is a huge community. Next time you surf the Tube, take a look at the different usernames associated with the videos; then take a look at the number of groups and you start to get the idea. It's kind of like a video commune. You can be totally anonymous even if you have a YouTube account. But if you post some really cool videos, you'll find that people leave comments on your stuff and subscribe to your channel. It's only polite to return the favor and thank your fellow Tubers for their comments.

But responding to comments is only the beginning. You can request to be a fellow Tuber's friend, join a group, subscribe to a channel, and so on. You may never meet the people you associate with on YouTube in person, but it's still fun. And let's face it, the world is a serious place. Adding some fun to your life is a good thing; it keeps you younger and relieves the stress in your life. So feel free to strike up a relationship with people who leave comments on your videos and leave comments when you watch a video you really like. You can also send messages to other Tubers. If you're not sure how to do it, we show you everything about the YouTube community in Chapter 6.

Creating the Perfect YouTube Video

Pixelated, blurry video is ugly and shouldn't be seen or heard. When you sift through the myriad of videos on YouTube, you may shake your head and ask the question: Why? We did the same, and that's why we're on a two-man crusade to stamp out ugly video. After all, if you've got something to show the world, and it has your username attached, it ought to be the best it can be.

Digital video is fun. However, many people who own camcorders don't even know how to get the video into their computers. Face it, if you can't get the video into your computer, you'll never get it on YouTube. But there's a lot more than getting the video into your computer. You need to render your video in a format supported by YouTube, and you need to do some editing. Let's face it, nobody except family members and a few close friends want to see the video where you forgot to stop recording after taping a scene and captured an additional two minutes of your shuffling feet.

In Chapter 7, we give you some tips on recording good video and how to get that video into your computer.

Let's say you want to kick your videos up a notch or two. Editing video isn't rocket science. You can easily add transitions between scenes or titles and credits with an application, like Windows Movie Maker or Apple iPhoto. Figure 1-8 shows a video being christened with an appropriate title credit in Movie Maker.

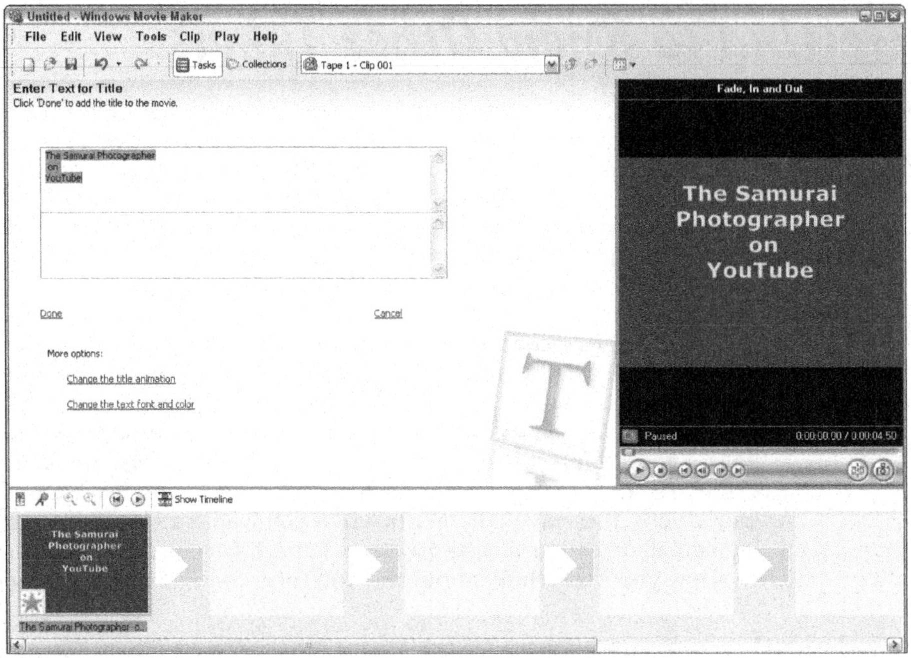

Figure 1-8:
Give yourself
credit when
you create
videos for
the Tube.

Creating Specialty Accounts

Are you a musician, celebrity, celebrity-wannabe, or a reasonable facsimile thereof? If so, YouTube likes people like you. In fact, they let you create special accounts. Yes, Virgina, the special accounts are still free, and your videos appear in the appropriate channel. For example, if you sign up for a Comedians account, all of your videos are found in the Comedians channel, which makes it easy for people who need a good laugh to find your material. Talk about having your cake and eating it too. Specialty accounts come in four flavors:

- ✔ **Comedians:** The hot spot to be if you're a performing comedian or an aspiring comedian. It's also the place to visit if you want a good laugh. These guys and gals will leave you in stitches. It's their job. Figure 1-9 shows the first page of people who have Comedians accounts.

- ✔ **Directors:** The hotspot if you're a videographer, aspiring actor, or a director wannabe.

- ✔ **Gurus:** The hotspot if you're a brainiac, and you want to pass your knowledge on to other Tubers. This is also an excellent place if you're an instructor of some sort and want to drive traffic to your Web site.

✓ **Musicians:** The hotspot if you're a musician, singer, recording label owner, or are involved in music in some other way. So if you have the notion to rock the boat baby, create a Musicians account. Who knows, MTV and Virgin Records may be surfing the Tube for talent and discover you.

YouTube also has a Partners account. But this type of account isn't available for mere mortals and the general Tuber population. Here you'll find companies, like CBS, Capitol Records, and VH1, to name a few. The name *Partners* leads the authors to believe that a partner must cough up cold, hard cash in order to get the account. But hey, somebody has to pay the bills so we Tubers can have our fun for free. The Partners channel is also an interesting place to visit when the partners crank out some serious videos. For example, in the CBS channel, you'll find interesting video clips about current events.

YouTube created a You Choose 08 channel, which serves as another platform for politicians who have thrown their hat into the ring for the 2008 Presidential Election. Now you can surf the Tube for fun, and then figure out which politician you'd like to see as the next President of The United States.

People have been discovered through the videos they've posted on YouTube. According to the YouTube founders, at least one person who posted a music video has signed a record contract. When you set up a specialty YouTube account and post a cool video, the world is your stage. If you think you're the next Mariah Carey, Jim Carrey, or Martin Scorsese, check out Chapter 9.

Figure 1-9:
Outta the way, knuckle-head, I have a joke to tell. Soitenly!

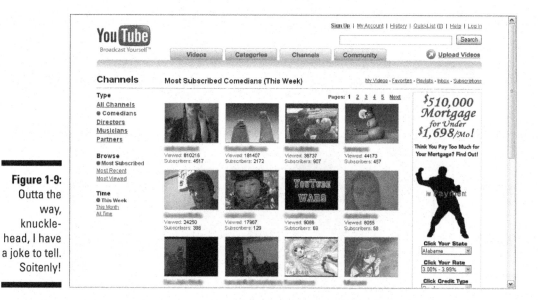

YouTube for the Entrepreneur

Do you have a product to sell or a message to tell? If you do, get your camcorder out, take a video of the product, or tape your message and upload the video to YouTube. You might find some prospects for your product or service by surfing the Tube. When you do create video to promote a product or service, make sure you add ending credits with the URL to your Web site or to the site where Tubers can actually purchase your product or service. Figure 1-10 is a YouTube video embedded in an eBay auction that's being previewed via eBay's Turbo Lister software.

You can also embed your product video in your Web site. What a deal, Lucille; full video to promote your product or service, and your site doesn't get the bandwidth hit. If you've got a warehouse full of products to sell, you can embed a YouTube video on your site's home page that shows site visitors your facility and the awesome merchandise you have available. We show you how to use YouTube to promote yourself or your products in Chapter 10.

Do you teach people how to use software applications, like Adobe Photoshop and Dreamweaver? Well, don't limit yourself to students in seminars. You can also be a guru online. In fact, YouTube has a Guru account, which is right up your alley, Sally. Being a guru online is different than being a guru in person. Instead of using a projector to display your computer screen to the audience, you use an application to capture video of every move you make while using an application. You can record audio at the same time. We show you how to create instructional videos in Chapter 7.

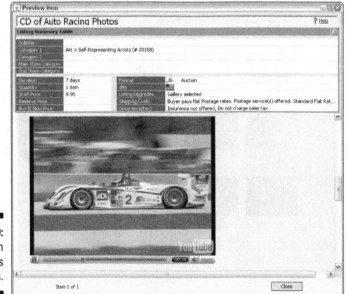

Figure 1-10:
An auction
that moves
bidders.

YouTube and the Copyright Police

Gobs of video get uploaded to YouTube every day. If you upload a video to which you don't own the copyright or haven't purchased rights to the video, you're in violation of the copyright law. YouTube does a pretty good job of policing its site. YouTube also gets feedback from users when a video isn't considered appropriate. If you upload a copyrighted video and YouTube catches you, it yanks the video and your account. YIKES! If the copyright owner of the video finds out, you could find yourself in deep water, which may require a life preserver in the form of an attorney. So be cool and respect other artist's materials. Don't upload copyrighted videos. We show you the skinny on what is and isn't cool to upload in Chapter 11.

A YouTube Parental Guide

Kids do the darndest things . . . including looking up inappropriate Web sites. If you have young children, monitor their computer usage. Even though YouTube does contain video not suitable for children, you can make YouTube a safe and enjoyable experience for your child as long as he is at least 13 years of age. In fact, you have to be 13 years of age to qualify for a YouTube account. We show you how to do this and more in Chapter 11.

Being a Model YouTube Citizen

In addition to making YouTube a safe experience for your children, we also show you how to play well with others. To be a model Tuber, you must respect the rights of your fellow video buddies. Our parents always told us not to say anything if you don't have anything nice to say. Well, we take that one step further and show you what we consider to be proper etiquette when commenting on other videos. Flaming (that is, saying nasty or derogatory things about other Tubers — or for that matter, anybody) is verboten.

If you're the shy, retiring type who likes to surf the Tube in relative anonymity, you can don the Tube veil of secrecy. You can share your videos with the world or just a few close friends and family, and either way, you can preserve your identity when you do so. And if you're interested in securing your privacy, don't forget about the content of the videos you're uploading. Sure, your YouTube contact information may be private, but what about what's in your video? We show you how to protect every aspect of your identity in Chapter 11.

Seeking the YouTube Experience

When we told our friends and relatives about this book project, we received mixed reviews. Some people thought the videos on the homepage of YouTube were the greatest thing since the release of the Xbox 360. Our older friends and relatives weren't quite as enthusiastic. But there's something for every-one on the Tube. You've just got to be an ambassador and show your friends how to find the stuff they want to see. That's what we show you in this book.

Not everyone finds all of the top-played videos interesting. In fact, you may find some of them repulsive. However, YouTube truly does have something for everyone. If you set up a YouTube account, you can have it your way. When you set up an account, follow some of our sage advice on how to search YouTube and start looking for videos that pique your curiosity. After you find something you like, you can save it as a favorite for future viewing and create video playlists. You can also leave comments for the users who upload videos you like. Chances are, they'll be your kind of people, too.

YouTube has so much more to it than meets the eye — or, for that matter, the ear. The intellectual highbrow type can find instructional videos on many topics. The artsy-fartsy kind can find video blogs from film festivals, videos from aspiring actors, and much more. The trick is to get past the home page and start surfing the categories and channels. Another place to look for your kind of video and your kind of people is in the YouTube Community section.

After you find what you like on the Tube, you can add the content to your channel. Each Tuber with an account gets his own channel, and many people like to make this space their own. When a fellow Tuber visits your channel, she sees the first page of your channel. Figure 1-11 shows the public view of a Tuber's channel. Fellow tubers can dive deeper into a channel by clicking the section links. A YouTube channel has the following sections:

- **Videos:** This section contains a list of videos the user uploads to YouTube.
- **Favorites:** This section shows thumbnails of videos the user selects as his favorites.
- **Playlists:** This section features playlists the user creates.
- **Groups:** This section shows groups that the user joins.
- **Friends:** This section shows the people the user adds as friends.
- **Subscribers:** This section shows a list of Tubers who subscribe to the user's channel.
- **Subscriptions:** This section shows a list of channels to which the user subscribes.

Figure 1-11:
A YouTube
channel
is a place
for your
video stuff.

The lists are comprised of thumbnail icons, which, after clicked, display the associated item. For example, if you click a playlist icon, you see the associated playlist.

The easiest way to make the Tube your way is to find some videos you like and then view the channel of the user who uploaded the clips. When the user's channel page is displayed in your browser, click through the sections and look at the playlists the user has created, the friends in her channel, the user's favorite videos, the videos she's uploaded, and so on. This gives you a good starting-off point. Within no time, you're subscribing to channels you like, creating playlists, and creating friends with other YouTube users. So if you're ready to start experiencing everything YouTube has to offer, keep reading.

Chapter 2

Registration, Please: Creating a YouTube Account

*W*hen you're registering a new account, YouTube doesn't demand excessive amounts of personal information from you. YouTube doesn't ask for your home address or your telephone number — and it does *not* ask for your credit card number. Compared to most other major sites, the YouTube registration requirements are appealingly non-intrusive.

But let's not kid ourselves: We all know that in this brave, new world of the Web, complete anonymity is a thing of the past. Whenever you register an account with any Web site, you're sharing your personal information. But you can feel safe with YouTube: Their terms-of-service disclosure assures you that they won't share your personal information with other Web sites or corporations.

Nevertheless, when you sign up with YouTube or any other Web site, you're "putting yourself out there" as they say; and with a Web site like YouTube, where you can share personal videos with a mass audience, it's worth taking a moment to think about the face that you want to present to the world.

Signing Up with YouTube

YouTube has an *open-door policy:* Anyone who visits the site can search the site and watch videos. You aren't required to register, to supply information about yourself, or to create a username and a password. That's a pretty good deal: One hundred million videos at your fingertips, and you're free to watch them in total anonymity.

If anonymity is appealing to you, the following is a list of things you can do on YouTube without registering or logging in:

- You have unlimited ability to search the YouTube video collection, including video groups.

- You can create a QuickList of videos that you want to save for later viewing.

- You can view the *history* of your session: a compendium of all the videos you've watched.

- You can share a video that you like by forwarding a link to friends' e-mail addresses.

- You can search through the Help section for answers to any questions you have about using YouTube.

Without registering or logging in, YouTube doesn't know who you are, and anything you save — such as a QuickList — is lost when you quit your browser or shut down your computer.

In addition to searching and watching videos, YouTube offers many fun and interesting features — commenting on a video, for example, or creating a list of your favorite videos — and to access those features you must first create an account.

The following is a list of YouTube features, which you must first register to access:

- Leaving feedback or commenting on a video

- Uploading your own video

- Flagging a video as inappropriate

- Creating specialty accounts, such as Director, Comedian, or Guru accounts

- Customizing your experience with subscriptions and playlists

- Creating your own channel

- Integrating YouTube with your personal Web site

These and other features truly enhance your relationship with YouTube, allowing you to customize your experience and interact with the YouTube community. After you register, your preferences — your favorite videos, your subscriptions, your search history, and so on — are all saved to your account page.

Choosing your username

Creating a username is a standard part of registering with any Web site. For example, if you're shopping online and want to purchase something from an online retailer, you must first create an account so that they know where to ship your goods — and how to bill you. Part of that process includes creating a username that you'll use to log in whenever you visit that site. No big deal, right?

Keep in mind, though, that YouTube is different. In the history of the Internet, never has anything been like it. YouTube isn't a retail site. YouTube isn't an auction site. YouTube is a video-sharing site, which is a wholly different thing. Why? Because it's personal. Viewing other people's videos is a very personal thing. Sharing your own videos with an audience of millions is an even more personal thing. Because of this, some of the procedures commonplace on other Web sites are worth a bit of rethinking on YouTube.

For example, your username. When registering at YouTube, you might want to consider creating a username that protects your anonymity. Using your full name as your username is in no way wrong or against the rules, but you probably don't want the millions of people who might watch your videos of you and your family to know your full name. This might not bother you, but many people don't want their full name out there, and creating a username that's anonymous is a much safer bet.

On the other hand, many users use YouTube for exactly that purpose: to get their name out there. Let's say that you're a musician or a comedian, and you're uploading your videos to YouTube to showcase your talent. In that case, you might very well want your username to be your full name. The same goes for your business. If you own a taxi service, for example, and you upload videos that advertise your business, it's probably a smart idea that your business and usernames are one and the same.

Opening your account

Registering with YouTube is quick and painless. You don't need to submit your address or your phone number, and YouTube doesn't ask you for a credit card number. Instead, YouTube requires that you submit a valid e-mail address and — surprise — your date of birth. Why your date of birth? Because YouTube is very specific in its terms of service that it doesn't consider itself to be a site that is appropriate for anybody under the age of 13, and it doesn't allow anybody under that age to register an account.

Signing up with YouTube begins at the home page of the site, www.youtube.com. When you arrive at this page as an unregistered user, the Sign Up link appears in bold at the top-right side of the page, as shown in Figure 2-1.

1. **Click the Sign Up link, as shown in Figure 2-1.**

   This takes you to the Join YouTube sign up page. (See Figure 2-2.)

2. **Enter your e-mail address.**

   You must enter a valid e-mail address to register.

3. **Enter a username.**

   To protect your privacy, it's not a good idea to use your full name as your username. The username that you enter must be different from the millions of other usernames registered already. If you enter a username that's taken already, you can't register until you change it to an original name.

4. **Enter a password in both the Password and Confirm Password fields.**

   It's a good idea to jot down your username and password in case you forget it.

5. **In the Country drop-down list, select the country where you live.**

The Sign Up link

Figure 2-1: The YouTube home page and the Sign Up link at the top-right corner.

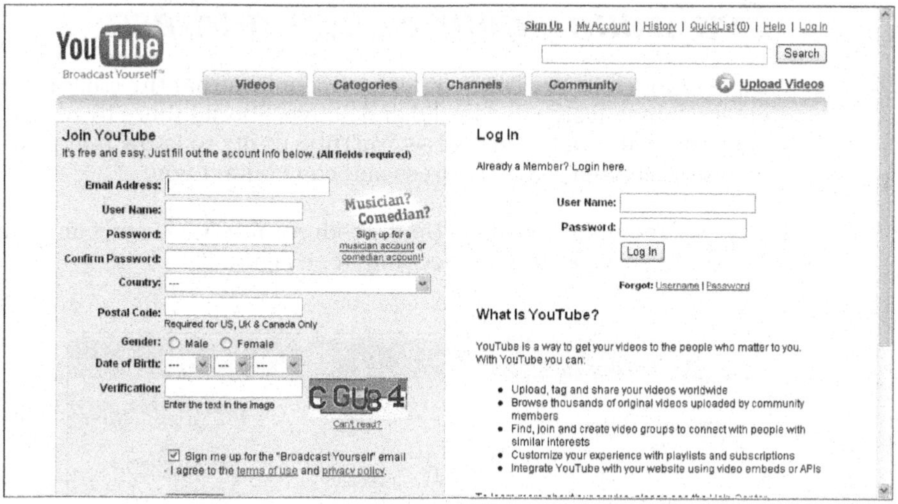

Figure 2-2:
The Join
YouTube
sign-up
page.

6. **Enter your postal code.**

    This is required only for citizens of the United States, U.K., or Canada.

7. **Click to select your gender.**

8. **Enter your date of birth.**

9. **Type the characters (letters and numbers) from the colored box into the Verification field.**

    YouTube wants to confirm that you're an actual human being and not a computer program creating false registrations. If you can't read the characters, click the Can't Read? link below the box to change to another image and color scheme.

10. **Check the box if you want to receive the YouTube "Broadcast Yourself" e-mail newsletter.**

    If you choose to receive it, YouTube will e-mail you the "Broadcast Yourself" newsletter on a regular basis. It's a cool little newsletter — not too wordy or overdone — that keeps you up to date with new features and happenings on YouTube.

11. **Click the Sign Up button.**

    If you leave any fields empty or if you choose a username that's taken already, YouTube refreshes the page with red warning notes identifying the fields that need to be corrected before you can register.

Confirming your e-mail address

It's very much in YouTube's interest to confirm that the e-mail address you enter when you sign up is valid and active. Should there be any issues with your account — good or bad — YouTube wants to know that it can identify you through your e-mail address and can contact you.

After you complete the Sign Up procedure, YouTube sends an e-mail titled "YouTube Service" to your account. (See Figure 2-3.)

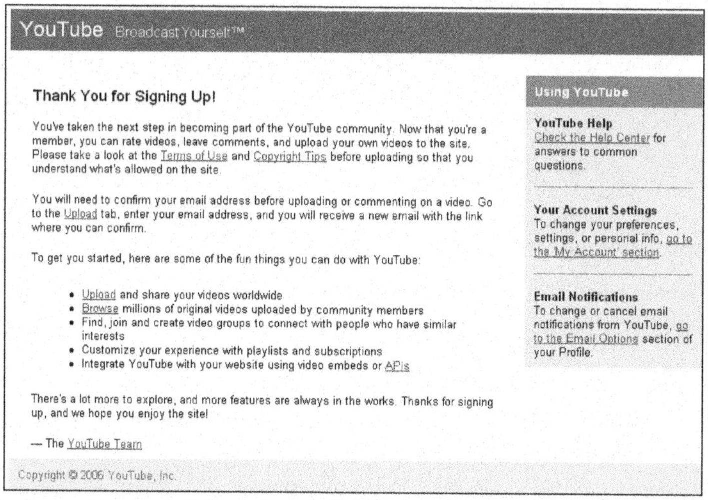

Figure 2-3: The YouTube Service e-mail.

This usually happens instantly after signing up, but it may take a few minutes. The e-mail welcomes you to the YouTube community and offers some highlights of the YouTube experience.

The second paragraph in the e-mail informs you that you must confirm your e-mail address before you can upload a video or comment on a video. Here's how:

1. **Click the blue Upload text link in the second paragraph.**

   This takes you to the YouTube e-mail confirmation page, as shown in Figure 2-4.

2. **Enter your e-mail address in the Send a Confirmation E-mail To: field.**

3. **Click Send Email.**

4. **Return to your e-mail Inbox and then open the e-mail from YouTube titled "YouTube Email Confirmation."**

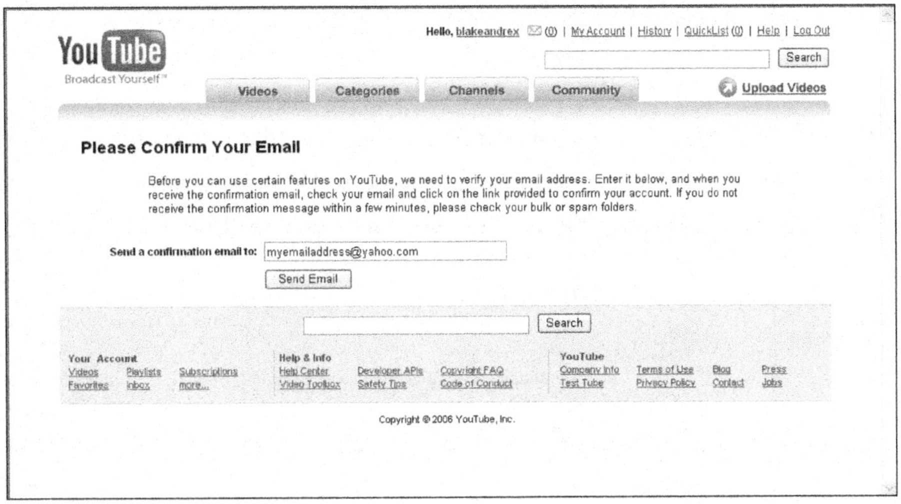

Figure 2-4:
The
YouTube
e-mail
confirmation
page.

5. **Click the blue Click Here text link.**

   This takes you to YouTube's video upload page, but you don't need to upload a video now if you don't want to. Your e-mail address is confirmed. You're now a fully registered member of the YouTube community and can access all features that are available only to members.

Jumping through Security Hoops

After you register, your username and password are YouTube's primary method for identifying you and allowing you access to your account. Therefore, it's important that you keep your password secret: With your username and password, anybody could log in to your account from any computer and have access to your personal YouTube property, such as family videos that you've designated as private.

Logging in

When you register an account with YouTube, YouTube automatically downloads a cookie to your computer. A *cookie* is short text-only string of computer code that YouTube uses to identify you whenever you return to the site using the same computer. For example, if you register with YouTube on your home computer, the next time you visit the site using that computer you're automatically logged in under your username. The cookie takes care of this. You know that you're logged in because your username appears in bold at the top of the page.

If you go to YouTube from another computer — that is, one without the cookie — you aren't logged in automatically. Logging in manually, however, is easy. Here's how:

1. **Click the Log In text link at the top-right corner of the page.**

   This takes you to the Login page. (See Figure 2-5.)

2. **Enter your username and password, and then click the Log In button.**

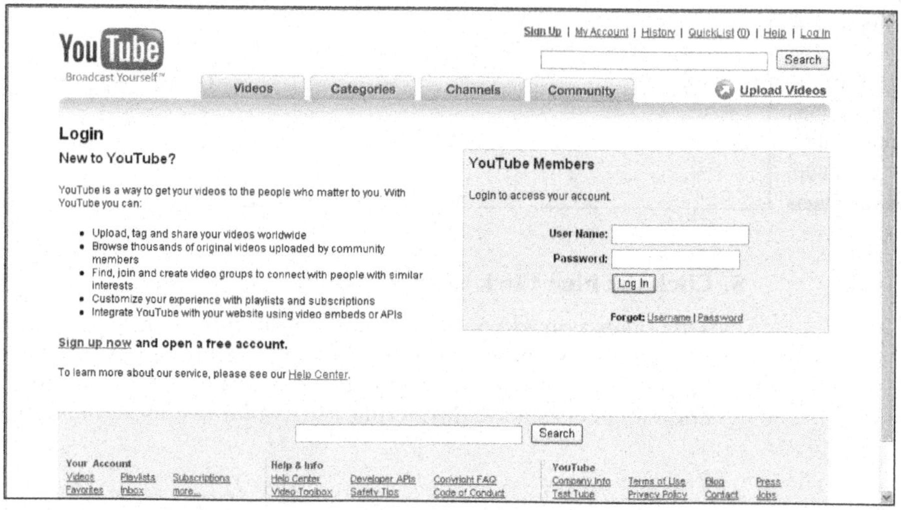

Figure 2-5: YouTube's Login page.

Getting help if you forget your username or password

When you first register with YouTube, jot down your username and password, especially if they're different from those that you use regularly on other Web sites. But if you forget either of them, it's really no big deal: Remember, YouTube has your e-mail address! To retrieve a forgotten password (or username), follow these steps:

1. **Click the Log In text link at the top-right corner of the page.**

2. **Click the Password text link next to Forgot: below the Log In button. (If you want to retrieve a forgotten username instead of a password, click the User Name text link instead.)**

   This takes you to the Forgot Password page. (See Figure 2-6.)

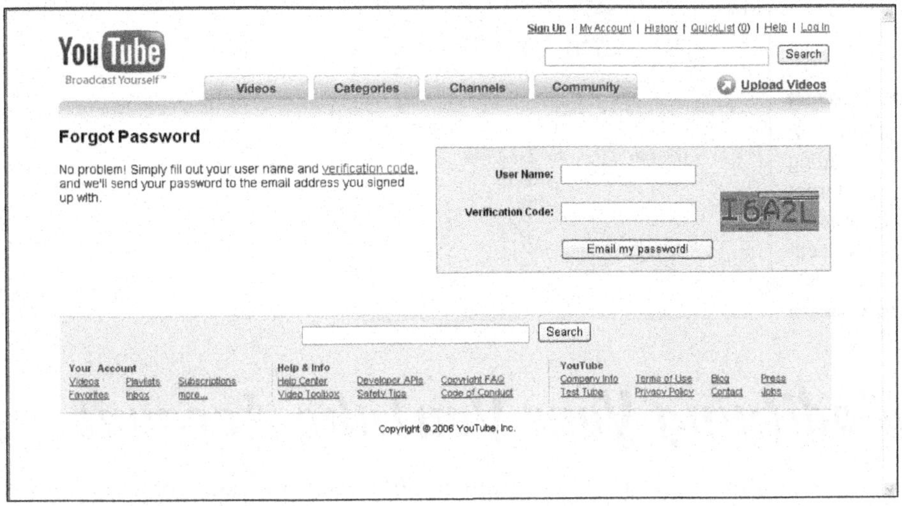

Figure 2-6:
The
YouTube
Forgot
Password
page.

3. **Enter your username.**

4. **Enter the verification code from the multicolored box.**

5. **Click the Email My Password! button.**

   YouTube sends an e-mail containing your password to your registered e-mail address.

Getting help if you can't log in

If you can't log in with what you're certain is your correct username and password, it's probably because you don't have cookies turned on in your browser preferences. If you're using Internet Explorer as your browser (chances are, you are) do the following to turn on cookies:

1. **In Internet Explorer, go to the Tools menu.**

2. **Click Internet Options.**

3. **Click the Privacy tab at top.**

4. **Click the Advanced button.**

5. **Set First- and Third-Party Cookies to Accept, as shown in Figure 2-7.**

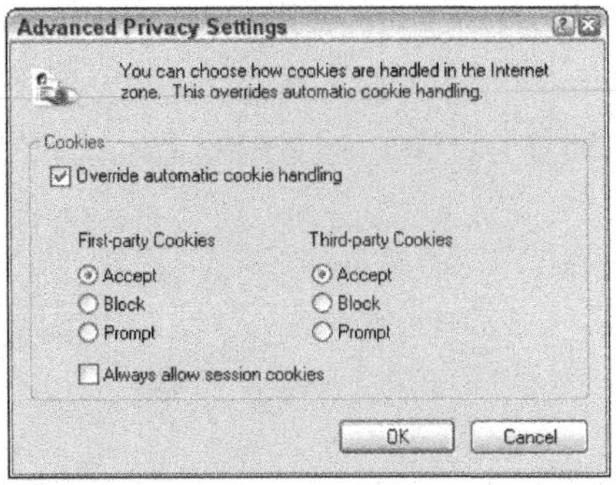

Figure 2-7:
Setting
Internet
Explorer to
accept
cookies.

Modifying Your YouTube Account

Things change. For example, you change jobs and get a new e-mail address. Or you finally break up with your I-just-can't-commit boyfriend and decide that you no longer want to use his dog's name as your password. When life's little changes come your way, some of them might require that you update your YouTube account. No problem.

Changing your e-mail address or password

You're free to change your password as often as you like. If your e-mail address changes — if you change employers, for example — you need to update your registered e-mail address with your new one.

1. **Log in to your YouTube account.**

2. **Click the My Account text link at the top of the page.**

3. **Click the Password & Email link in the Account Settings section at the bottom of the page.**

    This takes you to the Password & Email page, as shown in Figure 2-8.

4. **Enter your registered e-mail address or, if you're changing your address, enter your new e-mail address.**

5. **Enter your current password.**

6. **If you're changing your password, enter your new password and then retype it in the next field to confirm.**

7. **Click either of the Update buttons to the left to update your account with the new information.**

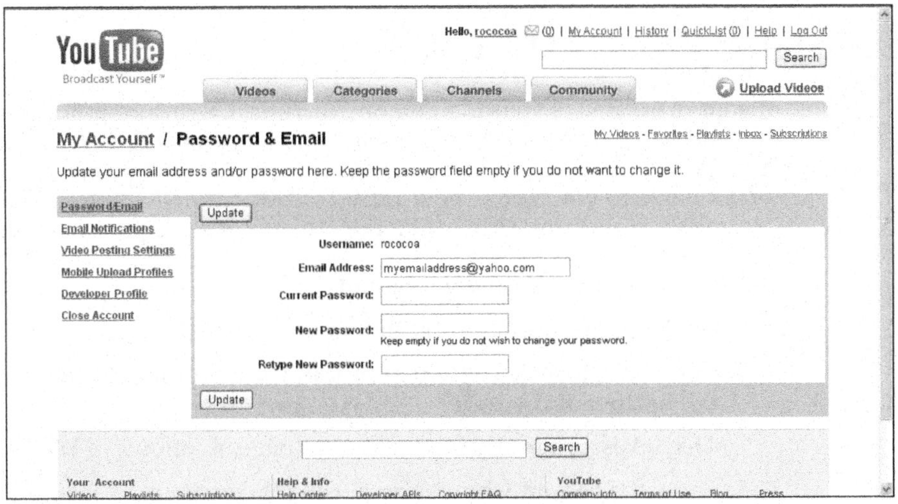

Figure 2-8:
Go to the
Password &
Email page
to change
your
password or
your e-mail
address.

Changing your username

The short answer to the question "How do I change my username?" is "You can't." In other words, you can't transfer all the unique qualities of your account — your favorite links, playlists, search history, and so on — from one account to another. The solution to the problem: Create multiple accounts.

Having more than one identity on YouTube can be desirable. Let's say, for example, you're a well-known lawyer, respected for your no-nonsense approach to your practice. And let's say, too, that you have a great video of your Sunday afternoon belly dancing performances at the local cultural center. If you wanted to create a video channel on YouTube for your law practice, you might not want your law videos sitting side-by-side with your belly dancing videos on the same page.

Fortunately, there's a simple solution. YouTube allows you to create multiple accounts with your single e-mail address. So our lawyer could easily create two accounts, one for her practice and another for her performance art. That way, her belly dancing fans would never be shocked and scandalized to discover that she's also a lawyer!

Closing Your Account

If your username is your identity on YouTube, closing your account means the end of that identity. All the unique qualities of your account — your groups, your subscriptions, your search histories, and so on — will no longer be available to you. That's your main consideration if you're thinking about closing your account. Other than that, the process is quick and simple:

1. **Log in to your YouTube account.**

2. **Click the My Account text link at the top of the page.**

3. **Click the Close Account text link in the Account Settings section at the bottom of the page.**

   This takes you to the Close Account page, as shown in Figure 2-9.

4. **Enter the reason why you're closing the account.**

   As with any breakup, the other party deserves to have some idea why you're leaving. If you're closing your account because you are unhappy with their service or had a bad experience on the site, that could be valuable information to the YouTube team for improving the site.

5. **Enter your current password.**

6. **Click either of the Close My Account buttons, and your account is closed.**

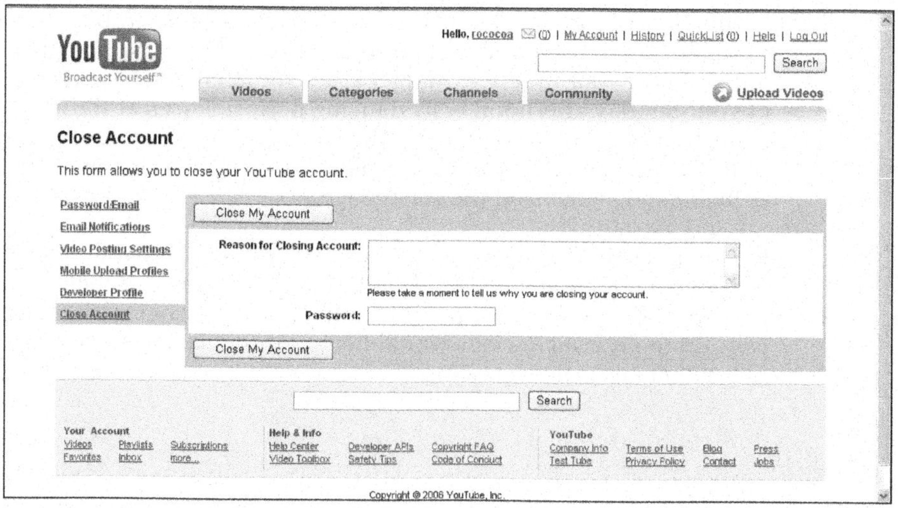

Figure 2-9: The Close Account page — when you're ready to say goodbye.

Chapter 3

A Guided Tour through the Tube

*Y*ouTube is already well known as a pop-culture phenomenon; a site where you can see video excerpts of your favorite TV shows, catch a red-carpet catfight between spoiled celebrity rich kids, or see a video replay of that game-winning goal at the World Cup.

But YouTube isn't just recycled pop-culture videos. So if you want to check out of the Paris Hilton and *Entertainment Tonight* isn't your idea of entertainment for tonight, rest assured that YouTube has much more to offer.

That's what this chapter is about. We click around the YouTube interface and check out what's up there. The main part of our tour takes you through YouTube's four main "tabbed" pages — Videos, Categories, Channels, and Community.

We show you some basic links that'll help you browse more effectively and find the videos that you want to see. We teach you how to power search by using the YouTube categories, and we look at some very popular channels. In the YouTube community square, you're introduced to groups, contests, and the amazing Colleges section. Finally, we show you how to get help if you need it and how to get company and contact information about YouTube.

So hop on our virtual tram and join us for the tour. Even if you're an experienced tuber, we feel quite confident that we can show you some smart tricks that you'll find useful and some cool things you haven't seen yet.

Viewing Top Videos

If you go to a bookstore, you know that they have thousands upon thousands of books for you to choose from. But you also know that the bookstore creates displays to promote books that they think you might find interesting: best sellers, controversial titles, award-winning series, and so on. YouTube's "Top Videos" section works in the same way — it's like a display that shows you what's getting watched by a lot of people on the Tube.

Top Videos is all about videos that are getting the most attention, but YouTube cross-references those videos in different ways. You can see a list of the videos that were the most watched today, or this week, or this month, or of all time. Instead of watching the most-viewed videos, you can go to the Most Recent page to view the newest video additions to the YouTube collection. YouTube cross-references videos in other great ways: You can watch the Most Discussed videos, or the Top-Rated videos, or the Most Favorited videos. It's up to you.

One of the many great things about YouTube is that it works by natural selection. For whatever reason, a video can become very popular, very fast. Sometimes, the reason is obvious: for example, a clip from the Super Bowl, concert footage of a reigning pop star, or a flash of political news from Washington. But then there are those other videos, the obscure ones from out of nowhere that — who knows why? — get passed around and before you know it, millions of people have seen them. Some are great. Some aren't so great. And some are just dumb. Whatever you might think of these videos, the YouTube *Videos page* is a new and truly fascinating thing: an instant snapshot of what millions of people around the world are all watching at the same time.

Finding newest videos: The Most Recent page

YouTube is adding new video to the site by the thousands every day. If you want to see what's new, all the newest videos are listed for you to browse through. Here's how you do it:

1. **Go to YouTube's home page at www.youtube.com.**

2. **Click the Videos tab at the top of the page.**

   This is the *Videos home page,* a central location for video browsing.

3. **On the left side of the window, click the Most Recent link in the Browse section.**

   This takes you to the Most Recent section of the Videos section. Figure 3-1 shows a screen capture of the random videos that were listed on the day and time we visited.

Figure 3-1:
The Most
Recent
page in the
Videos
section.

This page is updated every 30 minutes with the newest batch of videos to hit the site. If you upload a video, it's listed here as well. That's a good thing to keep in mind. If your goal is to get your video seen, this is prime real estate. Think of it as your video's official debut.

This page is all about browsing; it's like rummaging through a garage sale hoping to find a treasure. In terms of content quality, it's a crapshoot. You might be thinking, "Why bother with these videos when I can just go search for what I want?" Good point. These are just a bunch of random videos thrown together on a page for no other reason than that they were uploaded at the same time. But . . .

To best enjoy this page, you must *embrace* that randomness, as many people do. Tubers love this page because it's such a random — and often bizarre — snapshot of the population — the *world* population. Absolutely *anything* could end up on this page. This is where you might find that one-in-a-million awesome video that you'd never even *think* to search for. And another great thing: You're one of the first people to find it. You can be the YouTube treasure hunter and share your new finds with your friends and family.

The Most Recent page is a *batch-processed* page. That is to say, all the videos to hit the site — in say the last half-hour — are batched together and uploaded to the Most Recent page. A half-hour later, when the next batch appears on the Most Recent page, the previous batch is no longer featured. That's right, kid, fame is fleeting.

Browsing most-viewed videos: The Most Viewed page

Data collection and statistical reporting are such great things about the Internet, and YouTube has a lot of fun and interesting data to collect and report on. Every time a video is viewed, YouTube takes note, and the most-viewed videos are listed in one place for your browsing enjoyment. Here's how to get there:

1. **If you're not already there, click the Videos tab to go to the videos home page.**

2. **On the left side of the window, click the Most Viewed link in the Browse section.**

   This takes you to the Most Viewed section of the Videos section. Figure 3-2 shows a screen capture of the videos that were listed on the day and time we visited.

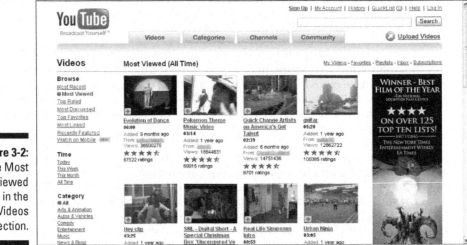

Figure 3-2:
The Most Viewed page in the Videos section.

First, note that a number of videos from the Most Recent page are listed here — this goes to show how many viewers your video can attract in the brief time that it appears on the Most Recent page.

The Most Viewed page is one of the most-viewed pages on YouTube, one that you'll want to come back to again and again. It's also one of the most interesting pages. Out of all the millions of videos on the site, these are the ones that are attracting the most eyeballs, which is a good indication that here you're likely to find videos worth watching.

Sexy sells, and many of the most-viewed clips get to be most-viewed because of racy content. That's a good thing to keep in mind if you have kids who surf the site. Remember, nothing extreme is allowed on YouTube, but you'll definitely find some R-rated content.

Browsing top-rated videos: The Top Rated page

After you watch a video on YouTube, as a registered user you can quickly and simply rate the video — from five stars for a great video to one star for, let's be polite about it, garbage. Just think about it, all those millions of users clicking all those millions of stars. And in the twinkle of an eye, YouTube can process all that data and show you which videos are the top ranked. Here's how you get there:

1. **If you're not already there, click the Videos tab to go to the Videos home page.**

2. **On the left side of the window, click the Top Rated link in the Browse section.**

   This takes you to the Top Rated page in the Videos section. Figure 3-3 shows some of the high-rankers that were listed on the day and time we visited.

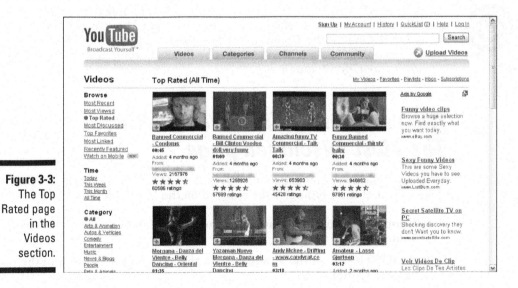

Figure 3-3:
The Top Rated page in the Videos section.

This is where things get really interesting. These videos — theoretically — are the cream that rises to the top. This is a great example of what the owners of YouTube mean when they say that YouTube is created not by the YouTube administration but by the YouTube community itself.

It's worth noting that the top four videos on this page are all from the same user. Now, we're not suggesting that he or she has some connection at YouTube and was able to make this happen artificially. That's not what's going on here, but clearly this isn't a coincidence.

The explanation is probably a combination of three things:

- The videos are high quality with a clear image and good sound. The content is fun, funny, and something that people would likely pass around to friends. People would also be likely to check out this user's other videos, which explains why more than one has risen to the top.

- The very fact that these are on the Top Rated page means that they're going to get lots and lots of hits, and many users will take the time to give them a rating.

- This user probably does his or her own public relations by passing around these videos to a long e-mail list of friends and family.

The Top Rated page is one of your best bets for finding quality entertainment on YouTube, and it's a smart place to visit often.

 YouTube doesn't rate videos, and it doesn't choose which videos are top-rated. Videos become top-rated because millions of people from all over the world like them enough to give them five stars. If you think about it for a moment, that makes the Top Rated page a really cool snapshot of what a random sampling of a world-wide audience thinks is good and worth watching. Pretty cool, don't you think?

Browsing most-discussed videos: The Most Discussed page

What are the videos that get people to respond, the ones that really get people talking — or at least typing? They're listed on the Most Discussed page.

1. **If you're not already there, click the Videos tab to go to the Videos home page.**

2. **On the left side of the window, click the Most Discussed link in the Browse section.**

These are the videos that spurred the most people to leave comments after viewing. This makes for a very interesting cross-reference of "top" videos. Unlike top-rated movies, these aren't necessarily videos that people like. And unlike most-viewed videos, these aren't necessarily the videos that everybody's watching. Instead, this category lists videos that get a rise out of people, videos that make people have an opinion — good or bad — and make them want to air that opinion.

The good-or-bad opinion angle is a big component that makes this category so interesting. In this list, you find videos that get lots of comments because they're fun, funny, outrageous, rude, insulting, unique, or obnoxious. These are the videos that generate debate, and that makes the Most Discussed page a great place to find provocative videos on YouTube.

Browsing top favorites: The Top Favorites page

Whenever you're watching a video on YouTube (and you're a registered user), you can mark that video as one of your favorites. YouTube refers to this behavior as *favoriting*.

When you favorite a video, the video is added to your account page, where you can access it again easily for repeat viewings. The *Top Favorites page* is a collection of the videos that are most favorited by YouTube users. Here's how to get there:

1. **If you're not already there, click the Videos tab to go to the Videos home page.**

2. **On the left side of the window, click the Top Favorites link in the Browse section.**

The Top Favorites page works hand-in-hand with the Top Rated page as a cross-section of the most well-liked videos on YouTube. How are top favorites different from top-rated videos? A video is listed as Top Rated based on the number of stars it achieves when ranked. Thus, the Top Rated page is a dependable list of videos that are well liked by a large number of people — limited to those tubers that rank videos. But not everybody takes the time to rank videos, so the Top Favorites page works as a nice conjunction — a list of videos that so many people have liked so much that they've saved them to watch again and again.

Be sure to remind friends, family (and your English teacher) that the word *favorite* is now a verb. I favorite, you favorite, he favorites, she favorites. "Yesterday, I favorited 22 videos on YouTube."

Browsing most-linked videos: The Most Linked page

Many people create links on other Web sites that connect to videos on YouTube. To see a list of the most-linked videos — and where the links are coming from, do the following:

1. **If you're not already there, click the Videos tab to go to the Videos home page.**

2. **On the left side of the window, click the Most Linked link in the Browse section.**

   This takes you to the Most Linked page. Note that a stat beneath each video thumbnail tells you how many links each video receives.

3. **Click any videos on the page that you find of interest.**

   This takes you to that video's page, and the video begins playing automatically.

4. **Click the More Stats link beneath the video window.**

   As shown in Figure 3-4, clicking this link reveals a list of the Web sites that are linked to this video.

Figure 3-4: Viewing a most-linked video's link information.

Browsing most-responded videos: The Most Responded page

The Most Responded page is pure YouTube — something completely new, something that didn't exist before YouTube. To see a list of the most responded-to videos, do the following:

1. **If you're not already there, click the Videos tab to go to the Videos home page.**

2. **On the left side of the window, click the Most Responded link in the Browse section.**

   This takes you to the Most Responded page in the Videos section. Figure 3-5 shows some of the high-rankers that were listed on the day and time we visited.

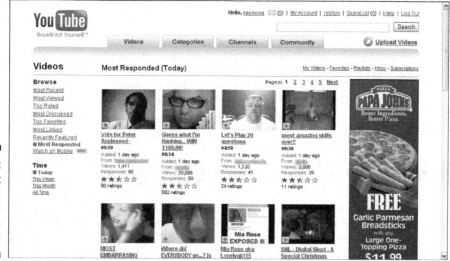

Figure 3-5: The Most Responded page in the Videos section.

Do you remember, in the early days of the Internet, the "new" phenomenon of online bulletin boards? It went like this: I post a text message online, you post a response, and other people can stop by to read our online conversation. The same discussion is going on in YouTube — but with videos! Think about that for a second — a video bulletin board. Or, if you prefer, a conversation between dueling videos.

As opposed to the *most-discussed videos* — those that receive the most text comments — the videos on the Most Responded page are those that spur the most people to upload a *video* response.

Top Favorites: Your click is counted

The Top Favorites page is a nice example of how you're really never alone on YouTube. When you rank a video, that's an action intended for the public: You're saying, "Hey, fellow tubers, here's what I think of this video." But favoriting a video is an inherently personal act. You're saying to *yourself,* "I like this video, and I want to watch it again sometime." So you click to add it to your favorites list. It feels like a private act. Wrong!

That click is registered by YouTube. The click is counted and shared as an anonymous statistic. Is that a bad thing? No. In fact, it's a good thing because it allows YouTube to create a really cool and useful page, like Top Favorites. But it's also a reminder that not much of what you do on YouTube is truly private. Big Brother is indeed watching . . . and he's taking notes!

If you're new to YouTube, creating and uploading your own video might sound like a big challenge and uploading a quickie video response to a video you just viewed might seem perplexing. Can it really be that quick and easy? The answer is . . . sure!

Many videos on YouTube are quick and simple productions that tubers make with a camera that's attached to — or embedded in — their computer. So posting a video response really can be quite easy. Whenever you watch a video, the Post a Video Response link is always available. Click it, upload your video, and just like that, you've responded to a video with a video of your own!

Browsing Videos by Category

With all those millions of videos in their library, it only makes sense that the YouTube gang makes a legitimate effort to *categorize* those videos — group them together in a way that helps users find videos in their field of interest. Thus, the *Categories page,* which is the YouTube library broken down into 12 distinct categories. If you haven't already been to the Categories page, ask yourself, which categories would you expect to find there?

You guessed "Sports" right? And you probably also guessed the "Comedy" and "Music" would also be represented in the categories list. But did you guess "Autos & Vehicles"? If not, you're going to be amazed at how many car, bike, plane, train, and speeding-drivers-who-are-totally-insane videos you'll find in this category.

One of the newer categories is Howto & DIY — not so easy to read, is it? DIY is "do it yourself" and that's what this category is all about: crafts, kits and home improvement videos hosted by amateur Martha Stewarts and Bob Vilas from far and wide.

The Categories page is more than meets the eye. At first, you might think of it only as a helpful place for searching, a basic breakdown of YouTube's video library. But as you discover more, you'll see that categories are a central component of a YouTube power search.

Browsing videos on the Categories page

The Categories page is a major component of the YouTube architecture and thus qualifies as one of only four tab buttons at the top of the site. Follow these steps to start checking out some interesting categories:

1. **Click the Categories tab to go to the top page of the Categories section, as shown in Figure 3-6.**

    On the left side of the page is a list of YouTube's 12 primary categories. In the main body of the page (you may have to scroll down) is a panel for each category, showing a thumbnail image of a featured video in that category.

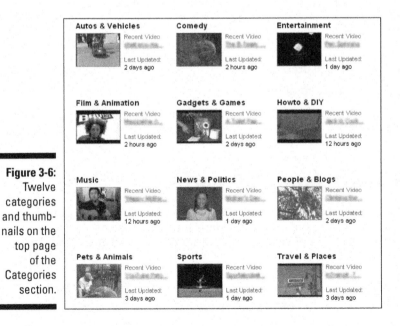

Figure 3-6: Twelve categories and thumbnails on the top page of the Categories section.

2. Click the Autos & Vehicles black text.

This takes you to the Autos & Vehicles category page, as shown in Figure 3-7.

Figure 3-7:
The Autos &
Vehicles
category
page.

3. Note at the top of the page is an "Editor's Pick" video for this category. Below that is the title "Featured Videos selected by YouTube Editors."

A Category page is one of the few video-collection pages on the site that isn't generated by random statistics — top-rated, top-ranked, and so on. Instead, these are videos hand-picked by the YouTube brain trust for your viewing pleasure.

4. Scroll to the bottom of the page.

Note the See More Autos & Videos link, which you can follow for more videos in this category.

Power searching categories

In the previous section, we looked at the top-rated search links — most-viewed, most-discussed, and so on — on the Videos page. You can use the top-rated links in conjunction with time parameters to power search any of the YouTube categories. Here's how you do it:

1. Click the Videos tab to go to the top page of the Videos section.

Note that, as shown in Figure 3-8, beneath the Browse section on the left is the Time section, and below that, a Category section listing all 12 categories.

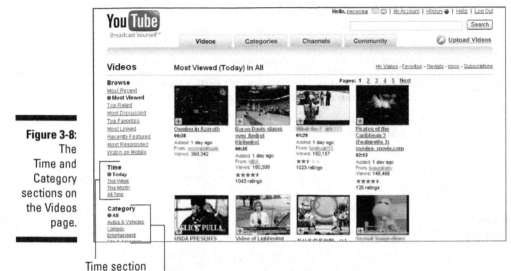

Figure 3-8:
The
Time and
Category
sections on
the Videos
page.

Time section

Category section

2. **Click Top Rated in the Browse section.**

   The page changes to show all the top-rated videos today. Note that the title of the page shows the word *Today* in parentheses.

3. **Click the Autos & Vehicles link in the Category section and then note the title change at the top of the page.**

   As shown in Figure 3-9, the page now shows today's top-rated videos in the Autos & Vehicles category.

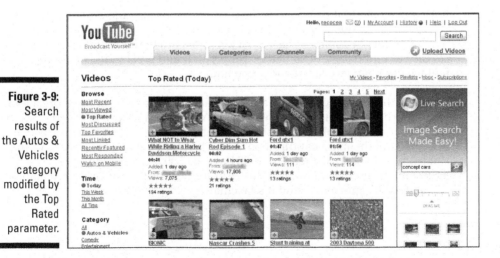

Figure 3-9:
Search
results of
the Autos &
Vehicles
category
modified by
the Top
Rated
parameter.

4. **Click This Month in the Time section.**

The search results change again. We're still seeing videos *only* in the Autos & Vehicles category, but the search results are defined by the Top Rated and This Month parameters.

5. **Click Most Viewed in the Browse section, click All Time in the Time section, and then compare your results to Figure 3-10.**

These are the most-viewed Autos & Vehicles videos throughout the history of YouTube.

Figure 3-10: Search results of the Autos & Vehicles category modified by the Most Viewed and All Time parameters.

Browsing the Autos & Vehicles category

If it's a machine that drives, flies, floats, hovers, or in some other way moves its way through this world, it's in this category. If you're a car enthusiast, you'll find lots of commercials for all kinds of cars in this category. If you're a *classic* car enthusiast, even better: Here you'll find great video of vintage cars, vintage car commercials, demos, you name it.

Anything that moves can crash, and this category has some of the more shocking, disturbing, and fascinating videos on YouTube. Yes, you guessed it, we're talking car crashes, plane crashes, boating accidents — you'll be amazed at how many of them are captured on video! If you're looking for a video of the Hindenburg, look no further. The 1960 Daytona 500 Superspeedway crash — the largest multicar crash in NASCAR history? It's here. Is this a morbid fascination? Absolutely. It's morbid. . . and it's fascinating.

One famous clip is "Greek Bike Accident 1," as shown in Figure 3-11. It's one of the most-viewed clips of all time. Now, before you go take a look, be warned: This is a *very* shocking video of a cyclist being hit by a car in an intersection on a road in Greece. Amazingly, the cyclist appears to be *completely* uninjured. Even more amazing, he appears to land on his feet and *immediately* begins yelling at the driver without taking even a second to absorb what has just happened to him.

Figure 3-11:
A shocking video of a bike accident in Greece; one of the most-viewed videos of all time in the Autos & Vehicles category.

This video is a very disturbing experience and a fine example of why YouTube isn't meant for kids. But it's also an undeniably fascinating 60 seconds of video, an incredible real-life moment captured and shared throughout the world on YouTube.

Fortunately, this category has a lot more than crash-and-burn videos. Check out Albert Einstein's demonstration of the flying car or watch footage of the new smart cars of the future that drive themselves.

This category is also good for a few laughs. "Real Life Frogger" is an unbelievable clip of a little car that runs a red light and speeds through an intersection so fast that it appears to drive *through* two other vehicles without hitting them. "Trouble Filling Up Gas" is a very funny video of a lady in Germany wrestling with a gas pump — and the pump wins.

And then there's the classic "India Driving," as shown in Figure 3-12. This is a simple video shot from a hotel room in India that's another of the most-viewed videos on YouTube. It starts out funny and then achieves some level of absurdist art as a melee of cars, trucks, buses, mini-buses, gas trucks, scooters, and pedestrians all compete for the right of way on a *very* busy street.

Figure 3-12: "India Driving," a true classic.

There are also clips named Greek Bike Accident 2, 3, 4, and so on. They definitely make you think twice about renting a scooter next time you go to Greece.

Browsing the Comedy category

You can guess what's in the Comedy category, right? Talented comedians with brilliant and incisive routines that will have you laughing at your computer screen on a daily basis. Well . . . sometimes.

The Comedy category isn't necessarily a collection of all the funny videos on YouTube; lots of funny videos are in other categories. Instead, you can think of the Comedy category as a collection of videos that are *intended* to be funny, videos whose sole reason for being is to make people laugh. People love to pass around videos that make them laugh, and that makes Comedy a very popular category.

This is definitely a pick-and-choose category; one man's junk is another man's treasure. Especially in this category, it's a smart idea to use the Top Rated or Most Viewed links to narrow your search to some of the true gems on the site.

Normally, we wouldn't feature a video named "Condoms" in this book; we'd search for another funny video with a more, shall we say, appropriate theme. But the fact that the top-rated video of all time in the Comedy category is indeed "Condoms" leaves us no real choice but to direct you to this YouTube hall-of-famer.

"Condoms" is shared by a user who specializes in somewhat risqué commercials from foreign countries. Despite its title, the "Condoms" clip contains no sex or anything that most viewers would find offensive. It is, however, wickedly cynical, very funny, and deserving of its lofty status on YouTube.

Browsing the Entertainment category

The Entertainment category is a wide-ranging collection of videos that can reasonably fall under the title of Entertainment. "*That's* entertainment?" You might find yourself asking that after viewing some of the not-so-spectacular offerings, but keep looking, as this category contains some of YouTube's most, um, *entertaining* videos.

The Entertainment category page refers to itself as a collection of "short movies and random weirdness." *Random* is the key word; you'll find all kinds of different videos in this section, everything from card tricks to men knitting, movie trailers and TV clips, a lady who levitates, and "Rebekah: The Human Can Opener" (that would be the "weirdness"). (See Figure 3-13.)

One really fun thing about this category is that a lot of kids and young people use it to upload videos of themselves performing — singing, dancing, playing an instrument, and so on — making this category something of an amateur talent show. Not all of it will bring you to tears, but lots of these kids are really talented. Check out "Robot Dance." Now that kid can move! And while you're there, you know you want to stop by for a peek at "Rebekah: The Human Can Opener." Don't try these things at home folks.

Figure 3-13: This seemingly normal woman is actually "Rebekah: The Human Can Opener."

Browsing the Film & Animation category

If you like Japanese anime, the Film & Animation is just chock-full of it. In addition, this category features a wide-range of videos that are artistic in nature. This includes stop-action animation videos, cartoons, line drawings, dramatic monologues by wannabe actors, and lots, and lots (and lots) of Japanese anime. You can also find some cool video of poetry slams in various urban locales.

One great feature about this category is stop-action animation. You'd be amazed at what people think of with a few dolls, some pen and ink drawings, a video camera, and a great imagination. One popular clip, "Star Trek Karaoke," brings the Enterprise crew to life. Another nicely done presentation is "No Boundaries," which features an animated snowman on a chalkboard that comes to life and interacts with the real world.

"3D Morphable Model Face Animation," as shown in Figure 3-14, is a very cool video from Germany that explains (in English) some of the principles behind vector-based facial-morphing animation software. The graphics are great, and the voice-over provides an easy-to-follow explanation of the concepts behind the programming.

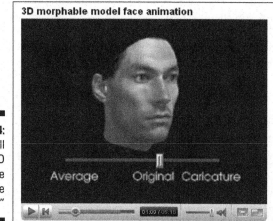

3D morphable model face animation

Average   Original   Caricature

Figure 3-14: A still from "3D Morphable Model Face Animation."

True talent always shines through, and the Film & Animation category is a showcase for talent. Check out "Drawing YouTube." At first, it appears to be simple sped-up footage of a talented young illustrator drawing a series of faces. But stay with it — there's a neat surprise when the video progresses. It turns out that the boy is drawing faces of tubers who have sent him videos of themselves. In the second half of the video, we get to see the faces that the boy's drawn and the actual faces of the people the drawings are based on. Send him a video of your face, and he'll draw you too! Now that's what we call interactive!

Browsing the Music category

Brace yourself: the Music category is one place where you can really get a sense of the overwhelming pop culture phenomenon that is YouTube. Think of the most random list of singers that you can, singers from any time, any genre. Burl Ives, Leslie Gore, Tony Bennett, Ernest Tubb, and Slim Whitman. Sit down and start watching; they're all up there. Musicians: Miles Davis, Yanni, Yo-Yo Ma, Eddie Van Halen, Chrissie Hynde, and Charo. Sit down and start watching; they're all up there.

The list is endless. If you like violins, videos of the world's great violinists are just waiting for you to find them. You can watch and listen to great performances of symphony orchestras from all over the globe. Listen to pop stars and great singers from any country of your choosing. Even if you took away every other category, YouTube as a video music library alone is a treasure. An *unprecedented* treasure.

A YouTube success story

ysabellabrave, as shown here, is a young lady from who-knows-where. She's posted dozens of clips on YouTube — no bells and whistles, just her singing into a video camera. And this girl can sing. She has everything a talent scout would look for: a great face, a unique voice, and tons of star quality. She already has a track record: An enormous fan base on YouTube, and she's a smart businesswoman. Her channel on YouTube is well produced and up-to-date. She provides links to her personal Web site, where you can see and hear more of her and — get this — send her a donation/gratuity via PayPal. Her real name is Maryanne, and she's a textbook example of how to use YouTube for all it's worth to broadcast yourself to the world.

Travellin' Man

00:41 / 02:16

The Music category is also a great place for you to be seen and show off your talents. The music industry is always looking for new talent, and YouTube is quickly becoming a platform where amateurs can get noticed. You don't need a recording studio, and you don't need thousands of dollars of equipment. You just need a video camera and talent.

Browsing the News & Politics category

Whenever there's controversy in the real world — and when is there not? — the clips often end up in the News & Politics category. Think of it as a current events channel — a place where you can go for videos of what's happening anyplace in the world.

The News & Politics category is one of the more serious collections on YouTube. Here you'll find many clips on 9/11 and its aftermath, conspiracy theorists, and debunkers. YouTube's been making headlines throughout the Iraq war with you-are-there videos shot by American troops and uploaded to the site. That is unprecedented — war footage not filtered through a journalist or news organization. The News & Blogs category is also the platform for the infamous Saddam Hussein execution video that was seen around the world.

It's not all heavy and depressing. You see a lot of Jon Stewart's face here, and Rosie O'Donnell's comments when she was on *The View* got a lot of airtime and are still very popular in this category.

Browsing the People & Blogs category

People. Now there's a broad term. This is a category of people: famous people, strange people, foreign people, funny people — pretty much all walks of life. Some of the more standout videos in this category are those of famous people, especially actors because singers and dancers are usually in the Music category and politicians and newsmakers are typically in News & Politics. So you see lots and lots of actors in these videos, though there is a lot of crossover.

If you love to travel, the People & Blogs category is a great way to see people from all over the world, speaking all kinds of languages in all kinds of settings.

This is where you also find YouTube's *video blogs,* video diaries uploaded by Tubers sharing their opinions on just about everything. Video blogging has become wildly popular on the Tube, especially for the already-famous Tubers. Many of the hot singers and comedians now post video blogs of themselves, not singing or telling jokes, but basically just talking about themselves, who they are, what they do. Many of them even give dating advice!

Many people upload their video blogs to this category rather than to News & Blogs — it just feels more personal.

Browsing the Pets & Animals category

If you like cute cats and playful puppies, browse some of these videos. Many of them are YouTube versions of Stupid Pet Tricks or Pets Do the Darndest Things. Many of them are also very funny. A video of a cat flushing a toilet became one of the most passed around and most-viewed videos on the site.

If you're an animal enthusiast, this category has more than just hijinks. Here you find great videos of animals in natural habitats, animals from all over the world. It's a great place to show your children videos of elephants, giraffes, and tigers. Any animal you can think of is represented.

Make a guess: Which animal can claim the title of the most-viewed video of all time in the Pets & Animals category? That would be "Sweet Tired Cat," who seems very sweet and definitely very tired. (See Figure 3-15.)

The Pets & Animals category is also a great place to meet other animal lovers and set up groups of shared interests. For example, many people who own and keep horses often get together through YouTube groups to share information and make friends.

Sweet Tired Cat

Figure 3-15: "Sweet Tired Cat," a YouTube superstar.

Browsing the Science & Technology category

This one is a strange collection — an odd assortment of videos that relate somehow to science and technology. Some of the best videos in this category are those of natural wonders and astronomy. You can find some great video of the Northern Lights, the Aurora Borealis, and St. Elmo's Fire. Comets and eclipses are other much-searched terms in this category.

You can also see some terrific footage of thunder and lightning storms, not to mention all types of natural disasters, earthquakes, hurricanes, tornados, and the like. Volcanoes and tsunamis also share a high-profile presence.

Another great way to search this category is to look for manufacturing videos, products that make you ask, "How do they do that?" You'll find some beautiful video on glass blowing or check out some of the videos on diamond mines and manufacturing. Fabrics, too, are fascinating, and you can see videos of lace makers and silk manufacturers. These types of searches not only deliver science and technology, they often take you on fascinating trips to foreign lands.

 As with any category, Science & Technology has its breakout celebrities. Albert Einstein, the Wright Brothers, and Jonas Salk all make cameo appearances, as do Jane Goodall and Dian Fossey. Modern-day doctors also get some airtime in this category, especially plastic surgeons with before-and-after videos.

Browsing the Sports category

The Sports category is like the Music category: vast. Think of the history of filmed and televised sports — all sports — and it's pretty much all here. The players, the superstars, the victories, the goals, the defeats — anything you can think of. This category is an online library of nearly 100 years of great sports moments and players, memories, and legends.

Browsing the Travel & Places category

Right from the start, travel and the Internet were a match made in virtual heaven. YouTube takes that another step further. Now you can see video of the places you're traveling to. Even hotels are getting into the game and uploading videos of the hospitality that they offer.

The Travel & Places category isn't only about actual travel, it's also about *virtual travel,* a trip around the world without ever leaving your home. See people from foreign lands. Watch videos from Cairo, the Great Barrier Reef, and the ruins of Rome. Or just head over to Utah. When you're traveling on YouTube, no place is too close or too far.

Checking Out the YouTube Channels

Imagine that you upload a lot of videos to YouTube, and you want to create a place where all those videos are collected together for people to watch. That place would be your channel on YouTube. You wanna be a YouTube star? Get yourself a channel.

Thank about that for a moment — your very own channel on YouTube, created by you, all about you and the videos you create. You can build an audience: People can subscribe to your channel. They can send you a message, and you can post a link to your personal Web site. You can *edit* your channel — add new videos, delete old videos. Essentially, it's your world, with a potential audience of millions.

Browsing the Channels page

Click the Channels tab on the YouTube home page to go to the Channels page, as shown in Figure 3-16. By default, the channels are listed in order of the number of their subscribers. In the figure, you can see that the miaarose channel has the most subscribers — 35,955 — for the week.

Figure 3-16: Something is always worth watching on the YouTube Channels page.

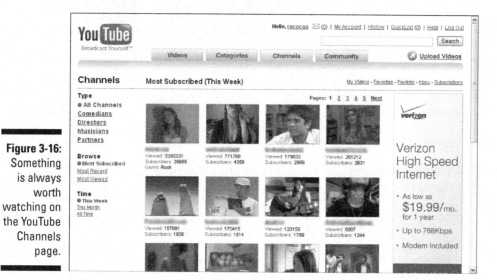

You can also use links in the left column to skew your search results by Most Recent and Most Viewed, and also by time parameters. For example, if you click All Time in the Time section, the search result gives you the most subscribed channels of all time. On the date that we searched, that list was led by YouTube *superstar* lonelygirl15. With 78,701 subscribers, she has nearly *twice* the number of subscribers as YouTube's CBS Television Network channel!

Browsing a channel

Click any channel listed on the Channels page to see that actual channel. Figure 3-17 shows the channel page of *Lonelygirl15,* the most-subscribed-to channel in the history of YouTube.

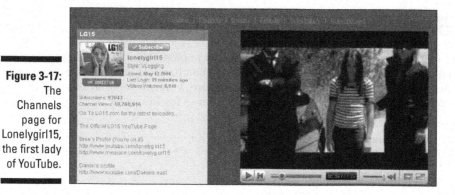

Figure 3-17: The Channels page for Lonelygirl15, the first lady of YouTube.

In the upper-left of the page is the signature thumbnail image of the channel — think of it like a traditional network icon, like the CBS eye or the NBC peacock. Beside the image is the Subscribe button. Click it, and you're the newest devotee to this popular channel.

The left column displays some basic statistics along with whatever text information the owner of the channel decides to share. On this page, that includes some links to related Web sites and a whole lotta background information on Bree. The right side of the page contains a collection of all the videos lonelygirl15 has added to her channel. So if you want to catch up on what has made this channel so popular — Lonelygirl15 was on more than a few year-end Top 10 lists in 2006 and was even interviewed by *The New York Times* — this is where you get the goods.

If you scroll down the page, on the left you see the Connect with lonelygirl15 section, which contains links to send her a message and also a link to her

Web site. Forget the Nielsen ratings and focus groups — on YouTube, your channel gets instant audience feedback.

Note the color scheme on Lonelygirl15's channel page: It's customized with an orange, brown, and pink color scheme. YouTube offers a number of cool options for customizing your channel.

Checking Out the YouTube Community Square

YouTube is most often thought of as a place with a lot of videos, which is of course true and something of an understatement. YouTube is also a place with a lot of *people*. Imagine for a moment the millions of people that are online on YouTube at any given time. The millions of people watching videos, commenting, favoriting, and sending messages. From this perspective, YouTube is more than just an online video depository: It's very much an online community of people, all of whom can communicate with one another and share information.

The Community page is where the many millions of people on YouTube go to befriend other people who share similar interests and perspectives. Click the Community tab to go to the YouTube Community page, as shown in Figure 3-18.

Figure 3-18:
The Community page brings together people who share common interests.

Browsing groups

The Community page is broken down into three sections, and Groups is the first. Groups are created by users, usually around a specific topic of interest. Some are rather general — sports fans, for example. Others are very specific, such as the group dedicated to rabid fans of *Family Guy,* the animated television series.

Click the See More Groups link in the Groups section at the top of the Community page. This takes you to the Featured Groups page, as shown in Figure 3-19. Listed in the middle are the featured groups that the title of the page refers to. They might interest you.

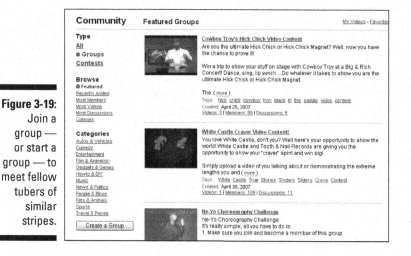

Figure 3-19: Join a group — or start a group — to meet fellow tubers of similar stripes.

What you're certain to find interesting are the links on the left side of the page. Though they're the same links that you've seen on the other major YouTube pages, it's important to remember that these links on this page search within Groups. For example, clicking the Autos & Vehicles link in the Categories section takes you to a list of groups that have formed around these topics. Here you'll find groups of classic car lovers, pilots and aircraft builders, motorcycle groups, boaters . . . it's a long list.

If the Groups section seems a bit hidden — it doesn't warrant its own tab at the top of the site — don't underestimate the power of Groups. Groups are a great way to power-search the site on very specific topics. They're a smart way to network with other tubers who share your interests. Groups offer you a place to create your own meeting space and bring together people that you want to get to know and share information that interests you. And if you're thinking strategically, Groups are a really smart method for networking and getting your videos seen by lots of people.

Browsing contests

Contests is the second section on the Community page; click the Contests link to go to the Featured Contests page, as shown in Figure 3-20.

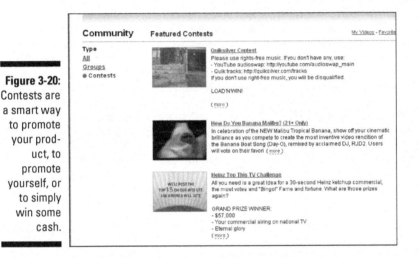

Figure 3-20: Contests are a smart way to promote your product, to promote yourself, or to simply win some cash.

Contests are an interesting niche that's developed for fun, profit, and promotion. Tubers create a channel for a contest and then other tubers send in videos competing to win the contest. That's the typical scenario.

Browsing contests can be a lot of fun because you never know what stunt somebody's going to think of next for a contest idea, and it's really fun to see the crazy videos people create to try to win. Figure 3-21 shows a very famous still from MsBlackBetty's video submission to become Miss Horrorfest 2006.

Figure 3-21: The famous still of MsBlack–Betty auditioning to be Miss Horrorfest 2006.

That's all fine and dandy, but we know what you're thinking: "Can I win money?" With so many millions of people trafficking YouTube every day, it didn't take long for businesses to come prospecting for opportunities. And yes, many businesses are happy to give away some money in exchange for your attention and a few thousand views on YouTube.

For the right product, running a contest can be a really smart promotion. In early 2007, just before tax season, H&R Block ran a contest to promote *TaxCut Online,* its do-it-yourself tax program. Users were asked to submit a short video explaining how they'd spend the "huge" tax refund they'd get by using the H&R Block software. The winning submission received a cash prize of $5,000. (They should have made the prize tax-free, don't you think?)

Figure 3-22 shows the contest's channel page. In addition to the cash prize, the winning video is featured on YouTube's home page for a full day in April. This indicates that the promoters of the contest did a business deal with YouTube to include this as part of the prize package. That was a smart move: For many tubers, being featured on YouTube's home page for an entire day is just as valuable — if not *more* valuable — than the $5,000!

Figure 3-22: Win $5,000! The contest page for H&R Block's TaxCut Online software program.

For you the viewer, hey, this is a pretty good opportunity, isn't it? A chance to win $5,000 and all you have to do is submit a 1-minute video? The odds are *way* better than winning the lottery, and you just might jump-start a movie career after your day in the sun on YouTube's home page.

Getting Info and Help

You're gonna have questions. YouTube, you will find, is a very well-designed and easy-to-navigate site. Somebody there has been blessed with the understanding that less is more, and YouTube is beautifully uncluttered. But at some point, at some time, you're gonna have questions. This chapter finishes our guided tour with a quick directory of where to find informational and help pages on the site.

Viewing your My Account page

To have an account page, you must first have an account, and you must first register to create an account. After you have, click the My Account link at the top of the page to go to your account page.

As shown in Figure 3-23, My Account is your personal home page on the site. Here you check for messages from friends, read comments that your videos receive, respond to invites from friends, and so on. While you search through YouTube, your account page is automatically updating and saving information of your favorite videos, playlists, subscriptions, and groups — everything you are and everything you do on YouTube is recorded here.

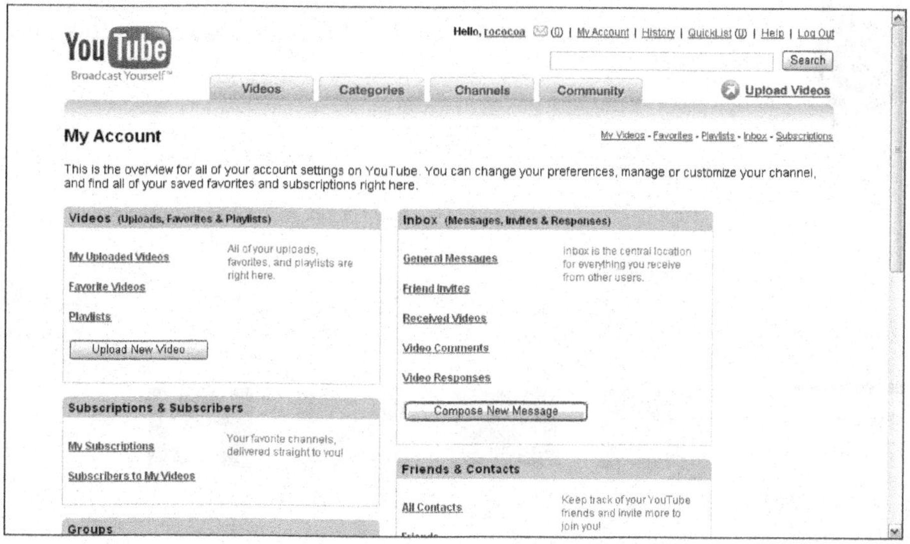

Figure 3-23: Your account page is your very own personal space on YouTube.

Viewing your Viewing History page

The Viewing History page, as shown in Figure 3-24, is accessed from the History link at the top of the site and shows a collection of your most recently watched videos. Unlike your Favorites page, where you actively choose to add videos that you like, your history page is updated *automatically* while you search YouTube. It can be very useful for quickly going back to view a video whose name you forget. On the other hand, it can also be very useful for someone else who uses your computer to view all the videos you've been watching and not necessarily talking about. So remember that your history page is *always* being updated, and the Clear Viewing History link is *always* there to erase that information.

Getting answers to general help questions

Help! You need somebody? Help! Not just anybody? Help! You need some YouTube help? Then click the Help link at the top of the page to go to the Help Center page, as shown in Figure 3-25. Here you find links and answers for many common questions about searching, watching and sharing videos, uploading videos, interacting with other users, account policies (such as account information and copyright guidelines), and other general questions. It's a fairly comprehensive collection of information that YouTube makes an effort to keep adding to and keep up-to-date. Then again, you won't ever need to go there because whenever you need help, you always have this book to help you through.

Don't overlook the Your Account and Help & Info links at the bottom of the Help page.

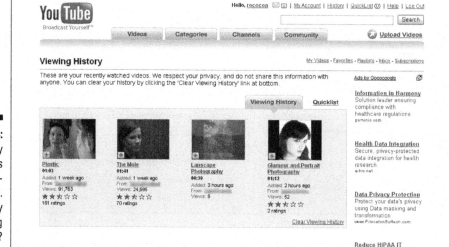

Figure 3-24: The History page traces your footsteps. Is anybody following you?

Getting the 4-1-1 on YouTube

YouTube has a YouTube section at the bottom of the Help page that contains a Company Info link. Click this link to go to the About YouTube page, as shown in Figure 3-26. More than just a bit of boilerplate, this page is a brief but interesting explanation of how YouTube defines itself and its vast community of users. It's definitely worth a quick read.

On the right side of the page are links to YouTube's press room, which contains a collection of press releases about the site. This is a very useful place if you're doing any research on the site.

The Contact Us page offers you an e-mail window to send a message to YouTube. The Advertising page offers another e-mail window and a form that you can fill out if you have an advertising budget of over $25,000 that you want to spend on YouTube. Both pages promise to respond to your queries, but don't be surprised that the person with the $25,000 to spend will probably get responded to faster.

YouTube is a wealthy, new company with a bright future and an even wealthier parent company, Google. Nice work if you can get it, and you can get a start on getting it by clicking the Jobs at YouTube link. Here you'll find lists of various job openings at various YouTube locations. If you're interested in working at YouTube, this is some pretty valuable information. Note too that, along with a competitive salary, full medical/dental benefits, and stock options (!), YouTube also promises free snacks and your very own YouTube t-shirt. What could be better than that?

Part II
So Many Videos, So Little Time

The 5th Wave   By Rich Tennant

"Your computer looks fine. I don't know why you're not receiving any video responses. Have you explored the possibility you may not have any friends?"

In this part . . .

In Chapter 4, we show you how to find your kind of video on the Tube. In Chapter 5, we show you how to customize your YouTube experience. Moving forward to Chapter 6, we show you how to become a part of the YouTube community.

Chapter 4

Searching the Tube for Your One-in-a-Million Video

Surfing the Tube is almost nothing like surfing the Hawaiian Pipeline, which, for those of you who don't know, is a Mecca for surfers with boards — not browsers. First and foremost, surfing the Tube is a heck of a lot safer: You don't have to watch for other surfers, dodge the occasional flying surfboard, or avoid any finned creatures that may be in the vicinity. Successfully surfing the Pipeline may take a lot of skill, but surfing the Tube and actually finding what you want takes only a little a bit. You don't need to be a rocket scientist to find what you want on the Tube, but you can find it a lot faster by adopting some of the techniques we present in this chapter.

Finding More Than One Way to Search YouTube

We're going to stick with our Pipeline metaphor for a while. After all, surfing the Tube is similar to surfing the Web, and the Hawaiian Pipeline is another form of surfing; albeit, inherently more dangerous. When you surf the Web, you can go to your favorite search engine to find what you want. And wouldn't you know it, YouTube is a Google company. For those of you who have been in a bubble for the last few years, *Google* is the Mother and Father of all search engines. When you use the Google search engine to find what you want, you type words in a text box that you think will return the Web pages that contain the information you require.

If you type the word **Pipeline** in the Google search engine, you'll get as a result thousands of Web pages that contain the word *Pipeline.* The results may be pages with information about gas and oil pipelines, magazines articles with the word *pipeline* in them, and so on. These pages are useless if you're looking for information on the Hawaiian Pipeline. However, if you refine your search, and type the words **Hawaiian Pipeline** in Google's text field, the results are much better: The first result on the first results page is a link to surfing the Pipeline. This is the basic way Web searches work.

YouTube searches work much the same way. Instead of randomly slogging though the millions of videos on YouTube, the folks that designed the site make it possible for you to search for videos that are of interest to you. But there's more than one way to surf the Web, and there's more than one way to surf the Tube. The upcoming sections show you how to spend your time finding cool videos on the Tube instead of searching for the proverbial needle in the haystack.

Searching YouTube's Video Vault

YouTube has a Google-like search engine built into its Web pages. In fact, a search text box appears in the upper-right corner of every YouTube page (see Figure 4-1). You type words into the text box, click Search, and get a page of results containing videos that pertain to the words you typed into the text box. To perform a simple search on YouTube, follow these steps:

1. **From any page on the YouTube Web site, type any words that you think are relevant to the videos you seek into the Search text box.**

   To perform a simple search, you can enter one word, a couple of words, or a full sentence.

2. **Click the Search button. (Or just press Enter or Return.)**

   The YouTube site refreshes, and you see icons for videos pertaining to the word or phrase you entered in the search text box.

So what happens after you click Search? YouTube searches the title, description, and tags of each and every video in its monumental vault of videos and serves them up on a results page. From this pool of results, YouTube sorts the videos by relevance. In other words, the more times the word you type into the search text box appears in the title, description, and tags of a video, the more "relevant" it is.

Search function

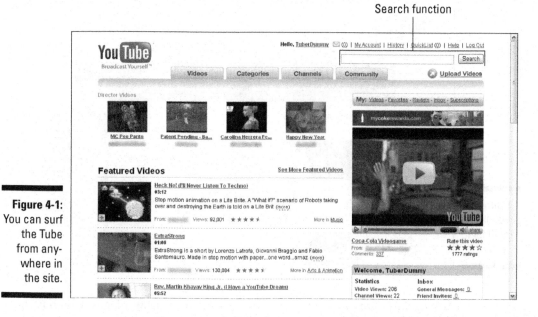

Figure 4-1:
You can surf
the Tube
from any-
where in
the site.

OK, where were we? Oh yes, "Pipeline." When we were writing this chapter, we typed the word **Pipeline** in the search text box just to see what would happen. The first video on the results page was a video of Stevie Ray and Jimmie Vaughan playing a song called "Pipeline" (see Figure 4-2) on a double-necked guitar, which, by the way, for those of us who like the Vaughan Brothers or appreciate good rock 'n roll/blues guitar, is way cool. You'll also find videos from the CNN show entitled *CNN Pipeline,* video clips of guitar virtuosos playing the surf classic "Pipeline" (made famous by the Chantays and the Ventures back in 1963 or so), and a few videos about the Hawaiian "Pipeline." I think you get the drift. If you want information about a specific topic, you have to get specific.

Improving your video's "relevance" with tags

Let that be a lesson to those of you who want your videos to be discovered on YouTube. If you want your uploaded videos to get a lot of attention (and who doesn't?), you should pepper the title, description, and tags with words that will make your video the cream-of-the-crop on the results page. For more information on adding relevant tags to your videos, see Chapter 8.

Tags are pieces of information about a video, such as the content within the video, brand names mentioned in the video, celebrities in the video, and so on. For example, if you're uploading a video of former Formula One World Champion Michael Schumacher driving for Ferrari in the Italian Grand Prix at the fabled Monza circuit, you'd enter tags, such as `Michael Schumacher`, `Ferrari`, `Italian Grand Prix`, `Monza`, and so on. You enter tags in a text field in the Video Upload page. Tags are covered in detail in Chapter 8.

Figure 4-2:
Well, you
asked for it,
you got it.

You can also narrow your search by looking in the right places, which is the topic of the upcoming sections in this chapter.

Changing Channels

YouTube has channels, lots of channels, but here are the six channels you find on the Channels page Type menu:

- ✔ Comedians
- ✔ Directors
- ✔ Gurus
- ✔ Musicians
- ✔ Partners
- ✔ You Choose 08

Each registered Tuber also has a channel all her own. A Tuber's channel has the same name as her username. If a user registers with a special account — for example, Comedians — her channel is found within the Comedians channel.

Don't get hung up on names. Sometimes the name of a user's channel gives you an idea of the content of that channel, but that's not always the case. It's just as likely that the name of the channel is absolutely worthless in determining what's in the channel.

One way to find videos that you like is to randomly surf one of the six channel types as follows:

1. **Log onto YouTube.**

2. **Click the Channels tab.**

   The YouTube Web site refreshes and shows the channels that have the most subscribers for the current week (see Figure 4-3). This is a crapshoot. The most subscribed channels may be of interest to you, or, in your humble opinion, they may be worthless drivel.

Figure 4-3:
Looking
for Mr.
GoodVideo
amongst
the most-
subscribed-
to channels.

3. **Click a user's channel.**

   The user's channel and videos are displayed.

4. **Click a video to play it.**

Another alternative is to click one of the actual channels:

1. **Log onto YouTube.**

2. **Click the Channels tab.**

   The YouTube Web site refreshes and shows the channels that have the most subscribers for the current week.

3. **Click the desired channel.**

   If you want to find videos of actors, click the Directors channel. Once again, YouTube serves up the user channels that received the most subscriptions for the current week, which in our example is from the

Directors channel. Figure 4-4 shows the most subscribed channels for the Directors category on the week that this chapter was written.

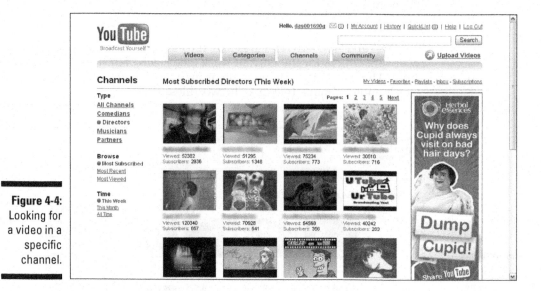

4. **Click a user's channel icon.**

   YouTube displays the user's channel and all the videos uploaded by the user.

5. **Click the video you want to play.**

   YouTube serves up a video; you supply the popcorn and soft drinks.

Searching for channels with keywords

Randomly searching through channels to find videos of interest can be a bit tedious, especially if you're looking for the perfect video during your 10-minute work break. If you need to cut to the chase, you can do so by finding user channels that pertain to the keywords you enter in the search text box. Here's how:

1. **From any YouTube page, enter the word or phrase that you think will return videos of interest to you.**

   The word or phrase that you enter is found in the video description, title, or tags.

2. **Click Search.**

   The YouTube site refreshes, and videos that pertain to the keywords you enter are displayed.

3. **Click Channels from the Search In menu.**

   YouTube refreshes and displays channels that contain the keyword or phrase you've entered. Figure 4-5 shows the results for the keyword *racing*.

4. **Click the user's channel icon.**

   YouTube displays the user's channel and an icon for each video uploaded by the user.

5. **Click the video you want to play.**

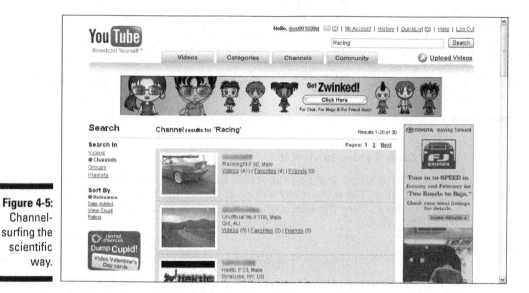

Figure 4-5: Channel-surfing the scientific way.

Searching for a fellow Tuber's channel

Some very popular Tubers are Internet legends. Some are just legends in their own minds. If you know a Tuber's username, you can search for all videos uploaded by the user and then get directed right to the Tuber's channel, where you can add comments to the channel, send a message to the Tuber, and so on. Now how cool is that? To search for videos uploaded by a user, perform the following steps:

1. **From any YouTube page, enter the username of the person whose videos you want to view.**

   If you don't know the full username of the person whose videos you want to view, enter as much as you can remember.

2. **Click Search.**

   The YouTube site refreshes with videos uploaded by the username you entered, as shown in Figure 4-6.

Figure 4-6:
Searching
for videos
uploaded by
a specific
user.

3. Click a video to view it.

At this stage, you can subscribe to the user's channel or view the user's channel. For more information on subscribing to a channel, see Chapter 5. You can view the user's channel by clicking her username, as shown in Figure 4-7.

Figure 4-7:
To view my
channel,
click my
username.

Indulging Your Special Interests with Groups

YouTube *groups* are communities revolving around a topic of interest. It might help to think of a group as a like-minded group of Tubers that like the same kind of video content. Any registered Tuber can create a group. After a group is created, any registered Tuber can join the group and upload her videos. You can conduct a search that reveals groups that pertain to the keywords you enter. Here's how:

1. **From any YouTube page, enter the word or phrase that pertains to the type of video group you want to find.**

   For example, if you want to find a group of Tubers who are into cooking, type the word **cooking** in the search text box.

2. **Click Search.**

   The YouTube site refreshes with videos uploaded by the username you entered.

3. **Click Groups.**

   The YouTube site refreshes and shows you the groups that pertain to the words or phrase you enter in the search text box. Figure 4-8 shows the results for the word *James Bond*.

Figure 4-8: Tip-toe through the YouTube groups.

4. Click a group icon.

The YouTube site refreshes and shows the home page for the group. Figure 4-9 shows the home page for a James Bond Group.

5. Click a video to view it.

YouTube serves up the video.

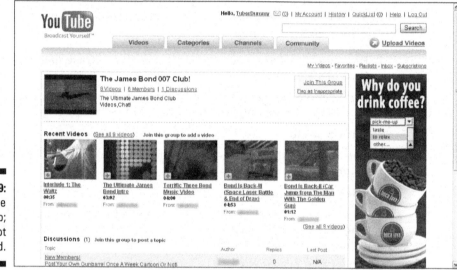

Figure 4-9: A YouTube group; shaken, not stirred.

You can also join a group. After you join a group you can add your own videos, participate in discussions, and more. We show you how to be a YouTube groupie in Chapter 5.

Searching through Playlists

Playlists are another kettle of fish. A *playlist* is a selection of videos that may or may not be related. Any registered Tuber can create a playlist. Responsible Tubers give their playlists titles that relate to the videos in the list. Irresponsible Tubers pick a title out of thin air. But that's what makes the Tube such an interesting place. You never know what you'll get when you click a channel, group, or playlist. To search through playlists, follow these steps:

1. **From any YouTube page, type the word or phrase that you think will return playlists of interest.**

   Try to think like a Tuber who'd take the time to assemble a cohesive playlist of related videos you'd like to watch and then enter the name you think he'd use. If you have a degree in psychology, this is easy.

2. **Click Search.**

   YouTube returns a list of videos from its vast vault that contains the specified word or phrase in the video title, description, or tags.

3. **Click Playlists.**

   The YouTube site refreshes, and you're presented with a list of playlists with titles containing your specified word or phrase. Figure 4-10 shows playlists that contain the word *Liszt*, as in Franz.

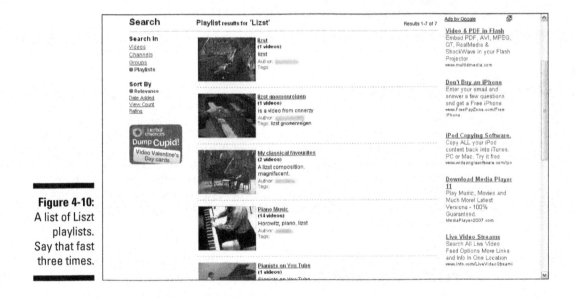

Figure 4-10:
A list of Liszt playlists. Say that fast three times.

4. **Click a playlist icon.**

   YouTube transports you to the playlist home page. Figure 4-11 shows a playlist with the word *Liszt* in the description.

   You can create your own playlists. We show you how in Chapter 5.

5. **Click a video to view it.**

Figure 4-11:
A piano
playlist from
the list
of Liszt
playlists.

Sorting a Search

If time is a major concern, don't surf the Tube. Because after you do one search, it inevitably leads to another and then another until you find yourself being sucked into the Tube. But if time is of the essence and you still want to surf the Tube, your first line of defense is an intelligent search. However, if you search for videos on a popular topic, such as recycling your cat's hair-balls, you may end up with several pages of results. In this case, your second line of defense is sorting the results, which is what we show you how to do in the upcoming sections.

Sorting by relevance

When YouTube returns results for words you enter in the search text box, they're sorted by relevance, which is the default method of sorting videos. It's not your fault, it's the fault of the Web design gurus at YouTube. When a search is sorted by relevance, YouTube arranges the video with the most relevant at the top of the heap. So what does *relevance*, in this context, mean?

Say, for example, you type the word **tuba** in the search text box and then click Search — or press Enter or Return for those of you who prefer the convenience of keyboard strokes. On the day this chapter was written, the word *tuba* returned the results, as shown in Figure 4-12.

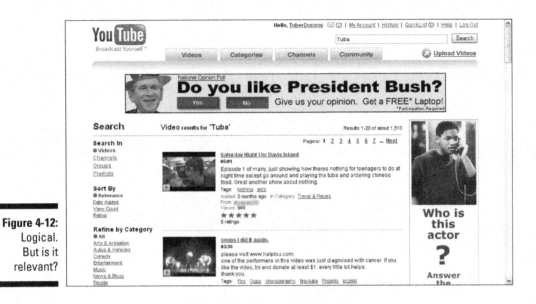

Figure 4-12:
Logical.
But is it
relevant?

It's not relevant to analyze why one video is more relevant than another. It's hidden in the YouTube search engine algorithm, although we have a sneaking suspicion it's the number of times the word or phrase you enter into the search text field appears in the title, description, and tags that were added to the video at the time it was uploaded. Smart Tubers pepper the title, description, and tags of the videos they upload with words that they think will cause their videos to be more relevant than those uploaded by other Tubers. And sometimes they get downright sneaky and add words that aren't relevant to the video at all, like the name of a sexy pop diva. These tricks will vault a video closer to the top of a search return. If the videos returned by the relevance sort aren't relevant to you, you can choose a different sort option, as we outline in the upcoming sections.

Sorting by Date Added

Do you like new stuff? Fresh, squeaky-clean, right-off-the-shelf-with-an-expiration-date-in-the-next-century stuff? If so, you can refine the results returned in a YouTube search so that the latest and greatest videos appear at the top of the results page. Here's how:

1. **From any YouTube page, type a word or phrase into the search text box.**

   Pick a word, any word that you think is relevant to the type of videos you like to watch.

   If at first you don't succeed in finding the videos you want to watch, type and type again another word or phrase into the search text field.

2. **Click Search.**

   YouTube displays icons of videos that are relevant to the word or phrase you specify.

3. **Click Date Added from the Sort By menu on the left side of the results page.**

   YouTube refreshes the results page with the most recently added video that pertains to your search at the top of the results list. Figure 4-13 shows the results for the word *tuba* when sorted by Date Added.

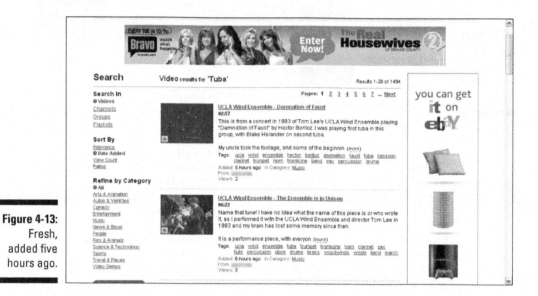

Figure 4-13: Fresh, added five hours ago.

Sorting by View Count

Sometimes the latest isn't the greatest. In fact, sometimes the latest can be quite awful. If you don't like the results that are returned by the default relevance sort or the Date Added sort, you can trust your fellow Tubers. I mean millions of viewers can't be wrong; can they? If you want to see the videos that pertain to your word or phrase of choice that have been viewed the most, just follow these steps:

1. **From any YouTube page, type a word or phrase into the search text box.**

   For consistency, we're going to stick with the word *tuba*.

2. **Click Search.**

   YouTube displays icons of videos that are relevant to the word or phrase you specify. Hmmm. A YouTube results page of videos of Tubers playing the tuba. The mind boggles.

3. **Click View Count from the Sort menu on the left-hand side of the results page.**

   YouTube shuffles the sort with the most viewed videos that pertain to your word or phrase at the top of the heap. Figure 4-14 shows our *tuba* search as sorted by view count. Yes, we watched the video. No, it contained nothing about tubas, but we assume we lost something in the translation because the title, description, and tags aren't in our native language. But it was viewed 179,175 times (including our viewing) in a week, received 232 comments, and was favorited 74 times. After reading a few of the comments, we assume the person who uploaded the video comes from Denmark. Does the fact that a tuba isn't present in this YouTube video signify that something is rotten in Denmark?

Favorited can't be found in any dictionary and will show up as an error if you type it in a word-processing application. YouTube is currently petitioning to Funk and Wagnalls to have the word added to the next edition of the English dictionary.

Figure 4-14: Our *tuba* was uploaded, viewed, and favorited.

Sorting by Rating

Truth in advertising is a wonderful thing. However, sometimes you get duped into watching a video that makes absolutely no sense to you even though it matches YouTube's test for relevancy, has been viewed a gazillion times, and was added yesterday. Do you close your browser and go off in a huff? Do you call 911 and ask for the video police? Before you frown in disgust and plan an assault on YouTube headquarters, you still have one fallback: Rating. To sort a search by rating, follow these steps:

1. **From any YouTube page, type a word or phrase into the search text box.**

   Tubas are big, brash, and sound great in parades, which is why we're looking for the perfect tuba video on the Tube.

2. **Click Search.**

   And once again we're confronted with pages and pages of video icons that may or may not have anything to do with the tuba.

3. **Click Rating.**

   The results are re-shuffled with the highest-rated videos at the top of the heap. Figure 4-15 shows our tuba search as sorted by rating. Yikes, the top-rated tuba video on the Tube only rates 2½ stars. Doug's cat Niki covered her ears when he played the video.

Figure 4-15: But it's the highest-rated tuba video on the Tube!

Sifting through a Category

Don't you just hate to be pigeonholed and put in a category? We know we do. We know we're originals and there are two broken molds with our names on them. But we're still categorized as geeks and authors. Oh well. But sometimes being categorized is a good thing; especially when it comes to video. You wouldn't upload a video of a prima ballerina into the Autos & Vehicles category, would you? (Never say never. A search on the word *ballet* in that category finds a 4×4 Mud Ballet video.) If your desk isn't in perfect order and your writing implements aren't sorted by size and popularity but you have categorized all of your files into neatly labeled folders, you'll be happy to know that you can modify your search results so that videos in only a certain category appear. Here's how to do it:

1. **From any YouTube page, type a word or phrase into the search text box.**

   You just know we're going to type the word **ballet** into the search text box, don't you?

2. **Click Search.**

   YouTube returns a neatly organized results page of videos that pertain to the word or phrase you specify. In our case the video's title, description, or tags contained the word *ballet*. However, we were looking for videos of ballet dancers, not videos of guys with the last name Ballet.

3. **Click the desired category from the left-hand side of the results page. (Because we're looking for ballet dancers, the desired category is the Arts & Animation category.)**

   YouTube shuffles the results and displays only videos that were uploaded to the category you specify. Figure 4-16 shows our results. However, if we wanted to view videos by the 1980s music group, Spandau Ballet, we could easily do so by clicking the Music category.

Figure 4-16: I had a date with a pretty ballerina . . . .

Refining Your Search to Target Results

YouTube is a blast, and we enjoy looking at entertaining videos. But we've also got a book to write and a publisher that wants it yesterday. So when we're doing research for the book, searching for compelling videos, and finding out all the cool things that can be done on YouTube, we have to cut to the chase and get it done. NOW. Otherwise, we wouldn't have time to write the book. The upcoming sections show you some of the tricks we use to quickly find what we want on the Tube.

Mixing and matching to find the perfect video

If you read this chapter from the start — we know who you are, we have influence in high places — you know there are a lot of ways to search the Tube. You also know that a lot of videos are on the Tube. The following list shows some techniques we discovered to find the videos we want to watch:

- ✔ **Current events:** To find videos about current events, click the Channels tab and then click Partners. CBS and Fox have channels on the Tube and post informative videos about current events.

- ✔ **Musicians:** To find videos of musicians, type the musician's or group's name in the search text box. After YouTube returns the first page of results, refine your search by clicking the Music category. This gives you the most relevant videos.

- ✔ **Sports celebrities:** To find videos about sports celebrities, type your hero's name in the search text box. After YouTube returns the first page of results, refine your search by clicking the Sports category.

- ✔ **Instructional:** To find instructional videos, type the name of the application or subject for which you want to find information. After YouTube returns the first page of results, click the Science & Technology category.

- ✔ **Similar categories:** If you find that you don't the get video you want after clicking a category, click a similar category. For example, if you're searching for videos about a comedian, your first choice would be to click the Comedy category after YouTube returns the first page of results. If you don't find what you want, click the Entertainment category. Comedians are entertainers. The same advice applies to musicians or musical groups.

After you fine-tune a search, you can refine it even further by clicking one of options from the Sort By menu.

Doing a tag-specific search

Millions of videos are vying for your attention on YouTube. Savvy Tubers add multiple tags to the videos they upload, which helps increase the chance that their video rates highly. The tags are listed whenever you play a video. These tags are also links that display all videos that have been uploaded with that tag. To do a tag-specific search:

1. **From any YouTube page, type a word or phrase into the search text box.**

   For this example, we did a search for the comedian David Spade.

2. **Click Search.**

YouTube returns results based on the word or phrase you entered.

3. **Fine-tune your search.**

   Remember, you can fine-tune a search by clicking one of the Search In options, sort the search by clicking one of the Sort By options, and further refine your search by clicking one of the Category options.

4. **Click a video icon.**

   YouTube serves up the video. Figure 4-17 shows a David Spade video that was uploaded by CBS. Notice that each tag is underlined, which means something happens when you click it. The category — Entertainment — and the Channel — CBS — are also underlined.

Figure 4-17: Click a tag, any tag.

Tags

If a video has more tags than will fit on a single line, a More link is displayed. Click the link to reveal all tags associated with the video.

5. **Click a tag.**

   YouTube refreshes the page and displays all videos that match the tag you clicked. At this stage, you refine the search by clicking one of the Search In options, sort the search by clicking one of the Sort By options, and further refine your search by clicking one of the Category options.

Click the Channel link to view the user's channel. Click the Category link to view the Most Viewed (Today) videos in the category.

Expediting Your Search with Chris and Doug's Tips and Tricks

But wait, there's more! When you write a book about a computer application, you have a tendency to experiment with things, stretch the envelope, and let your inner child run amuck. We took the same approach with this book and experimented with YouTube features and options. And we did discover a couple of things we'd like to share with you, Dear Reader. So take a few more minutes and read the following sections to find out how to tweak a YouTube search and to search for a video based on the audio within the clip.

Performing a "faux" Boolean search

If you've ever done a Boolean search at a search engine or in an application, like Adobe Acrobat, you know that you use operators to refine your search. With a search engine or application that has full-blown Boolean boogie capabilities, you can use the following operators: AND, OR, and NOT. When you do a Boolean search, each word or phrase in the search is in quotes.

The Boolean search comes from Boolean algebra, which uses operators to compare mathematical expressions. Boolean algebra was invented by George Boole, a British mathematician and philosopher.

For example, typing **"Dogs" NOT "Cats"** into a search engine that supports a Boolean search returns Web pages that contain information about dogs and not cats. You can't use the OR or NOT operators on YouTube, but you can use the AND operator. Follow this example to see how it works.

1. **From any YouTube page, type the name** George Harrison **in the search text box.**

   For those of you who may be too young to remember, George Harrison was known as "The Quiet Beatle."

2. **Click Search.**

   YouTube returns a list of videos with the name *George Harrison* in the video title, description, or tags. As of this writing, the search returned over 40 pages of George Harrison videos. That's great if you're looking for George Harrison videos, but what if you want to search for a specific video, say the video for the song, "Faster." If you type **Faster** in the search text box, YouTube serves up videos with the word *Faster* in the video title, description, or tags. To narrow it down to the video of George Harrison's song, "Faster," read on.

3. **Type** "George Harrison" AND "Faster" **in the text search box.**

4. Click Search.

YouTube displays all videos with *George Harrison* and *Faster* in the title, description, or tags, as shown in Figure 4-18. Talk about saving some time. Try our "faux" Boolean search whenever you want to quickly find specific videos.

Figure 4-18:
He's the master of searching faster.

Using the Podzinger search engine

When you perform a search on YouTube, the search engine looks for instances of the word or phrase you enter in the video title, description, and tags. Wouldn't it be cool if you could search the actual audio track of a video? Well we found a site that does search the audio of a video. Hmmm. You mean you're not impressed? Think about it. If you know a quote from a video you're trying to find, you can follow these steps to locate the video:

1. Enter www.podzinger.com **into your Web browser.**

2. Click the YouTube tab.

The browser refreshes, and you're presented with a text field just begging you to type something in it.

3. Type the quote you want to find.

The quote must be in quotation marks. You don't have to enter the whole phrase. We were looking for a video show of former Formula 1 World Champion Damon Hill, so we typed **"Damon Hill"** in the text field.

4. Click Zing It.

The page refreshes and returns videos in which the phrase appears. Depending on the phrase you type, you may also get some videos in which the phrase appears in the title, description, and tags. Podzinger returned several videos with Damon Hill in the audio. We played one, as shown in Figure 4-19. Notice that the quote appears to the right of the video thumbnail. It also lists the time and frame on which the quote can be heard.

Figure 4-19:
Zing It.

5. Click the icon to play the video.

The video appears in the Podzinger player. Notice the inverted triangle. This is the exact place in the video where the quote can be heard. The icons below the player enable you to get the HTML, which can be used to embed the video in a Web page or blog, get the URL where the video can be found, or e-mail the video to a friend. The first options have buttons that enable you to copy the HTML and URL to the clipboard. The option to e-mail opens a form in which you enter the e-mail address of the desired recipient and then compose a message.

Chapter 5

Customizing Your YouTube Experience

In This Chapter

▶ Saving videos

▶ Creating playlists

▶ Subscribing to a channel

▶ Changing your YouTube info

▶ Changing your channel design

*Y*ouTube is all about having fun and watching the type of videos that pique your curiosity. When you find something you really like, you may want to watch it again. If you're that kind of Tuber, you'll be happy to know you can save your favorite videos. Like many visitors of the Tube, your interests are probably varied. If so, you watch videos about a wide range of topics, which means you may end up with so many favorite videos that you have to sift through dozens before finding the one you want to watch. Those clever YouTube Web designers came up with a solution: the playlist. You can segregate videos into playlists that make sense to everybody, or to just you. After all, it's your Tube.

Some way-cool users on the Tube upload your kind of videos. Wouldn't it be nice to go to a YouTube portal where you can find your kind of videos? This is exactly what happens when you subscribe to a fellow Tuber's channel; a link to the channel is added to the Subscription section of your channel. That's right, Virginia, if you're a registered Tuber, you have a channel that other Tubers can tune in to. (Registering is covered in Chapter 2.) You can make your channel as unique as you are by customizing it. In this chapter, we show you how to customize your channel, subscribe to other Tubers' channels, save your favorite videos, and more. But if your eyes are a bit bleary from your last session on the Tube, douse them with Visine and read on.

Saving Your Favorite Videos

I love videos about Formula One racing and music. Chris likes videos of comedians and singers doing their thing. Yeah, we're different, which for you is a good thing. With different personalities and tastes, you get multiple viewpoints, which is like multiple personalities with none of the scary medical side effects. When you mark a video as a favorite, it's saved to the Favorites section of your channel. Other viewers — and for that matter, you — can watch their favorites when they visit your channel. To add a video to your favorites, follow these steps:

1. **Search for your one-in-a-million video.**

   We agree that looking for a favorite video is like looking for a needle in a haystack — that is, unless you follow the sage advice we present in Chapter 4. You *did* read Chapter 4, didn't you?

2. **Play the video.**

   Lay back and groove to the video, especially if it's a rainy day. While you're watching the video, figure out whether it actually deserves to be added to your favorites.

3. **If the video passes your litmus test for greatness, click the Save to Favorites link that's located beneath the video playback controller**.

   The Add Video to Favorites dialog box appears, as shown in Figure 5-1.

4. **Click OK.**

   An icon for the video appears in the Favorites section of your Channel.

Figure 5-1:
Yet another
favorite
video.

Have It Your Way with Your Own Playlist

Playlists are compilations of videos. A playlist can be played in its entirety, or you can pick and choose videos from the list to watch. We're logical kind of guys; you have to be when you write a book. We create a logical outline and then follow it so you get a book that makes sense. Therefore, we tend to apply similar logic when creating stuff like playlists. The videos within one of our playlists have a common theme, such as music or auto racing. You can be logical when creating your playlist or you can put together a hodge-podge of videos that appeal to you. Before you can add videos to a playlist, you have to create one. In the upcoming sections, we show you the different ways to create a playlist. We also show you how to create the playlist's red-headed cousin — the QuickList.

Creating a QuickList

When you're perusing the Tube, you may find several videos you want to watch. You can watch each video that appeals to you as soon as you find it. However, if you're pressed for time, you can create a QuickList of videos and play them later. As long as you don't log out of YouTube or close your browser, you can view the videos on your QuickList after doing more mundane tasks, like making money for your boss. However, if you take selections from a QuickList and save them as Favorites, or add them to a Playlist, you'll easily be able to find and view the video from your Channel next time you log on to the Tube. To create a QuickList, follow these steps:

1. **Log on to YouTube.**

   Go to www.YouTube.com and click the Log In link. On the Log In page, enter your username and password and then click Log In.

2. **Start surfing the Tube.**

   You can be scientific and search for videos or just take the hit-and-miss approach. Sometimes a good place to start is the home page, which has a list of featured videos. Each video icon has a plus sign (+) in its lower-left corner, as shown in Figure 5-2.

3. **Click the plus sign (+) icon of any video you want to add to your QuickList.**

   When you add videos to your QuickList, the number next to the QuickList link increases. (See Figure 5-3.)

4. **Continue adding videos to your QuickList.**

   There's probably a limit to the number of videos you can add to a QuickList, but we didn't find it. We stopped at 101. At that point, we figured it was no longer a QuickList, just a VeryLongList.

Figure 5-2:
If you click
the plus sign
icon, the
video is
added to a
QuickList. It
all adds up.

Plus sign icons

Figure 5-3:
He clicked
the plus sign
icon three
times.

5. **Click the QuickList link, as shown in Figure 5-3.**

   The YouTube site refreshes, and your QuickList is displayed, as shown in Figure 5-4. Notice that each video icon has a Remove button. From this view of the video list, you have the following options:

   • Click the Remove button to remove a video from the list.

   • Select the Remove Videos from QuickList as I Watch Them check box to remove the video currently being played from the QuickList.

   • Click Play All Videos to play each video in turn.

   • Click Save as a Playlist to save QuickList videos as a playlist.

     A QuickList disappears as soon as you log out of YouTube. A Playlist lasts forever, or until you cancel your YouTube account.

   • Click Clear QuickList to remove all videos from the QuickList.

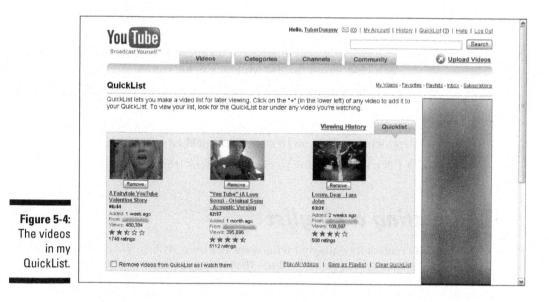

Figure 5-4:
The videos
in my
QuickList.

6. **Click a video icon.**

The video begins to play. The entire QuickList is displayed beneath the video currently playing, as shown in Figure 5-5. When you play a QuickList in this manner, you have the following options:

- Click the Play All button to play the QuickList in the order in which it was created.

- Click Play Next to play the next video on your QuickList.

Figure 5-5:
Quiet, I'm
watching my
QuickList.

- Click the icon that looks like a trash can to remove a video from the QuickList.

- Select the Remove Videos as I Watch Them check box to remove each video from the list while it's being watched.

- Click the Manage link to return to the view shown in Figure 5-4, which enables you to quickly remove videos from the QuickList.

- Click the Save link to open the Create/Edit QuickList dialog box, which enables you to save the QuickList as a Playlist.

- Click the Clear link to clear all videos from the QuickList.

Creating a playlist

You can create a new playlist whenever the urge strikes. We create playlists when we uncover a genre of videos that we never knew existed on YouTube. A playlist can be public — every Peter, Paul, and Mary on the Tube can see it; or private — only people on your Friends or Family list can view the playlist. You specify whether the list is public or private when you create it. In the upcoming sections, we show you every way to create a playlist.

Creating a playlist from the Video page

It's happened to us more than once. We stumble across a really cool video and think that we want to find similar videos. Then the blinding flash of insight comes, and we know this video will be one of many on a new playlist. To create a playlist while watching a video, follow these steps:

1. **Click the Save to Favorites link that's located beneath the video play-back controller.**

   The Save to Favorites dialog box appears.

2. **Choose New Playlist from the Add Video to Playlist drop-down list.**

   The Create/Edit Playlist dialog box appears.

3. **Enter a name for the playlist.**

   This is the name that's displayed for the playlist in the Playlist section of your channel.

4. **Enter a description for the playlist.**

   If you're logical, like the pointy-eared Vulcan from Star Trek, you can enter a fitting description for the videos in the playlist; you know, something more fitting than "My favorite videos."

5. **Enter tags for the playlist.**

   Tags are bits of descriptive information about the playlist. Tags can be multiple words. Each tag must be separated by a space. Because tags are also links, they can be used by the Tube community to find your playlist. Tags are also used as search criteria.

6. **In the Privacy section, click the Public or Private radio buttons.**

    This option decides whether every Tuber and his little brother can watch the video, or just those on your Friends or Family list. Figure 5-6 shows a playlist in the making.

7. **Click Save Playlist Info.**

    The playlist is saved and appears in the Playlists section of your channel.

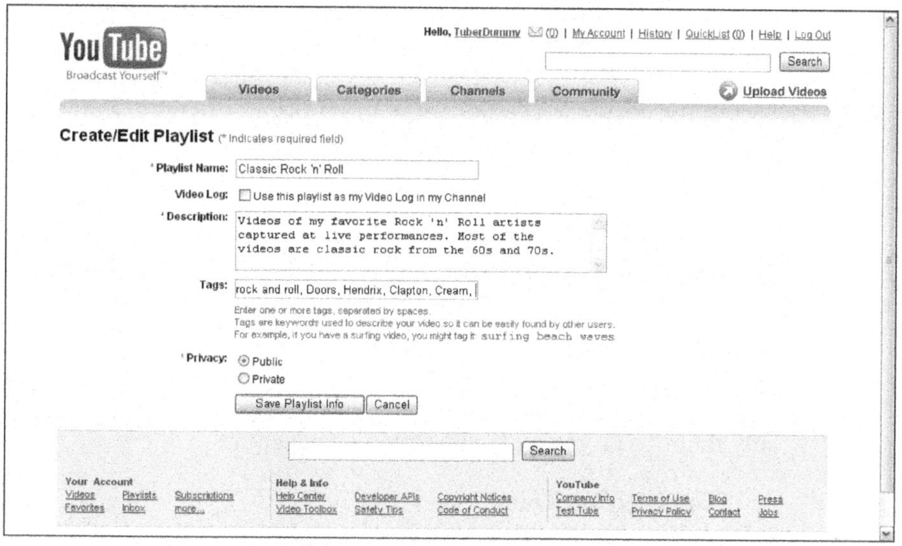

Figure 5-6: Creating a new playlist.

Creating a playlist from a QuickList

If you want to populate a playlist quickly, QuickList is the best tool. When we decide we want to create a new playlist of related videos, we use our tried-and-true Tube search tactics to create a list of likely suspects and then we create a Playlist from the QuickList as follows:

1. **Create a QuickList.**

    If you don't know how to create a QuickList, moisten your thumb and flip back a couple of pages to the section, "Creating a QuickList," earlier in this chapter.

2. **Remove the videos that you don't want on the playlist.**

    If you don't have enough time to review the QuickList, add all the videos to the playlist. If you don't like a video on your playlist, you can delete it while modifying the playlist.

  3. **Click the Save as Playlist link.**

  The Create/Edit Playlist dialog box appears.

  4. **Enter a name for the playlist.**

  This is the name that's displayed for the playlist in the Playlist section of your channel.

  5. **Enter a description for the playlist.**

  Enter a fitting description for the videos in the playlist.

  6. **Enter tags for the playlist.**

  Tags are information about the playlist that fellow Tubers can use to search for your playlist. Tags can be multiple words. Each tag must be separated by a space.

  7. **In the Privacy section, click the Public or Private radio buttons.**

  This option decides whether every Tuber and his little brother can watch the video or just those on your Friends or Family list.

  8. **Click Save Playlist Info.**

  The playlist is saved.

Creating a playlist from your account

You can also create a playlist for future use. When you create a playlist from your account, you start with a blank canvas to which you can add videos at any time. To create a playlist from your account

  1. **Log in to YouTube.**

  It's easy. Go to the YouTube Web site (www.youtube.com), enter your username and password in the appropriate fields, and then click Log In.

  2. **Click the My Account link.**

  It's to the right of your username. After clicking the My Account Link, your account page appears.

  3. **Click Playlists.**

  Your first playlist appears, as shown in Figure 5-7.

  4. **Click Create Playlist.**

  The Create/Edit Playlist dialog box appears, as shown in Figure 5-8.

  5. **Entire the required information.**

  YouTube doesn't let you create a playlist unless you enter a name and description for the playlist. We advise that you enter information in the Tags field as well. Tags are words that pertain to the video. Separate each tag with a space. Other Tubers can find your playlist by entering the tag in a YouTube Search text field and then choosing the Playlists option from the Search In menu on the results page.

Figure 5-7:
You've got
playlists.

6. Choose whether the playlist is public or private.

It's as simple as clicking the Public or Private radio buttons. If you choose to make your playlist public, anybody who surfs the YouTube video portal can view your playlist. If you choose the latter option, only registered Tubers on your Friends or Family list have access to the playlist.

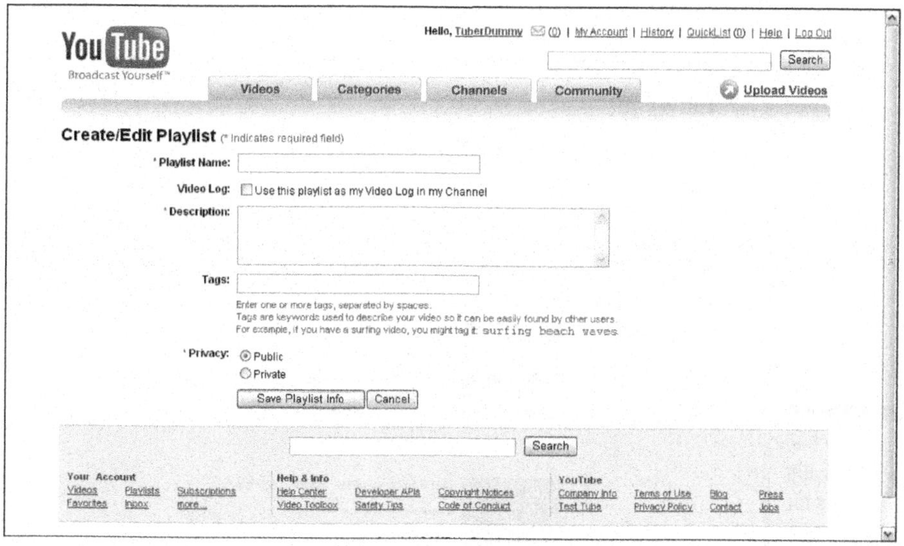

Figure 5-8:
Fill in the
blanks to
create a
blank
playlist.

Customizing a playlist

You can change a playlist at any time. There are several reasons you may want to change a playlist. You may grow tired of one or more videos on your playlist, or for some reason or another a video on your playlist may no longer be available. To modify a playlist, follow these steps:

1. **Log in to YouTube.**

   It's easy. Go to the YouTube Web site (www.youtube.com), enter your username and password in the appropriate fields, and then click Log In.

2. **Click the My Account link.**

   It's to the right of your username. After clicking the My Account Link, your account page appears.

3. **Click Playlists.**

   Your first playlist appears.

4. **Choose the playlist you want to modify.**

   A list of your playlists is displayed on the left side of your Playlists page. Figure 5-9 shows a playlist that can be modified. Notice that a number is to the right of each video in the playlist. The last video added to the playlist is number one on the hit parade.

5. **To change the name of the playlist, description, tags, or the playlist's status from private to public (or vice versa), click Edit.**

   The Create/Edit Playlist page appears, as shown in Figure 5-10. Modify the desired parameters and then click Save Playlist Info.

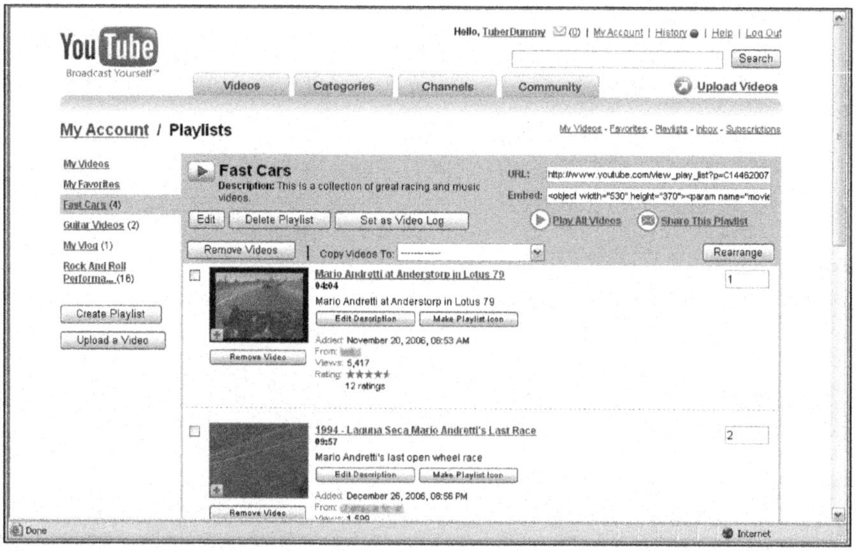

Figure 5-9: Modifying playlists for fun and profit.

Figure 5-10:
You can
modify a
playlist's
name,
description,
and so on.

6. **To remove a playlist from your channel, click Delete Playlist.**

   YouTube removes all records of the playlist from your channel.

7. **To rearrange the order in which videos on your playlist are played, enter the desired number in the text field to the right of the video and then click Rearrange.**

   YouTube puts the videos in the desired order.

8. **To remove one or more videos from the playlist, click the check box to the left of any video you want to remove and then click Remove.**

   The selected videos are removed from your playlist.

9. **To change the description of a video, click the Edit Description button beneath the video whose description you want to change.**

   The Edit Video Description page appears, as shown in Figure 5-11.

10. **Click the Use Custom Title and Description check box.**

11. **Enter the desired title and description in the appropriate text fields.**

    You can modify the title and description of the videos as they appear on your playlist. This however, doesn't modify the title and description of the video when it's viewed from the channel to which it was uploaded.

12. **Click the Submit button.**

    The video's title and description are changed in your playlist.

    You can also share a video from your playlist, share the entire playlist with Tubers on your Friends or Family list, or for that matter, share the playlist with anybody. For more information on sharing video and playlists, see Chapter 6.

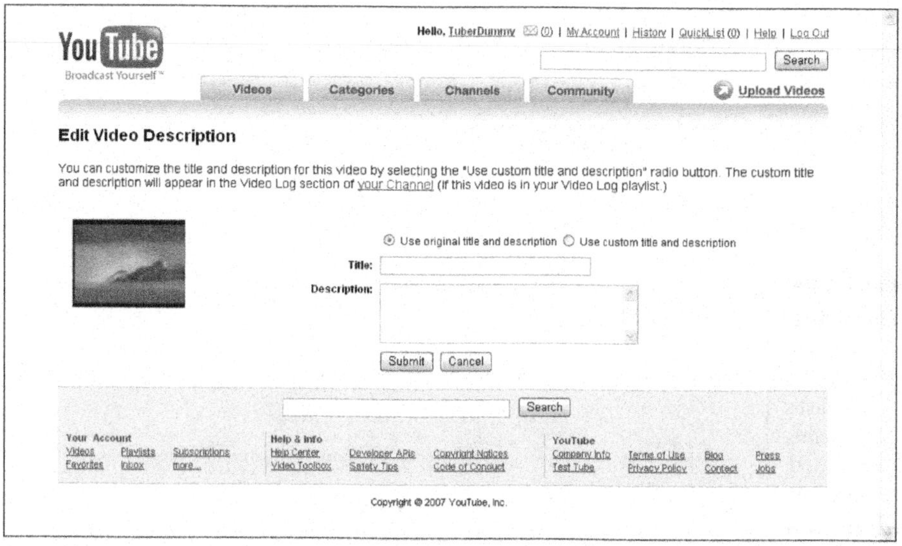

Figure 5-11:
You can
edit the
description
of any video
on a playlist.

13. **To copy videos to another playlist, click the check boxes of the videos you want to copy and then choose the desired playlist from the Copy Videos To drop-down list.**

    The videos are copied to the desired playlist. Note that you can also start a new playlist by choosing that option from the drop-down list.

    If a playlist gets a tad too large for your liking, copy half of the videos to a new playlist and then delete them from the original playlist on which they appeared.

14. **Continue modifying the playlist until it's just the way you like it.**

    If you have a lot of videos on the playlist you're modifying, you'll see the number of pages listed at the bottom of the Web page. You can use these links to edit, remove, or rearrange other videos on your playlist.

15. **Navigate to any other YouTube page after you finish modifying the playlist.**

    Your changes to the playlist are saved.

Adding videos to an existing playlist

After you create a playlist, you can add videos to it at any time. New videos are uploaded to YouTube every minute of every day. So, chances are, every time you visit the Tube you'll find new videos that are perfect for an existing playlist. To add a video to one of your playlists

1. **Go to YouTube and log in, please.**

   If the Tube doesn't know who you are, how can you expect to add videos to your playlists?

2. **Surf newly uploaded videos or search for videos of interest.**

3. **When you find a video you like, click Save to Favorites.**

   The page refreshes, and the Save to Favorites dialog box appears.

4. **Choose the desired playlist from the Add Video To A Playlist drop-down list (see Figure 5-12).**

5. **Click OK.**

   The video is added to the playlist.

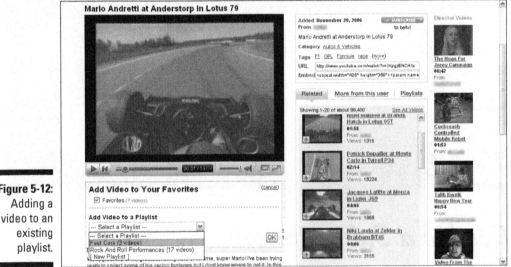

Figure 5-12: Adding a video to an existing playlist.

Channel Surfing

What's the best way to find interesting videos? Surfing the Tube! Of course, surfing is a random way of finding videos — you can find every type of video from a cat chasing her tail, to vlogs, to East European music videos. We've coined the technical term, *crap shoot* for blindly surfing the Tube. To find your type of video, here's what you do:

1. **Click the Channels tab.**

   YouTube displays a list of the channels most subscribed to for the current week.

2. **Click a channel that looks interesting.**

   YouTube displays the Tuber's channel, as shown in Figure 5-13.

3. **Play the videos.**

   To mosey back to the channel, click your browser's back button and then view more of the channel's videos. If you really like what you see, you can subscribe to the channel from the Video page. Or you can click one of the videos suggested by YouTube.

Figure 5-13:
Channel surfing for cool videos.

Get Me a Subscription

When you find a video you like by surfing channels, chances are the Tuber whose channel is linked to that video has more videos that are cool. If he's a frequent contributor to the Tube, you can subscribe to his channel and your subscription is added to the Subscriptions section of your channel. When you subscribe to a fellow Tuber's channel, and he uploads new videos, the next time you log in the new videos appear in the Your Subscriptions section on the YouTube home page. Now how cool is that?

You can subscribe to a channel from the Video page. We use this option when a video absolutely knocks our socks off. However, sometimes we prefer to be cautious and make sure the Tuber whose video we're watching isn't a one-hit wonder. In that case, we go to the Tuber's channel and sample some of her other offerings. If we like what we see, we leave a comment on her channel and subscribe to her channel from her channel.

Subscribing to a channel from the Video page

If you decide that you want to subscribe to a Tuber's channel after viewing a video, you can easily do so. This option is for those who often see a beautiful girl walking down the street and decide they've been struck by Cupid's arrow. Fortunately, your chances for success when subscribing to a channel that is great after looking at one video are better than actually trying to strike up a conversation with Ms. Pretty Woman and getting her to go on a date with you. To subscribe to a channel from the Video page, follow these steps:

1. **Find a video you really like.**

2. **Play the video.**

   While you play the video, pay careful attention to your senses. If you feel the hair on the back of your neck starting to stand up or if you feel your heart pounding in your chest, this may be a sign that you should subscribe to the Tuber's channel.

3. **Click the Subscribe button (see Figure 5-14).**

   The channel is added to the Subscriptions section of your channel.

Figure 5-14: Where else in the world can you get a free subscription?

The subscribe button

Subscribing to a channel from a channel

What you see is what you get. Sometimes that's true, and other times you can't read a book by its cover. When we decide it's best to err on the side of caution before subscribing to a channel, we go to the Tuber's channel and check out a few more videos before subscribing. Sometimes our suspicions prove correct because the channel has only one video. To subscribe to a channel from a channel, follow these steps:

1. **Find and play a video that piques your curiosity.**

2. **Click the Tuber's username to be transported to his channel.**

3. **Peruse the channel's videos.**

   Sometimes you can tell by the amount of videos in the channel, the frequency of upload, and the icons whether to dip your toe into the shallow end of the channel and subscribe; other times, you have to play a few more videos.

4. **Click the Subscribe button to subscribe to the channel.**

   The lovely orange Subscribe button becomes a dingy gray Un-Subscribe button. Figure 5-15 shows a channel chock-full of videos just waiting for Tubers with good taste to plunk down a subscription.

When someone subscribes to your channel, YouTube sends you an e-mail telling you the name of the lucky subscriber who has such good taste in video.

Figure 5-15:
A free subscription is one click away.

Subscribing to a tag

Tubers are no dummies when it comes to adding tags to their videos. And of course, they'll be even better at it after reading this book. Okay, we'll step off our soapbox and get back to the business of writing. If you like videos about a certain subject, chances are they all share a common tag. You can view videos about a subject by subscribing to a tag as follows:

1. **Log in to YouTube.**

2. **Click the Subscriptions link.**

   It's right below the Community tab preceded by My:. After clicking the link, the My Account/My Subscriptions page appears (see Figure 5-16).

3. **Enter a word in the Subscribe to Tags text field.**

   Enter the word that you think will deliver videos that contain blissful moments.

4. **Click Subscribe.**

   The tag to which you've subscribed appears on the left hand of the My Account/My Subscriptions page.

If you find a channel starts getting polluted or the Tuber doesn't upload videos as often as she used to, go to the channel and click the Un-Subscribe button.

Figure 5-16:
Subscribe to
a tag here.

Communing with a Group

YouTube's got groups, lots of groups. A group is a collection of individuals who have similar taste in video and related interests. We look for the groups that have lots of members and lots of videos. When you find a group that trips your trigger, join it. If you don't find a group that interests you, create one. We show you how to do both in the upcoming sections.

Joining a Group

There's a lot of video on the Tube; more than you could possibly hope to view in a lifetime. There are also a lot of videos that are not relevant to your tastes. That's why there's a Search text box on every page — it's one way to separate the wheat from the chaff. There's another way, though, to find the type of video you want to watch: Join a group. A *group* consists of Tubers who share common interests. Their videos are displayed on the group page. Before you join a group, you need to find one that piques your interest and then join it. To join a group, log on to YouTube and follow these steps:

1. **Log on to YouTube.**

   Go to the Tube, enter your username and password, and click Login.

2. **Click your username link that appears at the top of the page.**

   You're tuned in to your channel.

3. **Type the word or phrase that relates to the type of group you want to join in the Search text box on the top of any YouTube page.**

   This returns a list of videos that contain the word or phrase you typed in the video title, description, or tags.

4. **Click Groups from the Search In menu.**

   The page refreshes and lists the groups that contain the word or phrase you typed in the group title, description, or tags. Figure 5-17 shows the results from a group search using the word photographers.

5. **Click a group that looks interesting.**

   It's your oyster. However, if the group only has one member and one video, chances are you won't find what you're looking for. Figure 5-18 shows a photography group that caught Doug's attention.

6. **Click the Join This Group button.**

   Congratulations, you're a groupie. You are now a member of the group, and you're entitled to add videos to the group's YouTube page.

Figure 5-17: Searching for a group to join.

Figure 5-18: A group with lots of members and lots of videos.

To add video to a group you've joined, follow these steps:

1. **Log on to YouTube.**

   Go to www.youtube.com, enter your username and password in the appropriate fields, and click Login.

2. **Click your username link that appears at the top of the page.**

   You're tuned in to your channel.

3. **Click the Groups link.**

   The page refreshes and a list of your groups appears as shown in Figure 5-19.

4. **Click the applicable group icon.**

   Scotty beams you up to the group's page (see Figure 5-20).

5. **Click the Add Videos link.**

   A list of your videos appears (see Figure 5-21). Note that there are several links. You can add videos from:

   - **My Videos:** Click this link to display all videos you've uploaded.

   - **My Favorites:** Click this link to display a list of videos you've added to your Favorites list.

   - **My Top Videos:** Click this link to display videos you've uploaded in order of popularity. The most viewed videos appear at the top of the page.

   - **My Video Log:** Click this link to display videos you've added to your video log.

   - **Upload Videos:** Click this link to upload a video, add it to your channel, and add it to the group.

6. **Click the check box for the video you want to add to the group, and then click the Add To Group button.**

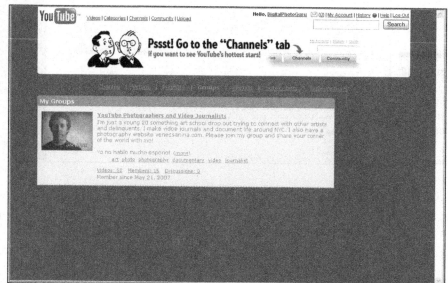

Figure 5-19:
A place for
my groups.

Figure 5-20: I'm a card-carrying member of this group.

Your video is added to the group and appears at the top of the group's page.

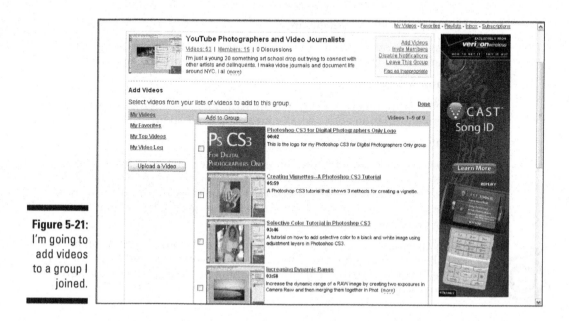

Figure 5-21: I'm going to add videos to a group I joined.

After you join a group, you can add your two cents to any discussion currently in progress. You can also start a discussion by clicking the Add Topic button and then following the prompts.

Creating a Group

So what do you do when you don't find a group with videos or discussions that you like? You create your own, of course. Creating a group is like uploading a video, but different. Just follow these steps:

1. **Log on to YouTube.**

   Use your favorite Web browser to navigate to the Tube, enter your username and password in the appropriate fields, and click Login.

2. **Click the My Account link.**

   You're transported to the My Account page.

3. **Scroll to the My Groups section.**

   It's way at the bottom of the page; you know, below the fold, just north of Tierra del Fuego.

4. **Click the Create a Group link.**

   The Create a Group page appears (see Figure 5-22).

5. **Enter a name for the group.**

   It's your group. However, we suggest you give the group a descriptive name that will give potential members an idea of what to expect.

6. **Enter a description.**

   Hello! Truth in advertising. The description should give potential members information about what your group is all about, Alfie.

7. **Enter tags for your group.**

   You can enter as many tags as you want. Remember to leave a space between each tag. Tags are words that are relevant to the type of video that will appear in your group. Tags are used by the YouTube search engine to direct potential members to your group. For a full course serving on tags, see Chapter 8.

If you want your group to be found, mirror the words you think people will use to find your group in the name, description, and tags. For example, if you're creating a group for fashion photographers, make sure those words appear in the name, description, and tags.

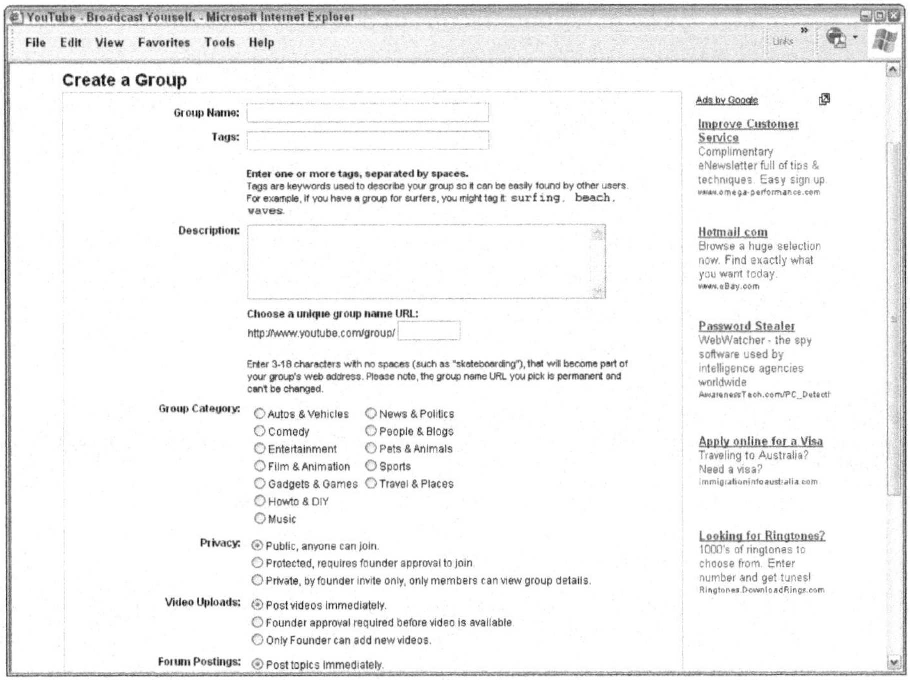

Figure 5-22:
Creating a
group.

8. **Enter a URL for your group.**

   You can send the URL to people whom you want to see your group, and potentially invite to join your group. Create a URL without spaces, as spaces confuse certain Web browsers. If you must separate words in your URL, type an underscore between them.

9. **Choose a category for your group.**

   It's a safe bet to use the same category you use when you upload your videos.

10. **Choose an option in the Privacy section.**

    You can make the channel public, protected (which requires permission by the founder, a.k.a, you, to join), or private for founder invite only.

11. **Choose an option for video uploads.**

    You can allow group members to post videos immediately, require permission by you before videos are added to your group, or enable only yourself to upload video. The latter option may limit the number of fellow Tubers that actually join your group.

12. Choose an option for forum postings.

You can allow members to post a topic without your permission, require your permission before posting a topic, or allow only the founder (that would be you) to post a new topic.

13. Choose an option in the Group Icon section.

Your options are to choose the video from which a frame is displayed as the group icon, or use a frame from the video last added to the group as the group icon.

14. Click Create Group.

Your group is created, but you don't have any videos there.

Creating a group is yet another way to meet fellow Tubers who share your interests, while at the same time creating more attention to your videos.

To add videos to your group, follow these steps:

1. Log on to YouTube.

Navigate to the Tube, enter your username and password in the appropriate text fields and click Login.

2. Click the My Account link.

The My Account page appears.

3. Scroll to the Groups section, and then click My Groups.

My Account/My Group page appears and displays a list of the groups you've joined and those that you own.

4. Click the group you just created.

The group information appears.

5. Click the Add Videos link.

A list of your videos appears. You can add videos from

- **My Videos:** Click this link to display all videos you've uploaded.

- **My Favorites:** Click this link to display a list of videos you've added to your Favorites list.

- **My Top Videos:** Click this link to display videos you've uploaded in order of popularity. The most viewed videos appear at the top of the page.

- **My Video Log:** Click this link to display videos you've added to your video log.

- **Upload Videos:** Click this link to upload a video, add it to your channel, and add it to the group.

6. **Click the check box for the videos you want to add to the group, and then click the Add To Group button.**

   The videos are added to your group.

7. **Click Manage Videos.**

   A list of group videos appears (see Figure 5-23). If you're requiring approval for videos to be added to your group, you access them by clicking the Videos for Approval link.

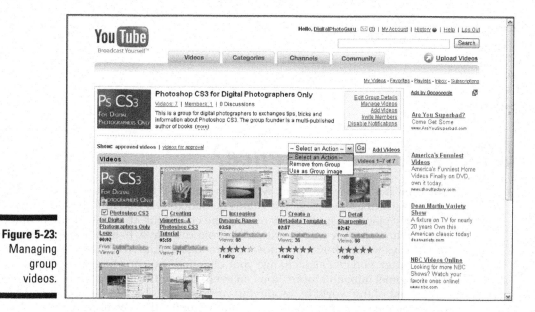

Figure 5-23: Managing group videos.

8. **Select a video and then choose an action from the Select an Action drop-down menu.**

   Your choices are: Remove from Group or Use as Group Image.

9. **Click Go.**

   YouTube applies the action to the video. Figure 5-24 shows a group that has been created and filled with videos. All it needs is some members.

Figure 5-24:
All the
group needs
is members.

What's Your Preference?

YouTube is a wonderful thing. Where else can you go and share your videos with the world as well as watch videos uploaded by a vast multitude of Tubers? Not many places that we know of. And the cool thing about the Tube is that you can have it your way — with fries, hold the mayo. In addition to all the other ways we've shown you how to personalize your YouTube experience in this chapter, you can also change your channel. You can change your personal info, channel info, and more. You can even change the way your channel looks to the rest of the world by modifying your current channel design. This is like changing your preferences for a computer application. Want to know more? Read on!

Changing your channel info

When you set up your YouTube account, you supply certain information that describes your channel and what visitors can expect to see when they view one of your videos. You can also specify which video is featured and so on. To modify your channel info

1. **Log in to the Tube.**

2. **Click the My Account link.**

   YouTube displays your account page.

3. **Scroll to the Channel Settings section of the page.**

   If you're a super geek who has dual monitors and a ridiculously large desktop size, you may not need to scroll down.

4. **Click the Channel Info link.**

   The My Account/Edit Channel Info page appears, which enables you to change your channel info (see Figure 5-25).

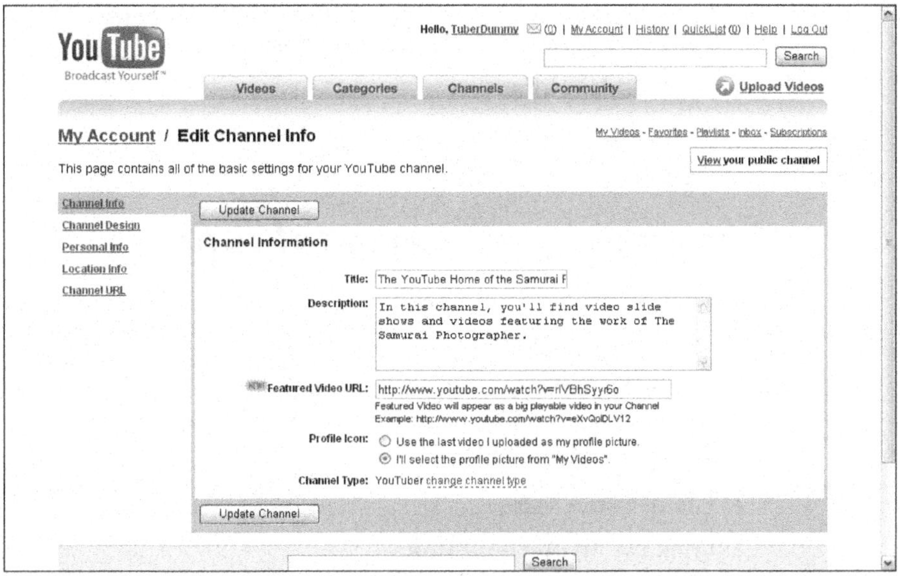

Figure 5-25: Time to give the old channel an overhaul.

5. **Modify the channel title and channel description.**

   If you've been hoodwinking other Tubers with false information, now's your chance to come clean.

6. **If desired, change the Featured Video URL.**

   This is the video that's featured on your page. To change this, you need to enter the URL to a different video that you've uploaded. The easiest way to do this is to open a new browser window and then play the video you want to feature. Copy the URL from the URL text field to the right of the video and then paste it in the Featured Video URL field in the page where you're modifying your channel info.

7. **In the Profile Icon section, choose whether to display an icon from the last video uploaded or whether to display an icon from other videos you've uploaded.**

   If you choose the latter option, you can specify which video is displayed as the Profile Icon by clicking the Make Channel Icon button below the desired video on the My Account/Videos page.

The video icon shows the frame that's displayed as a channel icon if you choose that video. To ensure that a certain image is displayed as a channel icon, import only that image and nothing else into a video editing application and then export the project as a video. The single image that makes up the video is displayed as the channel icon after you specify the video for that purpose.

8. **To change your channel type, click the Change Channel Type link.**

   The New Channel Type title appears. You can change your channel type by choosing one of the following options from the drop-down list: YouTuber, Director, Musician, Comedian, or Guru.

9. **Click Update Channel.**

   Voilà! Your channel is updated.

Changing your personal info

When you set up an account with YouTube, you supply some information about yourself. Fortunately, they don't ask for your credit card number, banking information, or dress size. You can determine how much personal information is displayed on your channel by modifying your personal info. For that matter, you can even add some personal information. To change your personal information

1. **Log in to the Tube.**

2. **Click the My Account link.**

   YouTube displays your account page and a whole lot of links.

3. **Scroll to the Channel Settings section of the page.**

   It's way down on the southern section of the page.

4. **Click the Personal Info link.**

   The My Account/Edit Personal Info page appears with a lot of text fields, more than can be displayed in a single image (see Figure 5-26).

5. **You can modify or add information in the following areas:**

   • **Personal Information:** In this section, you decide whether to display your name (or a bogus moniker), change your gender listing (yikes!), list your relationship status, display your age, add personal info about yourself, and display your Web site URL.

   • **Professional Information:** In this section, you can display information about your occupation(s), and the company(s) for which you work, or in the case of Bill Gates, the companies you own.

   • **Student Information:** In this section, you have one text field in which you can list the schools you've attended. Many people can truthfully enter "School of Hard Knocks" in this field.

- **Interests:** In this section, you can show people how eclectic you are. You can enter information about your interests and hobbies; favorite movies and shows; favorite music; and favorite books. Sybil didn't have enough categories for all her interests. Most other people are okay with the choices available in this section.

6. **Click the Update Channel button.**

   Your personal info is no longer personal — at least on the Tube.

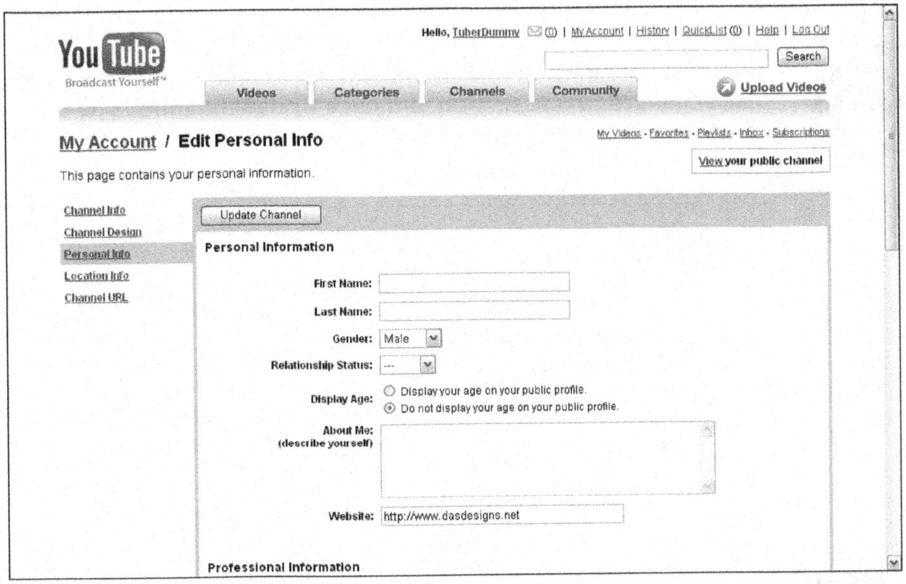

Figure 5-26: My personal info. Will it be truth or fiction?

Changing your location info

Every Tuber was born somewhere and currently lives somewhere. If you don't, you may be a figment of your own imagination. You can post information about where you were born and where you currently live on your channel by following these steps:

1. **Log in to the Tube.**

2. **Click the My Account link.**

   YouTube displays your account page and more sections than you'd care to tackle on a Sunday afternoon.

3. **Scroll to the Channel Settings section of the page.**

   For most people, the majority of the page is below the fold. If it isn't, you have a humongous — or as the late Ed Sullivan would say, *really big* — desktop.

4. **Click the Location Info link.**

   The MyAccount/Edit Location Info page appears with text fields that enable you to enter information about the location in which you live (see Figure 5-27).

5. **Enter or modify your hometown, current city, current postal ZIP code, or choose a country from the Country drop-down list.**

6. **Click Update Channel.**

   Your location information, whether it's truth or fiction, is added to your channel.

If you're making wholesale modifications to your Channel Settings, after you make changes to one section and click Update Channel, you can modify another section by clicking a link on the left side of the page.

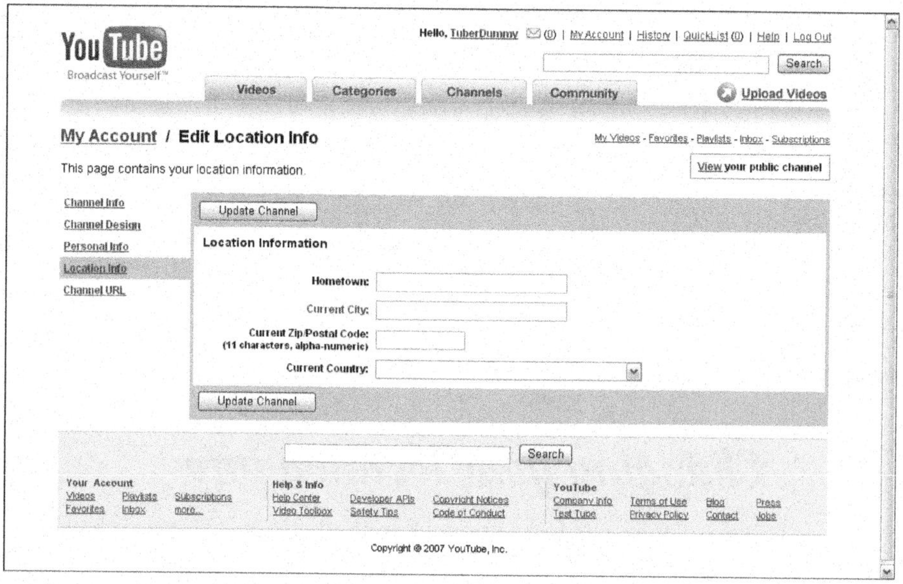

Figure 5-27:
This week, I'm fairly sure, I'll be in Monaco.

Changing your channel URL

The URL (Uniform Resource Locator) is the browser equivalent of a phone number: Enter the correct URL, and your browser serves up the Web page you're looking for. Enter the *wrong* URL, and . . . you get the picture. Every Web page has its own URL. It's like an extension for a company with lots of employees and departments. Accordingly, every YouTube channel has its own URL: for example, `www.youtube.com/profile?user=yourusername`. You can, however, change your channel URL to a custom URL as follows:

1. **Log in to the Tube.**

2. **Click the My Account link.**

   YouTube displays your account page and links you can click to change information, see your videos, view your channel, and so on.

3. **Scroll to the Channel Settings section of the page.**

   It's just south of Tierra del Fuego — um, we mean the Groups section.

4. **Click the Channel URL link.**

   The My Account/Customize Channel URL page appears (see Figure 5-28). A custom URL doesn't come without rules and regulations. First and foremost, the URL can consist of only letters and numbers. That's right, no spaces, forward slashes, or anything else that can be deciphered as HTML code. Another rule is that the custom URL can't be currently in use. I mean, that would be like having two identical phone numbers; wouldn't it?

5. **Enter the Custom URL in the text field and click Save URL.**

   You've saved your custom URL. Somehow this doesn't give you the same fuzzy feeling you get when you donate to Save the Whales, but you will have a custom URL that amazes your friends and fellow Tubers.

When someone clicks your profile, they don't see your custom URL. Until you send the custom URL to someone or send it as a link, that person doesn't see it. Only when he enters that custom URL into his browser address field or clicks the custom URL link will he be tuned in to your channel loud and clear.

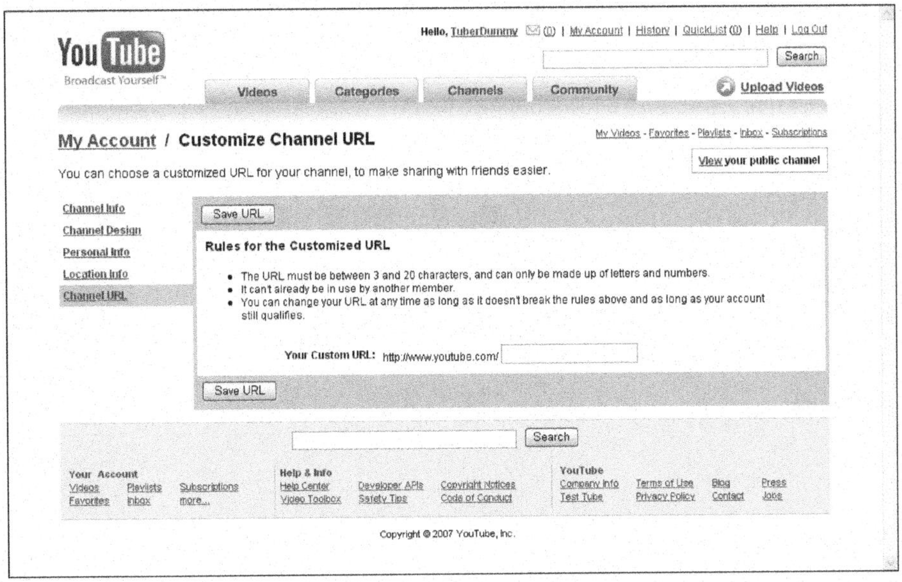

Figure 5-28: I'm gonna get me one of them custom URLs.

Customizing Your Channel's Look

The classic look for a YouTube channel isn't very personal. In fact, you might say the default look is downright boring. You can change the way your channel looks by changing its design. When you change your channel's design, you can change the colors, choose which items are displayed, display a background image on the page, and more. To customize your channel design, follow these steps:

1. **Log in to the Tube.**

2. **Click the My Account link.**

   YouTube displays your account page and links you can click to change information, see your videos, view your channel, and so on.

3. **Scroll to the Channel Settings section of the page.**

   It's just south of the Groups section.

4. **Click the Channel Design link.**

   The My Account/Customize Theme page appears (see Figure 5-29).

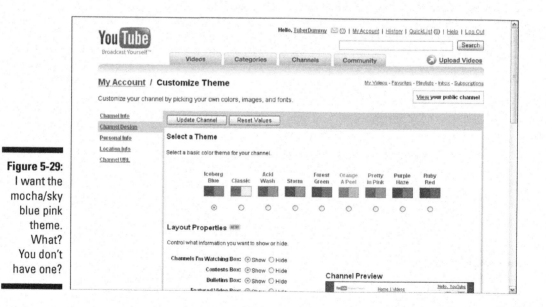

Figure 5-29:
I want the mocha/sky blue pink theme. What? You don't have one?

5. **In the Select a Theme section, select the color combination that suits your personality and fancy.**

   If you're a child of the 1960s, check out Purple Haze — 'scuse me while I kiss the sky.

6. **Choose the desired options in the Layout Properties section.**

   This section determines what visitors to your channel see. For example, if you don't want everybody in the world to know what channels your watching, click the Channels I'm Watching Box: Hide radio button.

   If you want your vlog displayed prominently at the top of your channel, hide the Featured Video Box and Videos Box.

7. **If you really want to trick out your channel, in the Advanced Colors section, click the Pick link next to a listing and then choose the desired color.**

   After choosing a color, the hexadecimal value for the color is listed in the text field. If you know how to specify a hexadecimal value for a color, you can enter that value to use that color for the design element you choose to modify.

   Hexadecimal values for colors are a combination of six alphanumeric values. The first and second values represent a shade of red; the third and fourth values represent a shade of green; and the fifth and sixth values a shade of blue — the standard red, green, and blue are used to define a color for monitor viewing. The hexadecimal scale uses the letters A–F and the numbers 0–9. If you do the math, that's 16 possible values for each slot. Pure black is hexadecimal #000000 and pure white is hexadecimal #FFFFFF. Pure red is #FF0000, pure green is #00FF00, and pure blue is #0000FF. That works out to 256 possible shades of red, green, and blue, and 16,777,216 colors, one of which is sky blue pink. That's a whole lot of colors.

   If you choose custom colors and your theme starts looking a ghastly shade of ugly, click one of the default color themes or click Reset Colors.

8. **To display an image as the channel background, enter the URL of the Web site where the background image can be found.**

   For example, `http://www.mysite.com/images/bg.gif`, will display an image called `bg.gif` as the page background. The image won't be scaled to fit the background; it will occupy an area equal to its native dimensions.

9. **Click the Repeat Background Image: Yes radio button to tile the image across the background.**

   This option works well if you have a small square image, such as a seamless pattern. The tile option makes it appear as if the background is a single image sized to fit.

10. **Choose a face from the Font drop-down list to changes the default font.**

   Your choices are Arial, Times New Roman, Georgia, and Verdana.

   When you make changes to your channel theme, the preview updates in real time.

11. **Click Update Channel to apply your modifications.**

   Figure 5-30 shows a channel decked out in the beautiful Purple Haze theme. Unfortunately, because this book is in black and white, you just have to imagine how beautiful it is.

Figure 5-30:
Whatever it
is, this
channel
puts a spell
on me.

Chapter 6

Joining the YouTube Community

In This Chapter

▶ Networking with others on YouTube

▶ Sharing your experiences

▶ Getting rid of the bad stuff

*V*ideos. YouTube is most well known for and most commonly identified with videos — which makes good and proper sense given that YouTube is, after all, the Internet's first video-sharing Web site. YouTube is about videos, but YouTube isn't *only* about videos.

You may remember us saying many times in this book that YouTube is a community, and you may have thought, "Yeah. A community. A bunch of people sharing and watching videos. Cool. Got it. Next." But when you really spend some time clicking around the Tube and trying out its features, it dawns on you just how extensive — and how *interactive* — the YouTube community is. The YouTube community isn't just a concept — it's a *real* thing.

People talk to people on YouTube; people meet people on YouTube. They make friends and bond over shared interests and goals. The three major features that make YouTube an interactive community are *commenting, channels,* and *groups.* We take a good look at these features in this chapter — all from the perspective of Tubers meeting other Tubers. We also show you how to keep away from the Tubers you don't want to know — the ones who annoy you. Yes, they're out there, too!

YouTube has become synonymous with videos, but YouTube is just as much about social networking and making friends. YouTube is something like the first video-version of *MySpace* or *Facebook,* two hugely popular social networking Web sites. The idea of YouTube as social networking via video is quite an amazing concept to consider. As Doug likes to say: YouTube + MySpace = YouTopia!

Networking with Other Tubers

Communication goes both ways on the Tube: You can contact other Tubers, and they can contact you. When you register with YouTube, you create a username and an account. With your account automatically comes your personal channel. When other Tubers want to contact you, they send a message to your account via links on videos that you upload or links on your channel page.

Now, if you never upload a video of your own, you might never hear directly from other Tubers. But after you upload a video, you'll be surprised at how many people will indeed watch it and how many of them will send a message to you.

As we said, communication goes both ways on the Tube. Even if you don't upload videos, you can interact with other Tubers by sending them messages. And chances are, they'll message you back.

Posting a text comment on a video

If you start watching a lot of videos on the Tube, you'll find that sometimes you just can't contain yourself: You just *have to* post a comment. Maybe it's because the video is so great — the images are so beautiful, the singer is so talented, or the comedian is so funny — that you want to thank the person who posted it and give them a pat on the back. Or, maybe the video is controversial and sparks a discussion — a discussion that makes you want to put in your two cents. Or maybe the video is just plain revolting, nasty, or maddening, and you can't help but give the poster the proverbial piece of your mind. In any case, commenting on a video is an essential component of the YouTube experience, a great way for you to get yourself heard and to interact with other Tubers. The following steps tell you how to do it:

1. **Search and find a video you think is interesting or thought-provoking — good or bad.**

2. **Scroll down to the Comments & Responses section, just below the video window.**

   If you like, you can read through some of the comments other users have posted about this video.

3. **Click the Post a Text Comment link.**

   When you click the link, a comment window appears, as shown in Figure 6-1.

4. **Type your comment in the window.**

Figure 6-1:
Post a text comment to put in your proverbial two cents.

5. **Click the Post Comment button.**

   A window pops up thanking you and telling you that your comment has been posted. Don't expect you comment to appear immediately, however. Refresh the page after a few minutes, and it should be there.

Posting a video response

So here's something new: Respond to a video with a video of your own! When a simple text comment just doesn't do the trick, you can post a video response to any video on YouTube. If creating and uploading a video just to respond to a video sounds like an awful lot of work, remember that many new-model computers come equipped with built-in video cameras, and Web cams that sit on top of your monitor have become commonplace. For many Tubers, creating a video is a quick and easy thing — and video responses have become the hip, new way to talk back. Here's how you do it:

1. **Search and find a video you want to respond to.**

2. **Scroll down to the Comments & Responses section, just below the video window.**

   As shown in Figure 6-2, if a video has received video responses, thumbnails of those responses appear in the Comments & Responses section.

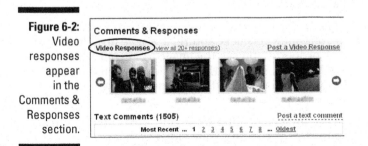

Figure 6-2:
Video responses appear in the Comments & Responses section.

3. Click the Post a Video Response link.

Clicking the link takes you to the Video Response page, as shown in Figure 6-3. You can post a video response in three ways, each represented by its own link in the three sections of the page:

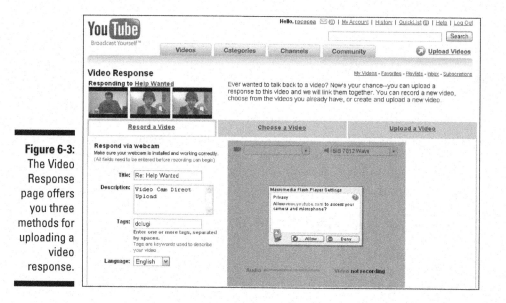

Figure 6-3: The Video Response page offers you three methods for uploading a video response.

- **Record a Video:** Record a new video with your Web cam or built-in video cam. This is the default choice.
- **Choose a Video:** Choose a video that you've uploaded already as your response video.
- **Upload a Video:** Upload a new video as your response video.

4. If you want to record a video response with your Web cam, enter a title for your video, a description, and at least one tag.

For more information on tags, see Chapter 8.

5. If the Macromedia Flash Player Settings dialog box appears, as shown in Figure 6-4, click the Allow button.

When you choose the Record a Video option, you record video and audio directly into YouTube via QuickCapture. If you've installed a Web cam and it's working properly, you see the image from your Web cam (probably your own beautiful mug!) in the main window on the page. If you don't see that image, you may need to choose a different video source from the Video drop-down list.

6. When you can see the picture coming from your own camera, click the Record button to start recording your video response.

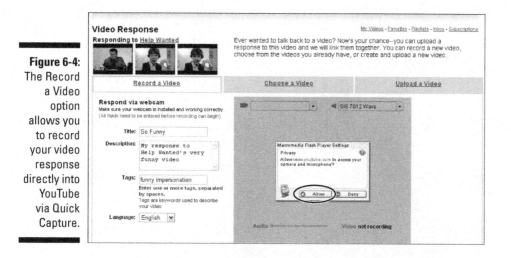

Figure 6-4:
The Record
a Video
option
allows you
to record
your video
response
directly into
YouTube
via Quick
Capture.

7. **After you're finished, click the Done button if you're happy with what you've recorded or click the Re-Record button if you want to record it again.**

   When you click the Done button, your video is uploaded automatically to YouTube as a video response.

Regardless of which of the three methods you choose to post a video response, if your video isn't posted immediately or relatively soon, that may be because the owner of the video that you're responding to has set up preferences that allow him to view and approve video responses before they're posted.

Remember too that any one of your videos can be used as a video response to *only* one other video at any given time. This is to prevent crafty users from using the video response feature to disseminate hundreds of copies of their videos throughout the Tube and thereby, increase their viewings. Therefore, if you use a video as a response to Video A and then use the same video as a response to Video B, your video no longer appears as a response to Video A; it's removed automatically.

Rating a video

Some Tubers upload some incredible videos — videos that move you, make you laugh, or just flat-out amaze you. One of the best ways to reward another Tuber's efforts is to take a moment to give them a high rating. When you rate a video on YouTube, you're making a difference because videos with high ratings get better positioning and greater visibility in YouTube searches, especially when you skew a search with the Top Rated search parameter. (See Chapter 3 for more about top-rated searches.) Here's how you do it:

1. **Search and find a video that you want to rate.**

2. **Float your cursor over the stars beneath the video window, as shown in Figure 6-5.**

When you float your cursor over the stars, they change to show the five ratings available:

- One star — Poor
- Two stars — Nothing special
- Three stars — Worth watching
- Four stars — Pretty cool
- Five stars — Awesome!

3. **Click when you see the rating that you want to apply.**

Messaging another Tuber

Don't misread the title of this section: We're not talking about giving another Tuber a *massage*. We're talking about sending a *message* to another Tuber. This is as opposed to posting a *text comment* — which is a public response available for anyone to see. When you message another Tuber, your message is sent directly to their account as a private communication. Here's how you do it:

1. **Search and find a video whose owner you want to send a message to.**

2. **Go to the video poster's information section, as shown in Figure 6-6.**

    The section is available for every video posted on YouTube.

3. **Click the username text link — beside the word "From" in the upper-left corner of the section — to go to the poster's channel page.**

4. **On any user's channel page, scroll to the Connect With . . . section and then click the Send Message link to send the user a message.**

The poster's information section

Figure 6-6:
The video poster's information section.

Checking your messages, video comments, and video responses

Your account page is the central location for all activity that occurs in relation to your account, including general messages, video comments, and video responses. Any time that any Tuber sends you a message or comments on one of your videos, that information is listed on your account page.

When a user sends you a message, you can reply to the message if you like or you can simply delete it. It's very important you make the distinction that messages aren't e-mails. Let's say that your username is JaneSmith, and I send you a message. This means that I've gone to your channel — *JaneSmith* — and clicked the Send Message link. I am sending you this message *through* YouTube, and you read it *through* YouTube. The important distinction is that I never found out your *real* e-mail address, and you're not reading it through your real e-mail address. This is only a YouTube message sent between YouTube users; it's not an e-mail.

This distinction is important because your e-mail address is private. YouTube never publishes your e-mail address on the site, and no other user has access to that information. To send a YouTube message, follow these steps:

1. **From any page on YouTube, click the My Account link at the top of the page to go to your account page.**

   Whenever you have unread messages, a red envelope icon appears beside your username at the top of any YouTube page, along with the number of unread messages.

2. **Go to the Inbox section and then click General Messages.**

   The General Messages window, as shown in Figure 6-7, lists all the messages that other users have sent you.

3. **Click the underlined text link in the subject section to read the full message, or click any of the Reply, Delete, Block User, or Spam links to take that action.**

   Clicking the Spam link reports to YouTube that the message you received isn't a "real" message — it's *spam,* some sort of message trying to sell you something or asking you to do something not related to YouTube.

   This window offers you two great options regarding comments and messages. The first is the option to have a notification e-mail sent to you when a comment is left on one of your videos. The second gives you the option to permit only your contacts to send you messages. You probably shouldn't choose the second option — why block potential friends that you have yet to meet from contacting you?

4. **Click the Video Comments link in the left column to see a list of all the comments that Tubers have left to any of your uploaded videos, as shown in Figure 6-8.**

Figure 6-7: The General Messages window lists all messages sent to you from other Tubers.

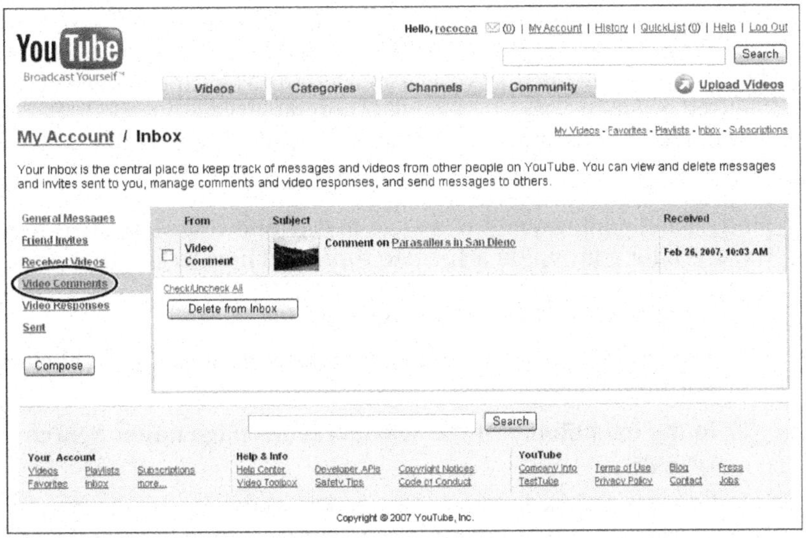

Figure 6-8:
The Video
Comments
window lists
all com-
ments other
users have
posted to
any of your
videos.

5. **Click the underlined text link in the subject section to go to your video and read the full comment.**

6. **To delete the video comment, click the box to the left to place a check mark and then click the Delete from Inbox button.**

7. **Click the Video Responses link in the left column to see a list of all the video responses that Tubers have left to any of your uploaded videos.**

Don't confuse video comments and video responses with messages. These are three different things. *Video Comments* are text messages that other users post to comment on your videos. *Video responses* are videos that other users upload to respond to your videos. *Messages* are simple text messages that other users send to you privately via the Send Message link in your channel.

Joining a group

With all the millions of people who surf the Tube, it only makes sense that many of them are people that you'd like to meet — people whose passions and hobbies are similar to yours. Groups are a great way to meet with and interact with those people.

Like any group that might form in the "real" world, YouTube groups are created based on a specific subject or interest. For example, you'll find groups of Tubers who are classic car aficionados, film buffs, cat lovers, and so on. Whatever topic you can think of — *The Simpsons,* poodle breeding, movies in which Shelley Winters drowns or dies wet — you can either find a group for that topic or create one yourself.

What happens in groups isn't much different from what happens on YouTube in general: You watch videos, share videos, post comments, and send messages. The key to groups is that you're sharing the YouTube experience with a more focused group of users — a smaller community within the larger YouTube community — users who congregate around a topic of shared interest and enthusiasm.

Finding and joining a group is easy. In the following steps, we show you how to search for a group on a specific topic and how to join that group:

1. **Go to the YouTube home page and log in.**

2. **Type** Miniature Pinscher **in the Search field and then click the Search button.**

3. **In the left column of the search results page under Search In, click Groups.**

    When you click Groups, you're narrowing your search results only to those groups that contain your search criteria in their description tags. In this case, as shown in Figure 6-9, the search results show that one group has been created for and about Miniature Pinschers.

   All group listings show the number of videos and the number of members associated with the group.

Figure 6-9:
Search
results
within
groups for
Miniature
Pinschers.

4. **Click the name of the group — Miniature Pinschers — to go to the group page, as shown in Figure 6-10.**

    At the top of the group page is a thumbnail image, which represents the group. Beside the thumbnail is a description of the group and information that this group contains 14 videos, 17 members, and 1 discussion.

    The Recent Videos section shows thumbnails of some of the videos that have been uploaded to this group. Below this section is the Discussions section, where one of the members has posted a topic for other users to read and comment on.

5. **Click the 17 Members link.**

Figure 6-10:
The
Miniature
Pinschers
group page.

The results, as shown in Figure 6-11, list all the group members. If you like, you could message any of these members to discuss miniature pinschers or anything else that you might have in common.

6. **Click the Join This Group link in the yellow box at the top of the page.**

When you click to join a group, the only visible result is that you get a message saying you've joined the group. However, behind the scenes, YouTube has identified you as a member of this group. The group and a link to the group appear on your Account page under My Groups. Also, you're notified of any new activity within the group — for example, when someone uploads a new video. This is a great way to keep in touch with other users who are sharing videos and discussing topics that you're interested in.

Figure 6-11:
A list of the
members
of the
Miniature
Pinschers
group.

Starting a group

Sometimes, you just gotta be proactive. If you search for and can't find a group based on a specific topic that you find interesting, you can always start your own group. Just follow these steps:

1. **From any page on YouTube, click the My Account link at the top of the page.**

2. **On your account page, scroll to the Groups section and then click the Create a Group button to go to the Create a Group page, as shown in Figure 6-12.**

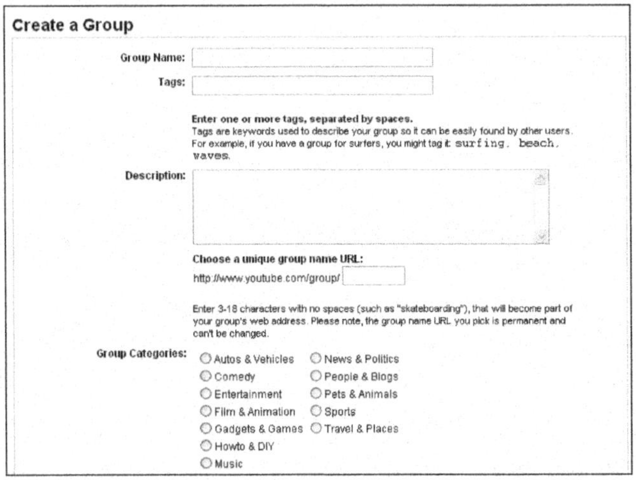

Create a Group

Group Name:

Tags:

Enter one or more tags, separated by spaces.
Tags are keywords used to describe your group so it can be easily found by other users. For example, if you have a group for surfers, you might tag it: surfing, beach, waves.

Description:

Choose a unique group name URL:
http://www.youtube.com/group/

Enter 3-18 characters with no spaces (such as "skateboarding"), that will become part of your group's web address. Please note, the group name URL you pick is permanent and can't be changed.

Group Categories:
- Autos & Vehicles
- Comedy
- Entertainment
- Film & Animation
- Gadgets & Games
- Howto & DIY
- Music
- News & Politics
- People & Blogs
- Pets & Animals
- Sports
- Travel & Places

Figure 6-12: The Create a Group page is where your group gets started.

3. **In the Group Name field, type the name of the group.**

4. **In the Tags field, type words — separated by spaces — that could be used in a search for this group.**

5. **In the Description field, type one or two sentences that convey the group's concept, main topic, or central idea.**

6. **In the URL field, type the name of the group as a single word with no spaces.**

   Creating a group is akin to creating a Web page on YouTube, so much so that it even has its own URL that other YouTube members — and even nonmembers — can bookmark and link directly to.

7. **In the Group Categories section, click the category that most relates to the group concept.**

8. **In the Type section, choose which type of group you want to create regarding new members.**

When you create a group, you have three choices regarding new members:

- **Public groups:** You can make your group a public group — anyone can join.

- **Protected groups:** In this type of group, the group founder or owner is alerted when someone asks to join and can approve or disapprove that member.

- **Private groups:** In this type of group, new members can join only by invitation.

Of the three, public groups offer the most opportunities for meeting new people on YouTube that you wouldn't otherwise meet.

 9. **In the Video Uploads section, choose how you want members to be able to upload videos.**

    In a group, members often upload videos to share with other members. The Video Uploads section allows the founder of the group to determine how free group members are to upload videos. Constraining video uploads to the approval of the founder as a way to keep the group on-topic and to eliminate random videos uploaded by members who really aren't interested in the group topic isn't a bad idea.

10. **In the Forum Postings section, choose how you want members to be able to post topics for discussion.**

11. **In the Group Icon section, click the Let Owner Pick the Video as a Group icon.**

    When you start a group, it's a good idea for you to choose which video thumbnail serves as the group's icon. If you're serious about your group, you want to keep that icon consistent and recognizable for other members of the group.

12. **Click the Create Group button.**

Sharing Your YouTube Experiences

Much of YouTube is centered on family and friends: You see something you like on the Tube, something that's interesting, something that makes you laugh, and you want to tell your friends or your family about it. (You'll find many things on the Tube that you want to show to your friends but probably not your Mom.)

What works really well is that your interest in sharing your fun YouTube experiences falls right in line with YouTube's interest in finding new users and getting current users to surf the site as often as possible. So, of course, YouTube has created a number of features that allow you to urge your friends and family to go to the site and have a look at the videos that you've been looking at.

Creating a list of contacts

You'll meet a lot of people on YouTube, some of whom you'll want absolutely nothing to do with, but many of whom you'll want to stay in touch with. As part of its social networking system, YouTube allows you to quickly and easily create a list of contacts — other users who you meet along your way.

YouTube uses the term *contacts* to refer to all the users you choose to add to your main list of people that you want to stay in touch with or perhaps contact sometime in the future. Contacts can be broken down into subcategories, such as family and friends, which we discuss in the following section. But first things first, you must invite someone to be a contact.

In the following steps, we invite Doug to be a friend:

1. **Type** TuberDummy **in the search field and then click the Search button.**

   Your search yields a list of the videos that Doug (TuberDummy) has uploaded, including his great photography portfolio and a video of his nephew Colin Hughes, who is a gifted guitar player.

2. **In the left column of the search results page under Search In, click Channels.**

   When you click Channels, you narrow your search to only channels that contain the name TuberDummy. Because only one channel has this name, you've found Doug's channel.

3. **Click the TuberDummy text link to go to Doug's channel page, as shown in Figure 6-13.**

   Because Doug is a super-suave James Bond-type of guy, you'll note that he's surrounded by beautiful women in glamorous tropical settings. It's a rough life, but someone's gotta live it.

4. **In the Connect with TuberDummy section, click the Add as Friend link, which takes you to the Friend Invitation page, as shown in Figure 6-14.**

5. **Click the Add As drop-down list arrow and then choose Friends.**

6. **Click the Send Invite button.**

   After you click the Send Invite button, that person isn't added automatically to your Contacts list. The person you invite must accept your invitation to be a friend before her username appears in your Contacts list.

7. **Click the My Account link at the top of the page.**

8. **Scroll to the Friends & Contacts section on the right and then click the All Contacts link to go to the Friends & Contacts page, as shown in Figure 6-15.**

Figure 6-13:
Tuber
Dummy's
channel
page: Too
hot to
handle.

The Add As Friend link

As shown in the figure, TuberDummy is listed in the All Contacts list.
Note that the status of the TuberDummy contact is listed as Pending. It
remains as such until Doug confirms that he wants to accept your invite
to be his YouTube friend.

Figure 6-14:
The Friend
Invitation
page —
where all
YouTube
friendships
begin.

Creating a Friends list and a Family list

On YouTube, everyone who accepts your invitation as a friend becomes a contact and appears on your All Contacts list. In addition to All Contacts, YouTube automatically creates two other default lists with every new account: Friends and Family. Your Friends list and your Family list are subsets of your All Contacts list. They can each contain users that are mutually exclusive or, more likely, that overlap between the two lists.

Figure 6-15:
Tuber
Dummy in
the All
Contacts list.

Because of YouTube's choice of terms, the distinction between your All Contacts list and your Friends list can get slightly confusing. Here's the deal: When you want to invite someone as a contact, the YouTube interface says that you're inviting someone as a *friend*. However, when they accept your invitation, they are added automatically to your All Contacts list, *not* your Friends list. So, when you go to your Friends list, that user isn't listed there.

Why would you want to create different lists of your contacts? Here's an example: Let's say you shoot some video of your kids at the playground and you upload it to the Tube. Now, you want to let your contacts know that the video is up there. But not all your contacts, right? You don't want to tell every stranger that you've met on YouTube to go and watch your family videos. Most likely, you want to let the grandparents, aunts, uncles, and in-laws know, and that's easy to do when you've isolated those contacts into your Family list.

On YouTube, no user who accepts your invitation to be a *friend* is added automatically to your Friends or Family list; they're added only to your All Contacts list. It is you, and only you, who add contacts to your Friends list and your Family list — by copying them from your All Contacts list. Here's how you do it:

1. **From any YouTube page, click the My Account link at the top of the page to go to your account page.**

2. **Scroll to the Friends & Contacts section and then click the All Contacts link to go to the Friends & Contacts page.**

   Note that on the left side you see links for your three default contact lists: All Contacts, Friends, and Family.

3. **Click to place a check mark in the box beside TuberDummy, as shown in Figure 6-16.**

Selecting a contact

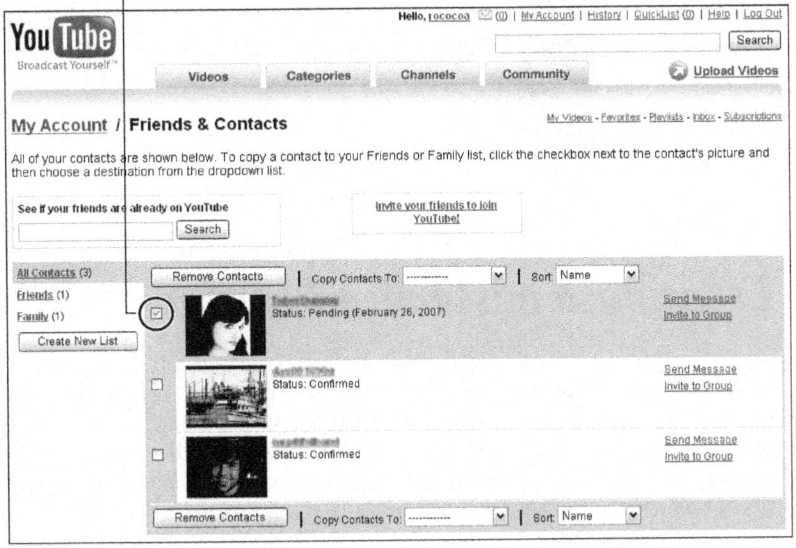

Figure 6-16:
Click to
place a
check in the
check box
to select a
contact
within
the list.

TuberDummy is Doug's username and will appear in your All Contacts list if you complete the previous section in this chapter.

To do anything to a contact in a contact list — copy it, delete it, and so on — you must first select it by clicking a check into its check box.

4. **Click the Copy Contacts To: drop-down list arrow and then choose Friends.**

   When you choose Friends from the list and release your mouse, the screen refreshes and the check mark beside TuberDummy disappears. Note that you're still looking at your All Contacts list.

5. **Click the Friends link on the left side of the window.**

   As shown in Figure 6-17, TuberDummy is now a contact within your Friends list. TuberDummy is still listed within your All Contacts list as well.

6. **Follow the same steps to copy a contact to your Family list or to any other list you create (see the following section).**

Creating a customized contact list

You're not just limited to the three default contact lists — All Contacts, Friends, and Family. Feel free to create as many you like, depending on how you use YouTube and what works best for you. For example, if you want to create a list just for co-workers or if you're a comedian, you might want to create a list of only those Tubers who subscribe to your channel. Feel free to create as many customized contacts lists as you like. Just follow these steps:

1. **From any YouTube page, click the My Account link at the top of the page to go to your account page.**

2. **Scroll to the Friends & Contacts section and then click the All Contacts link to go to the Friends & Contacts page.**

3. **Click the Create New List button.**

   A pop-up window appears asking that you enter a name for a new contact group.

4. **Type** Co-Workers **in the field and then click OK.**

   Co-Workers appears in the contacts list beneath the three default lists.

5. **Click the Co-Workers link.**

   As shown in Figure 6-18, the Co-Workers list is empty; no contacts have been copied to this list.

Figure 6-18:
By default,
new contact
lists contain
no contacts.

Deleting a contact list is as easy as creating one. In these two steps, you'll delete the Co-Workers contact list that you just created.

1. **Click the small blue X beside the Co-Workers link.**

   A pop-up window appears asking if you're sure that you want to delete this contact list.

2. **Click OK.**

Removing a contact from a contact list

Removing a contact from a contact list is as easy as transferring contacts between lists. Here's what you do:

1. **From any YouTube page, click the My Account link at the top of the page to go to your account page.**

2. **Scroll to the Friends & Contacts section and then click the All Contacts link to go to the Friends & Contacts page.**

3. **Click to place a check mark in the box beside any contact you want to delete from this list.**

4. **Click the Remove Contacts button.**

Forwarding a link to a video

One of the most fun things to do on YouTube is to share what you find. Simply put, many gems are on this site — many crazy, funny, shocking, outrageous, and unexpected videos that you feel you just have to share them with people you know.

YouTube loves it when you share what you find. For YouTube, that means more page views. This means that you're giving other users a reason to come back to the site and watch a video. YouTube likes it when you share a video so much that it gladly allows you to forward a video link even to people who *aren't* already registered users on YouTube. In fact, YouTube likes that the best because, by doing so, you're advertising YouTube, maybe to people who've never even visited YouTube! The following steps show you how to forward a video link to someone you know:

1. **Search and find a video that you want to forward to a friend or friends.**

2. **Click the Share Video link beneath the window.**

   A pop-up window appears, as shown in Figure 6-19.

3. **(Optional) You can enter your first name and a message in their respective fields.**

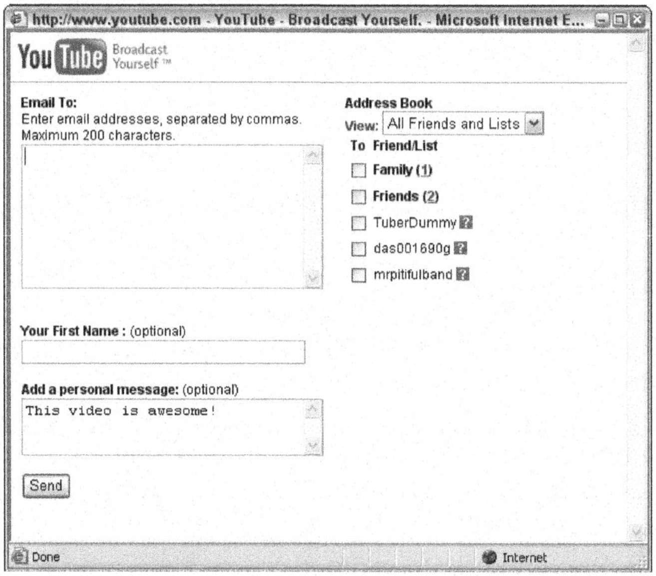

Figure 6-19:
Use the
Email To:
window to
forward a
link to family,
friends, or
other
contacts.

4. **If you want to send a video link to one or more e-mail addresses (outside the YouTube community), enter those e-mail addresses in the Email To: window, separated by commas.**

   Note that you're limited to 200 characters. Therefore, you can use this window to forward a link to approximately 12–15 e-mail addresses.

5. **In the Address Book section on the right, click the View: drop-down list arrow and then choose Friends.**

   As shown in Figure 6-20, all the contacts that you've copied to your Friends list appear individually beneath the menu. (For space reasons, we're showing only two contacts in the figure; your window likely shows more contacts.)

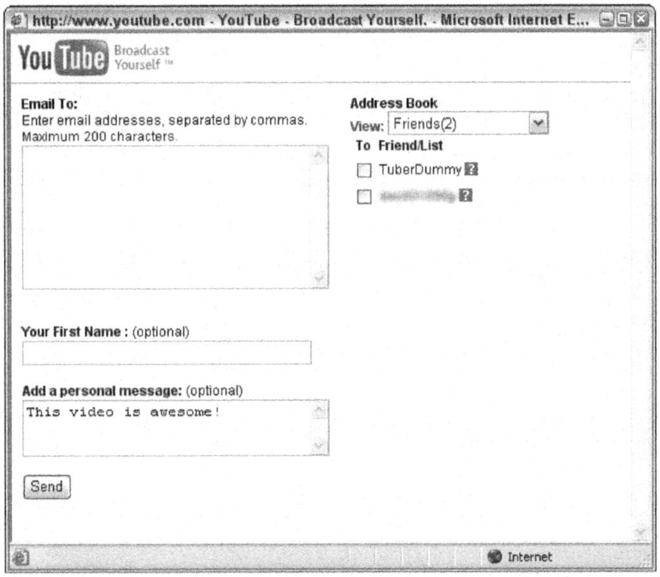

Figure 6-20:
Viewing contacts within the Friends contact list.

If you don't recognize a contact by name, clicking the question mark icon beside a contact's name opens a window showing that contact's channel page.

6. **Click to place a check mark in the check box beside the first contact at the top of the list.**

   Note that the contact appears in the Email To: window.

7. **Click the Send button.**

   YouTube sends a link to only the single contact that you specify.

Sharing a playlist

In the preceding section of this chapter, we discuss sharing a video with friends, family, or other contacts. Let's take a giant step forward: Imagine sharing an entire playlist!

A *playlist* is a collection of videos that you've assembled — usually because you like them and want to watch them again. *Favorites* — the list of videos that's created when you click Save to Favorites when watching a video — is the default playlist, but you can create as many playlists as you like. For example, if you like videos of airplanes and other flying machines, you can create a playlist called Flying Machines to contain videos that fall only under that category.

In Chapter 5, we showed you how to create a playlist. Once you've done so, if you have playlist that you're particularly proud of and want to share it with a friend, doing so is as easy as sharing a single video. Here's what you do:

1. **From any page on YouTube, click the My Account link at the top of the page and then click the Playlists link in the Videos section of your account page.**

2. **In the left hand column, click the link for the playlist that you want to share.**

3. **In the blue bar at the top of the playlist page, click the Share Playlist icon.**

   A pop-up window appears, as shown in Figure 6-21.

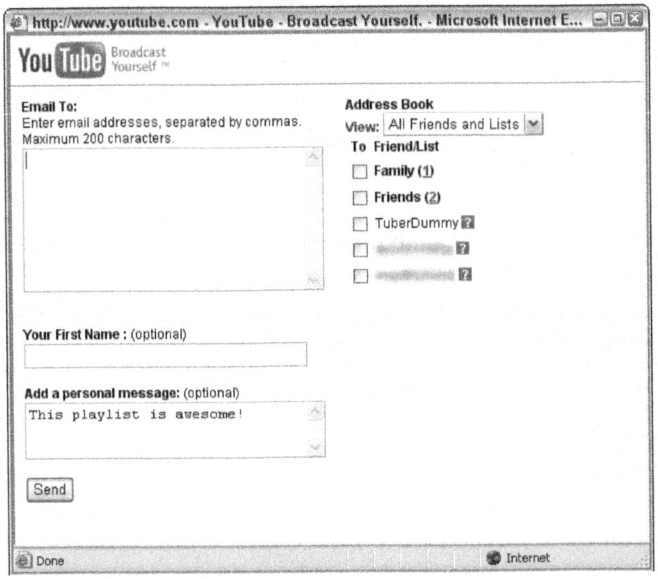

Figure 6-21:
Use the Email To: window to forward a playlist to family, friends, or other contacts.

4. **(Optional) You can enter your first name and a message in their respective fields.**

5. **If you want to send a playlist link to one or more e-mail addresses (outside the YouTube community), enter those e-mail addresses in the Email To: window, separated by commas.**

   Note that you're limited to 200 characters. That means you can use this window to forward a link to approximately 12–15 e-mail addresses.

6. **In the Address Book section on the right, click the View: drop-down list arrow and then choose Friends.**

   All the contacts that you've copied to your Friends list appear individually beneath the menu.

   If you don't recognize a contact by name, clicking the question mark icon beside a contact's name opens a window showing that contact's channel page.

7. **Click to place a check mark in the check box beside the second contact in the list, as shown in Figure 6-22.**

   Note that the contact appears in the Email To: window.

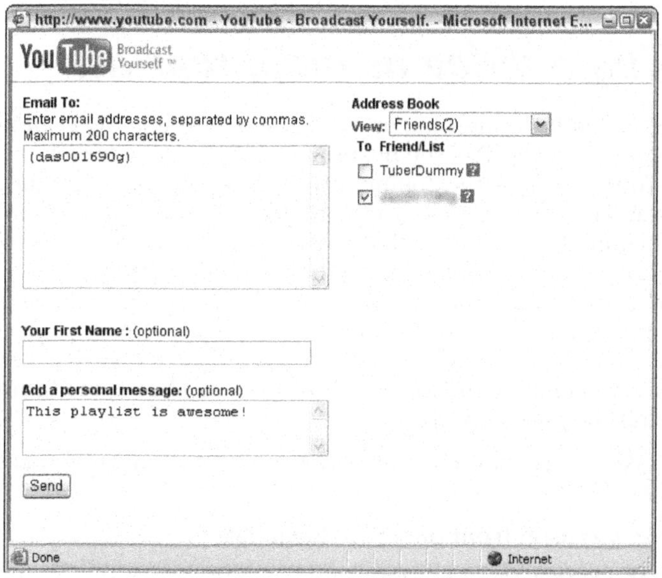

Figure 6-22:
Selecting a
contact to
receive a
link to a
playlist.

8. **Click the Send button.**

   YouTube sends a playlist link to only the single contact that you specified.

Weeding Out the Bad Stuff

By far, most of your YouTube experiences are good experiences: fun, funny, fascinating, and maybe even shocking (in a good way). But it's also quite likely that, at one time or another, you'll have an experience that's not so great. Someone might post a comment saying that a video you uploaded is lousy or offensive, or that you're a terrible person. Or, you might be watching a video and find yourself absolutely outraged at what you see. Or, you might be reading through a list of posted comments and find one or two that are so rude and so crude, that you just can't contain yourself.

Things that offend you on YouTube fall into two distinct categories:

- Offensive content or behavior that — though objectionable to you — is allowed under YouTube's terms of service.

- Offensive content or behavior that's a violation of YouTube's terms of service. (See Chapter 11.)

In the following sections, we give you some ideas and show you some options for dealing with the not-so-good YouTube experiences that you might encounter.

Flagging a video as inappropriate

If you're offended by something on YouTube that you know is allowed under YouTube's terms of service, the best thing you can do is forget about it and move on. YouTube is a large community, and as with any community, you'll see things and hear things that you don't like. If, on the other hand, you encounter content or behavior that you think is a violation of YouTube's terms of service, report it by flagging the video as inappropriate. *Flagging* is a very smart method that YouTube has developed to essentially allow the community to police itself. To flag a video, follow these steps:

1. **Click the Flag as Inappropriate button — as shown in Figure 6-23 — beneath the video window.**

    This takes you to the This Video is Inappropriate window, as shown in Figure 6-24.

2. **Choose a reason from the drop-down list.**

3. **Click the Flag This Video button.**

Figure 6-23:
If you think it's just wrong, click the Flag as Inappropriate button.

Figure 6-24:
When you flag a video as inappropriate, you must give YouTube a reason why you think it is so.

When you flag a video as inappropriate, don't expect it to be removed instantly from the site. Videos in question are presumed innocent until YouTube decides they're guilty. YouTube takes flagging very seriously and claims to work around the clock — 24 hours a day, 7 days a week — processing flagged messages from the YouTube community. When you flag a video, the YouTube administration team views the video, and if it does indeed violate the terms of service, they remove the video from the site.

Don't worry about repercussions or retaliations from the user who posted the video that you flagged. That user isn't informed that it was you who flagged the video.

Blocking another user from contacting you

Interacting with other Tubers — on occasion — introduces you to people you'd rather not meet. Unpleasant interactions generally come at you from two directions — comments and messages. If you post a video and find that someone has posted a rude, crude, or just plain-old stupid and unrelated comment, you can block that user from ever leaving comments on your video again. Perhaps even more important — especially if you have kids surfing the site — a blocked user can no longer send messages to your account. Both of these types of blocks are very powerful for keeping out unwanted influences. Here's how to do it:

1. **Click a user's username to go to that user's channel.**

2. **After you're on their channel, go to the Connect With . . . section, as shown in Figure 6-25.**

3. **Click the Block User link.**

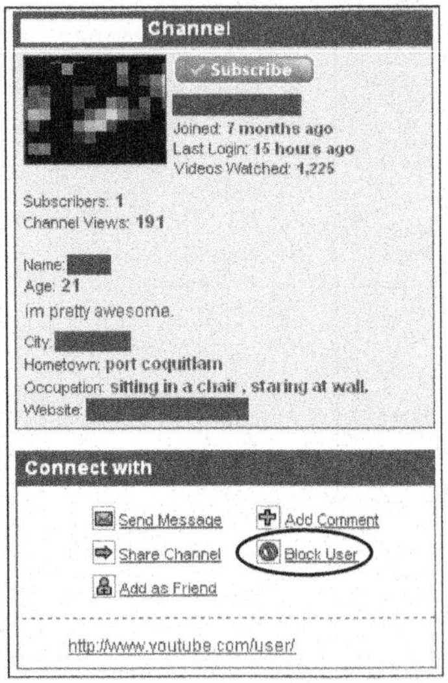

Figure 6-25: Blocking another user.

When you block a user, that user isn't notified by YouTube that you've done so. If that user ever tries to contact you again, he'll get a message saying that the message won't be delivered until you accept him as a contact, which you won't; you won't even know that he's tried to contact you, because he's blocked.

Blocking a user won't automatically remove that user's comments from your video; you'll need to do that yourself by clicking the delete link beneath the comment.

Filtering user comments

"Flaming" fights and "cyberbullying" are two new types of bad behavior in the Internet age, and on YouTube, this bad behavior happens mostly through comments posted on videos.

Posting comments is a huge component of the YouTube experience, and it's the most-used method of interaction for the YouTube community. If you're viewing a popular video, don't be surprised to find hundreds or even thousands of comments posted to the video. You'll also see that many comments actually have little or nothing to do with the video but are instead responses to other comments. And other comments are responses to responses. So the comments window for any given video can become an interactive bulletin board with all kinds of users sharing all kinds of opinions and comments.

And sometimes, it gets ugly.

If you upload a video and someone posts a comment to your video that you don't like, you can always delete it quickly and easily by clicking the Delete link beneath the comment. Poof. It's gone.

If you want to be more proactive in deciding what does or doesn't get posted to your videos, you'll be happy to know that YouTube offers you some cool options for filtering that feedback.

To specify comment preferences for videos you've uploaded already, do the following:

1. **Log in to your YouTube account.**

2. **Click the My Account link at the top of any YouTube page and then go to the Videos section at the top left of your account page.**

3. **Click My Uploaded Videos at** www.youtube.com/my_videos.

4. **Find the video that you want to change and then click the Edit Video Info button for that video.**

 5. Scroll to the Allow Comments section, as shown in Figure 6-26.

Allow Comments: ○ **Yes, with Approval:** Allow comments to be added to this video after you have approved them.
○ **Yes, Automatic:** Allow comments to be added to this video immediately.
○ **No:** Don't allow comments to be added to this video.

 6. Choose which of the three options you want to apply for comments to this video:

 • To require your approval before a comment is posted, click Yes, with Approval.

 • To allow comments without your approval, click Yes, Automatic.

 • To disallow any comments, click No.

YouTube refers to choosing the Yes, with Approval option as turning comments "kinda" on.

 7. Click the Update Video Info button at the bottom of the page.

Rather than having to go back and specify comment preferences for each video that you've uploaded already, make your preference choice at the time that you upload a video. Simply scroll to the Allow Comments section like you do in the preceding steps and choose your preference.

Part III

Broadcasting Your Video to the World

In this part . . .

We show you how to create good video with your camcorder, edit it, add a bit of panache to it, and upload it to YouTube. If you're a musician, actor, comedian, or videographer, we show you how to get your 15 minutes of fame on the Tube.

Chapter 7

From Camcorder to YouTube

*I*f you create your YouTube videos with a camcorder (or a digital camera that can capture video) this chapter's for you. In this chapter, we show you tips and techniques to capture clean video with your camcorder. We also cover the blatantly obvious, like pressing the record button when you're finished recording a scene. But that's only half the equation. After you create a video, you have to get it into your computer and then repurpose it into a format that you can upload to the Tube. We show you which video formats can be uploaded to the Tube and give you a smattering of information, such as frame rates, codecs, and other terms. Not to worry, we don't get overly technical.

We also show you how to capture video from your computer applications. If you're an instructor or have a YouTube Guru account, you capture video to show other Tubers how to use the application. Of course, this is the carrot you dangle to get Tubers to your Web site and then turn them into clients. Other topics of discussion include optimizing video for the Tube and then uploading it.

Recording the Perfect Video

If you've surfed the Tube for a while, you've seen your share of bad videos. Nothing is worse than trying to watch a movie that looks like it was shot by a cat wired on catnip. You know what we're talking about: zooming in too quickly, panning from side to side at the speed of light, and so on. If you don't pan and zoom smoothly, your video looks like an amateur shot it. And even if you are an amateur, you don't have to let fellow Tubers know. In the upcoming sections, we show you techniques to record good quality videos that people actually want to view.

Recording video with a camcorder

Video camcorders are wonderful devices. Many of them are small enough to fit in a purse or fanny-pack. Your camcorder has a method for zooming in and out, and other features, such as adding special effects with camcorder menu commands, recording the date on the video, and so on. Your camcorder may also have features such as a thread for attaching a tripod, a jack for attaching an external microphone, and threads on the lens for attaching accessory filters. The following tips ensure you shoot the best quality video your device is capable of capturing:

✔ **Don't use digital zoom.** When you use digital zoom, the camcorder uses the highest available optical zoom and then crops the image to a smaller part of the scene. In essence, the camcorder is redrawing pixels, which inevitably results in poor quality.

✔ **If you're recording a subject that's backlit, the background is brighter than your subject. If you let the camcorder set the exposure, your subject will be dark and the background will be perfectly exposed.** In this case, set the exposure manually or use the camcorders backlit exposure feature if so equipped. The background is overexposed, but your subject is properly exposed.

You can also compensate for backlighting by bouncing light on your subject. You can create a makeshift reflector with a car windshield shade. Many sunshades have a silver finish on one side and gold on the other. Have a friend or family member position the shade so that it's out of frame and bounces light back on your subject. Use the gold side of the sunshade to bounce warm light on your subject.

✔ **If you're recording a subject that's in heavy shade, such as a person under a beach umbrella, and the rest of the scene is brightly lit, your camcorder will average the exposure for the scene and you won't be able to see any detail on your subject.** When this is the case, zoom in on your subject, set the exposure manually, and then zoom out and record the scene.

When you manually set exposure to record an adversely lit scene, make sure you change the exposure when lighting conditions change or switch to auto-exposure when you finish recording the scene.

✔ **When recording a night scene, manually set the focus on your subject.** Camcorders set with automatic focus have a tendency to focus on the brightest subject in a scene, which may cause the focus to go out of whack when bright lights, such as car headlights enter the scene.

✔ **When panning a scene with different light levels, manually set the exposure so that the brightest part of your scene isn't overexposed, and you still have detail in the shadow parts of your scene.** If you don't manually set exposure, your camcorder changes exposure when you pan to a part of the scene that has a different light level, which often causes the video to be momentarily too bright or too dim while the camcorder processor is trying to sort it all out. Remember, your camcorder processor is like a computer. It can't predict what you'll record next. But if you plan ahead of time, you'll know exactly what you're recording and can set up the camcorder to record the scene perfectly.

✔ **Don't pan too fast or too slow.** If you pan too fast, you can't see details, and the resulting video will look amateurish. If you pan too slowly, your video will be boring and your audience will fall asleep or find another YouTube video to view. Panning too quickly can also confuse the camcorder auto-focus, resulting in several seconds of blurry video while the camcorder processor catches up.

✔ **When you pan, hold the camcorder level.** If you're doing a lot of panning, a tripod with a level and a head that enables you to pan smoothly is a definite plus. You can also become a human tripod by spreading your feet slightly and holding your arms close to your side. If you're panning a fast-moving object, such as a moving car, the panning motion should come from the hips, not the arms.

✔ **Mount the camcorder on a tripod when you're interviewing someone.** If you don't have a tripod handy, place the camcorder on a stable surface and then compose the scene. Make sure you position the camcorder so that the object being used to steady the camcorder isn't visible in the frame.

Practice makes perfect with any skill, and panning is no exception. To hone your panning skills, capture video of neighborhood kids riding their bikes past you. When you can capture good video of kids on bikes, graduate to cars traveling down your street.

✔ **When you zoom in or out, don't zoom too fast or too slow; otherwise, your video looks like it's shot by a gerbil having an acid flashback.** Most camcorder zoom controls enable you to regulate the speed at which you zoom in or out. Practice zooming until you know the capabilities of your camcorder and can smoothly zoom in or out.

✔ **Don't break the time code on your tape.** The *time code* is a method of measuring the amount of time and frames that elapse as the tape is recorded. The time code is measured as *hh;mm:ss;ff*, where *h* is hours, *m* is minutes, *s* is seconds, and *f* is frames. For example, the time code 00:05:13;09 is 5 minutes, 13 seconds and 9 frames into the tape. If you break the time code, your capture software stops when it encounters a broken time code, thinking it's the end of the tape. Many people like to rewind their camcorders and preview what they've recorded already, which often leads to a broken timecode. When a timecode is broken, the video capture application thinks the recording has ended. To prevent this, record several seconds of black frames before rewinding or recording a new scene. You can easily do this by replacing the lens cap and recording 5 or 10 seconds.

✔ **Use an external microphone when at all possible.** You get better quality sound without any mechanical noise from the camcorder motors that advance the tape.

✔ **Use a pop filter on your external microphone.** A *pop filter* helps reduce wind noise and also safeguards against distorted vocals when pronouncing words with "plosives," like the letter P. You can use a thin sock for a makeshift pop filter.

If you're recording video in windy conditions, and you don't have an external microphone with a wind filter (also known as a pop filter), enable your camcorder's wind cut feature if your camcorder is so equipped. This feature is a menu command on most camcorders.

✔ **If you must follow a subject while taping her, use a shopping cart as a makeshift dolly.** Mount the camcorder on a tripod and set it in the shopping cart. If you handhold the camcorder while recording video, the camcorder bounces up and down while you walk. Watching a video of this caliber is almost as bad as being seasick. In lieu of a shopping cart, you can use something else with wheels, such as a wheelchair.

✔ **If you're recording a video from inside a car, mount your camcorder on a tripod on the passenger seat.** Secure the camcorder with the seatbelt and then fasten two bungee cords to the bottom of the tripod and secure them on the seat frame. You can use your camcorder remote to start and stop recording. If you use this technique, make sure to keep your eyes on the road. If you want to capture video in heavy traffic, have a friend sit in the back seat with the remote. Tell your friend when you want to start and stop recording.

✔ **Don't shoot video in bright sun in the middle of the day.** This results in harsh unflattering shadows. Shoot early in the morning or late in the afternoon when the light's golden and the shadows aren't harsh. If you're forced to shoot video in the middle of the day, find an area with even shade.

✔ **Compose your scenes.** If you're a photographer, you may be familiar with the "Rule of Thirds" in which you imagine a grid with nine squares superimposed over your scene. Position your *subject,* or the center of interest, where the gridlines intersect and you'll create more compelling videos.

✔ **Shoot additional scenes to flesh out your finished video.** For example, if you're conducting an interview of a person in Chinatown, capture several scenes that capture the magic and ambience of Chinatown. You can splice these into the video to add interest to your subject's audio commentary.

✔ **Don't record the date and time in your video.** This looks unprofessional and detracts from your subject. If you must record the date for reference, record three seconds of video of the scene with the date displayed. You may also want to record some audio to establish the purpose of the video. Then use your camcorder menu commands to disable displaying the date and record the good stuff.

✔ **Shoot a few extra seconds of video at the start and end of a scene.** The extra footage gives you more leeway when editing your video.

Accessorize your camcorder

When you purchase a camcorder, you may feel you have everything you need to record compelling video for the Tube. NOT! You'll also need some accessories to maintain your camcorder and protect it. The following is a list of items you should consider when accessorizing your camcorder:

- **Camcorder Case:** Purchase a case that's large enough to house your camcorder, extra tapes, and any other accessories you plan on purchasing, such as an external microphone.

- **Extra Batteries:** Nothing's worse than running out of power when you're in the middle of beautiful scenery that you want to record for posterity.

- **Battery Charger:** If you're going to be recording on the road, you might consider purchasing a unit that charges camcorder batteries via power from a car cigarette lighter.

- **Head Cleaning Tape:** Your camcorder head picks up residue from the tape and other debris. A dirty head isn't conducive to crystal clear video. Follow the head cleaning tape manufacturer's instructions for cleaning instructions and how often you should clean the head.

- **Lens Cleaning Kit:** Your camcorder lens picks up atmospheric pollutants that affect the clarity of your video. A good lens cleaning kit contains a microfiber cloth that can get rid of any *schmutz* (technospeak, for dirt and visible gunk) on your lens, including your fingerprints.

- **Skylight Filter:** A skylight filter that screws into the accessory threads of your camcorder lens reduces the bluish cast found in daylight and warms the colors in your video. In addition, the filter protects the lens. Replacing a scratched skylight filter is a lot cheaper than replacing a scratched lens.

If you're purchasing a camcorder to record videos that you'll be editing and uploading to the Tube, make sure the camcorder has a method for downloading the video to your computer. Many camcorders use DVD for the recording media. Videos recorded to DVD are convenient because you can watch them on your TV. However, you may not be able to download the video from the DVD to your computer in a format that can be edited with video-editing software. Ask the salesperson for details or refer to the camcorder manufacturer's Web site.

Recording video with your digital camera

There's no substitute for a good camcorder when you want to create compelling video. You can, however, create video with your digital camera if your camera has a movie mode. The video isn't broadcast quality. However, if you have a good camera with precision optics, you can create video suitable for monitor viewing or from the Tube. Here are a few suggestions for capturing good video with your digital camera:

- ✓ **Choose the highest frame rate at which your camera is capable of capturing video.** If you have an inexpensive point-and-shoot camera, the only option you may have is 15 fps (frames per second). If you own a more advanced camera that gives you the option to record at 30 fps, use it because you'll get smoother video.

- ✓ **Choose the highest frame size possible.** If you have an inexpensive camera, your only option may be a frame size of 320 × 240 pixels. If your camera has the option to capture video with a frame size of 640 × 480 pixels, use it.

- ✓ **Use high-performance memory cards.** When you capture video with your camera, your camera captures a sequence of images and converts them to video. A faster memory card enables you to capture the maximum number of fps that your camera is capable of, which results in smoother video.

- ✓ **Pan smoothly and slowly.** If you pan too quickly, you'll end up with jerky motion and blurred video because the camera can't process the images fast enough.

- ✓ **Zoom in on your subject before recording.** Most digital cameras don't have the option of zooming while recording video.

White balance and other delights

The dials and menu commands on your camcorder may seem intimidating to anyone who is the least bit techno-phobic. Let's face it, they're even intimidating to card-carrying geeks like us. Every camcorder is different. Here are a few options on digital camcorders that you should get to know on a personal basis. And if you're not sure where to find these options on your camera, you can always try reading the manual.

- ✓ **Audio Input Level:** This option enables you to control the audio input level of an external microphone. When you enable this option on most camcorders, you see a meter on the camcorder LCD display that shows the left and right channel sound level. Set the input level so the audio peaks aren't clipped. Your camcorder manual contains details on how to precisely set the audio input level.

- ✓ **Backlight:** If your camcorder has a backlight setting, use it when you're recording a scene in which the background is considerably brighter than your main subject. This setting can compensate for scenes, such as taping a couple walking down the beach with the setting sun in front of them.

- ✓ **Spot Light:** If your camcorder has a spot light setting, use it when you're recording a subject that's lit by a bright light, such as a comedian or a singer on stage.

✔ **Exposure:** If your camera has an exposure setting, you can manually set exposure for your scene. This option is handy when you're recording a scene with different light levels. You can manually set exposure so your main subject is properly exposed.

✔ **Focus:** Many camcorders have a focus ring that you use to manually focus on your main subject. Manual focus is useful when you're dealing with changing light conditions. Your camcorder may also have an Infinity focus setting, which is useful when you're recording a landscape. When you set focus to infinity and pan the camcorder, your camcorder isn't tricked into focusing on a nearby object that pops into the scene.

✔ **Menu Commands:** Camera menu commands vary, depending on the camera manufacturer and the price of the camcorder. More expensive cameras have more bells and whistles, hence more menu commands; not to mention, a thicker manual. With menu commands, you can change display options for your LCD viewer, change record mode from standard play to long play, change microphone input level, change audio mode, and so on. In order to figure out the advanced features of your camcorder that can be accessed through menu commands, we suggest you try the manual.

✔ **White Balance:** The human brain has a built-in filter that enables us to perceive white as white no matter what the lighting. Digital camcorders also have a built-in function that's used to record white objects as white. However, under mixed lighting conditions, the automatic white balance may be tricked into recording video that has a green tint or other color-cast. You can be absolutely sure that white is white by manually setting the white balance of your camcorder. Some camcorders have settings for outdoor and indoor. You can choose the setting that best matches the lighting conditions under which you're capturing video. Other camcorders have a setting that enables you to manually set white balance by zooming in on an object that's white and then pushing the White Balance button.

From Source to Desktop

After you create what you feel is the perfect video with your camcorder, you have to get it into your computer. Unless you own a camcorder that records video to DVD or memory card, your camcorder records to a cassette tape. Recording to DVD may sound like an advantage, but we prefer tape because it's easier to get your raw footage into the computer and then slice and dice it to create a video fellow Tubers enjoy.

Camcorders that record directly to a self-contained hard drive are more expensive than camcorders that record to tape, but do offer the advantage of faster data transfer from the camcorder to your computer.

If all you've ever done is connect your camcorder to the TV and play back the footage, you know how gnarly raw video can be. Even a pro misses the record switch after shooting a scene and captures several minutes of his feet scurrying across the ground.

If you've never edited video before because you didn't know what software to use, you're in for a surprise. If your computer has the latest Macintosh or Windows operating system, the software you need to turn your raw footage into a finished product is included with the computer operating system. If you own a PC and Windows XP or Vista, you find Windows Movie Maker lurking about on the Accessories menu. It you've taken a bite of the Apple and have one of the latest Macintosh operating systems, you have iMovie. With either application, you can create professional, quality videos for home viewing or for the world to see on the Tube. We show you how to work with both in the upcoming sections.

Starting a new project in Movie Maker

If you own a PC and you feel the need to create a video, your first step is to create a project in Movie Maker. After you create a new project, you're ready to capture video, compile the clips on the timeline, add transitions, and much more. To start a new project in Movie Maker, follow these steps:

1. **Choose Start⇨Programs⇨Accessories⇨Windows Movie Maker.**

   The Window Movie Maker application launches.

2. **Choose File⇨New Project.**

   A new project is created with the default options. After you create a new project, it doesn't look like anything happened. However, any video clips you add to the timeline are included as project data. No matter how much you slice or dice the video, the changes are recorded with the project and your original video is untouched.

Video editing uses a lot of your processor's resources. It's a good idea to save a project early, and save it often, especially if you're multi-tasking and have your e-mail application as well as YouTube open while working on a project. You never know when a computer conflict might lock up Movie Maker tighter than Fort Knox, causing you to lose your carefully crafted video.

Starting a new project in iMovie

If you own a Mac, your first step to compiling your raw footage into a movie is to create a new project in iMovie. *iMovie* is a video-editing software package that comes standard when you purchase a Macintosh computer. After you create a new project in iMovie, you're ready to import, or *capture,* video from your camera and then use the software to edit your clips and apply transitions and other effects.

To start a new project in iMovie, follow these steps:

1. **Double-click your Mac's hard drive.**

   By default, your Mac's hard drive is named Macintosh HD, but you can always rename it.

2. **Double-click the Applications icon on the left and then double click the iMovie (or iMovie HD) icon to launch the software.**

   On a Mac, you can also double-click the iMovie (or iMovie HD) icon in the application dock to launch the software.

3. **On the application splash screen, as shown in Figure 7-1, click the Create a New Project button.**

Figure 7-1: iMovie's splash screen, which is where you create a new movie.

This opens the Create Project dialog box, which you use to name and save your new project.

4. **Type** Dummies iMovie 1 **in the Project text box, click the Create button, and then save the project to your location of choice.**

   Actually, you can type any title you want. But if you want to make a Dummies movie in iMovie, have at it.

5. **The main window in iMovie, as shown in Figure 7-2, opens automatically when you create the project.**

   You're now ready to capture video to edit in the Movie Timeline beneath the view window.

Video editing is a memory-intensive operation and challenges your Mac processor. It's a good idea to save your project often, especially if you're multi-tasking with YouTube open while you're working.

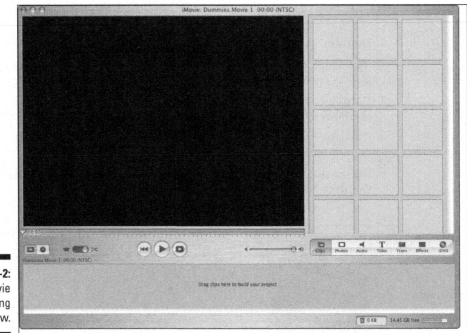

Figure 7-2:
The iMovie
main editing
window.

Capturing video with Windows Movie Maker

Windows Movie Maker is quite an impressive application. It has everything you need to turn your raw footage into a finished movie. If your camcorder has a FireWire (IEEE 1394) or USB port, you simply connect it to a FireWire or USB card on your computer and Movie Maker does the rest. You can also capture video with an analog capture card. If you choose the latter and want to capture the audio as well, you need a sound card capable of receiving signals from external sources.

When you capture video to your hard drive, you use over 200MB of hard drive space for each minute of video you capture. If you only have one hard drive on your system, and you're capturing a lot of video, you run the risk of running out of hard drive space and creating a non-recoverable system crash. It's a good idea to invest in a second internal hard drive, or an external hard drive, and use this drive for video capture.

To capture video with Movie Maker, follow these steps:

1. **Turn on your camcorder, switch to video playback mode (known as VTR mode on most devices), and connect the cables from your camcorder to your capture device.**

Windows makes an annoying noise and alerts you to the fact that you have a device connected to your computer. Depending on how your system's configured, a window may open that gives you options. If one of them is to capture video with Windows Movie Maker, choose that option. Alternatively, you can close the window and launch Windows Movie Maker manually, which we show you how to do in the next step.

2. **Choose Start⇨Programs⇨Accessories⇨Windows Movie Maker.**

   Windows Movie Maker opens (see Figure 7-3).

3. **Choose Capture Video from the Movie Tasks section.**

   The Video Capture Wizard appears. Your camcorder is listed as one of the options (see Figure 7-4).

   Alternatively, you can connect your camcorder to your computer after launching Movie Maker to automatically launch the Video Capture Wizard.

4. **Select your camcorder or capture device and then click Next.**

   The Captured Video File section of the Video Capture Wizard appears (see Figure 7-5). Notice that many methods of capturing video from the computer are used to capture this screenshot.

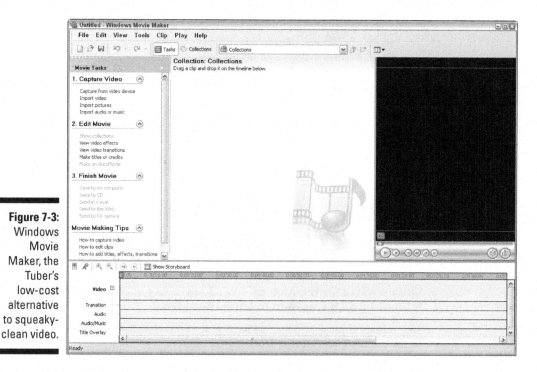

Figure 7-3: Windows Movie Maker, the Tuber's low-cost alternative to squeaky-clean video.

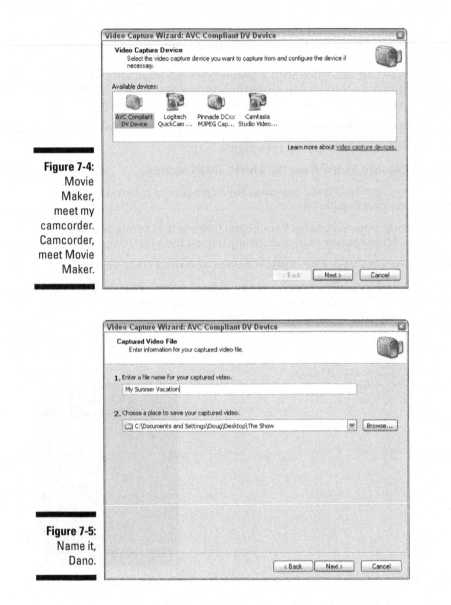

Figure 7-4:
Movie
Maker,
meet my
camcorder.
Camcorder,
meet Movie
Maker.

Figure 7-5:
Name it,
Dano.

5. Enter a name for the footage you're capturing and then browse to the folder in which you want to store the video.

We're logical kind of guys, so we use a name that makes sense when we open the files six months from now.

6. Click Next.

Lo and behold, the Video Setting section of the Video Capture Wizard appears (see Figure 7-6).

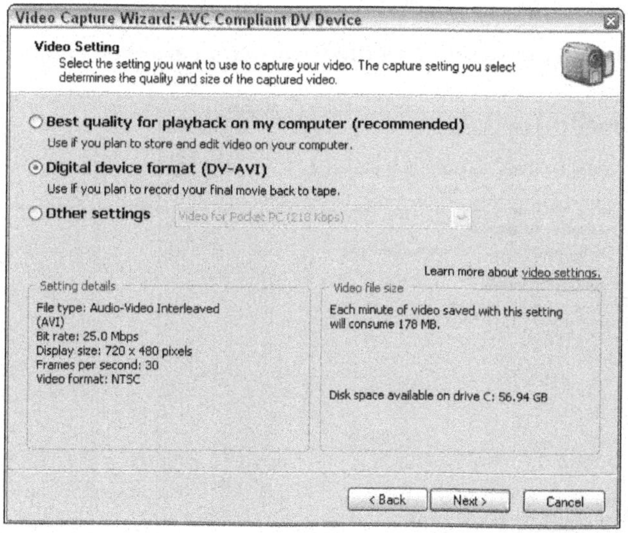

Video Capture Wizard: AVC Compliant DV Device

Video Setting
Select the setting you want to use to capture your video. The capture setting you select determines the quality and size of the captured video.

○ **Best quality for playback on my computer (recommended)**
Use if you plan to store and edit video on your computer.

⊙ **Digital device format (DV-AVI)**
Use if you plan to record your final movie back to tape.

○ **Other settings**   Video for Pocket PC (218 Kbps)

Learn more about video settings.

Setting details
File type: Audio-Video Interleaved (AVI)
Bit rate: 25.0 Mbps
Display size: 720 x 480 pixels
Frames per second: 30
Video format: NTSC

Video file size
Each minute of video saved with this setting will consume 178 MB.

Disk space available on drive C: 56.94 GB

< Back   Next >   Cancel

Figure 7-6:
Choose a capture setting.

7. Choose the desired video setting.

The setting you choose determines the quality of video with which you have to work.

- **Best Quality for Playback on My Computer:** If your hard drive doesn't have copious amounts of unused gigabytes, select this setting. This converts the captured footage to the WMV (Windows Media Video) format.

- **Digital Device Format (DV-AVI):** If you'll eventually burn the video to DVD, choose this setting. This option applies minimal compression to the captured video. The resulting video is the proper size (720 × 480 pixels) and frame rate (29.97 fps) for broadcast quality video.

If you choose the Digital Device Format capture option, you use approximately 179MB (megabyte) of hard disk space for each minute of video you capture.

8. Click Next.

The Capture Method section of the Video Capture Wizard appears (see Figure 7-7).

9. Choose the desired capture method.

You can choose to manually capture parts of the video or capture the entire tape. We always choose the latter. Video capture is 1-to-1. If you record an entire 60-minute tape, you end up with about 62 minutes of video, which takes 62 minutes to capture. Manually capturing video takes a bit longer, but it allows you to choose the sections you capture, which eliminates the need to delete them from your hard drive after capture.

10. **Click Next.**

The Capture Video section of the wizard appears (see Figure 7-8).

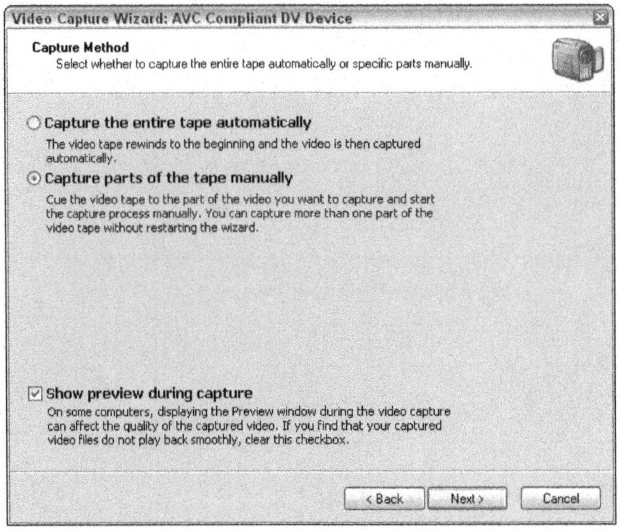

Figure 7-7:
Okay, here's the plan: We capture video for the Tube.

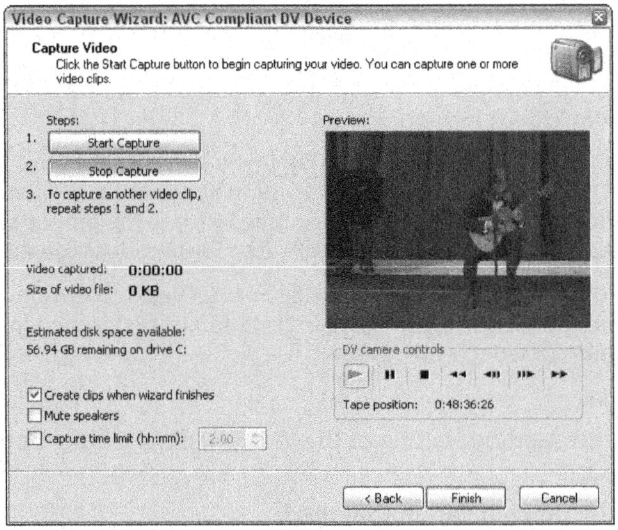

Figure 7-8:
Gentlemen, start your capture.

11. **If you choose to capture the entire tape, step away from your computer and do something else. If you choose to manually capture clips, you must be at the helm.**

If you choose to manually capture your video, this section of the wizard has a Start Capture and Stop Capture button plus VCR-like controls. You begin playing the tape and then click the Start Capture button to capture footage. When you see something you don't like, click the Stop Capture button. If you choose the Create Clips when Wizard Finishes option, Windows Movie Maker creates individual clips for each section you capture.

In this section, you also have an option to mute the speakers while Movie Maker is capturing your video, and you can specify the maximum number of minutes of video Movie Maker captures.

12. **Click Finish after you capture the desired clips.**

    Windows Movie Maker saves the clips to your hard drive with the name you specify appended by the number of the clip. The clips are saved as a *collection,* from which you can assemble the final video. The first frame of each captured clip appears as a thumbnail in the collection.

Capturing video with iMovie

A big step in any video-editing project is accessing your raw footage on your camera and transferring it to your computer. In video-editing lingo, this is referred to as *capturing* video.

Working on a Mac, you use iMovie to capture video from your camcorder, and that captured video is transferred directly into your iMovie software.

To capture video with iMovie, follow these steps:

1. **Connect your video camera to your Macintosh computer via a FireWire cable.**

2. **Verify that your camcorder is turned on and then set the camera mode to VTR.**

    If your camera doesn't have VTR mode, try using either Play or VCR mode.

3. **In your iMovie software, click the mode switch to set iMovie to camera mode, as shown in Figure 7-9.**

4. **Use the playback controls to view your raw video footage in the iMovie monitor.**

5. **Find the location in the video playback where you want to start importing and then click Import.**

    When you click Import, iMovie HD begins capturing the video footage.

    Rather than click Import, you can press the Spacebar.

6. **Click Import again when you want to stop capturing.**

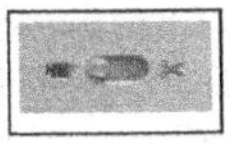

Figure 7-9:
Setting the
mode switch
in iMovie
to capture
video.

While iMovie is importing your video, the software is preset to automatically break up your video footage into individual clips wherever it finds a *scene break* (wherever the recording was interrupted when you were shooting). To disable this preset, click iMovie HD on the menu bar, click Preferences, click the Import icon, and then deselect the Start a New Clip at Each Scene Break check box.

If you own a camcorder that has an internal hard drive or uses memory cards to capture video, it won't allow you to "capture" video. Instead, it transfers video from the camera hard drive or memory card to a folder on your hard drive. This is much faster than capturing video. However, the quality may not be as good as tape because some models compress the video before saving it.

Creating your first movie in Movie Maker

So you want to be the next big star on the Tube? Well, to achieve that lofty goal, you have to upload some video; preferably something entertaining and unique. After you create a project and capture video, you're ready to create your first movie with Movie Maker. To create a movie in Movie Maker, follow these steps:

1. **Choose Start➪Programs➪Accessories➪Windows Movie Maker.**

   Windows Movie Maker launches, and you're ready to make some movie magic.

2. **Choose File➪Create New Project.**

   Alternatively, you can press Ctrl+N.

3. **Capture or import video.**

   To capture video, connect your camcorder to an IEEE 1394 port, also known as a FireWire port, choose File➪Capture Video, and then follow the prompts (as we outline in the section "Capturing video with Windows Movie Maker," later in this chapter). To import video, click Import Video to open the Import File dialog box. You can import the following video file formats into Movie Maker: AVI, MPG, M1V, MP2, M2V, MPEG, MPE, WM, WM, and WMV. A collection is created for each video clip you import.

4. **Click Collections.**

   The video collections you import in to Movie Maker are displayed as icons in the left column of the workspace (see Figure 7-10).

5. **Select a video clip from a collection and then press the Play button.**

   The video clip plays in the Playback window (see Figure 7-11).

6. **Drop the clip on the timeline.**

   While you drag the clip from the Collections bin, a dimmed-out icon of the clip appears. Release the clip on the timeline, and it snaps to the tail of the last clip you added to the timeline.

7. **Continue adding clips to the timeline.**

   You can add as many clips as you want to the timeline. If you have a normal YouTube account, your video needs to be less than 10MB and no longer than 10 minutes.

8. **Click the Rewind Timeline button and then click the Play Timeline button.**

   Your movie plays in the preview window.

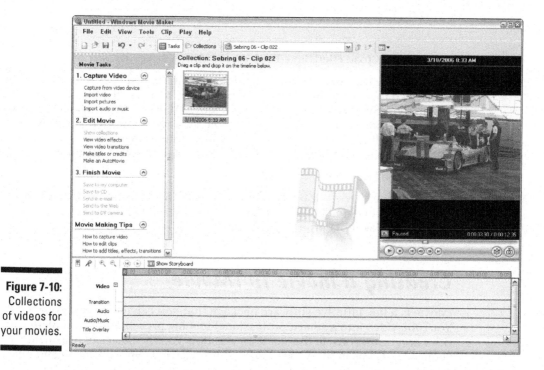

Figure 7-10:
Collections
of videos for
your movies.

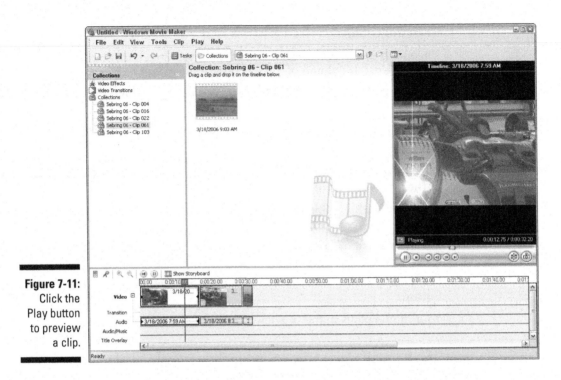

Figure 7-11:
Click the
Play button
to preview
a clip.

9. **Choose Close File⇨Save Project.**

   The Save Dialog box appears. Enter a filename and specify a destination in which to save the file. When you save a Movie Maker file, the file is saved in the MSWMM (Microsoft Windows Movie Maker) format. The file isn't a movie that can be played. The file's the information needed to reconstruct the timeline and any other gingerbread you may have added, such as transitions and titles. We cover transitions and titles in Chapter 8.

10. **Choose File⇨Save Movie File.**

   The Save Movie Wizard appears, as shown in Figure 7-12. The wizard is covered in detail in the section, "Optimizing video for the Tube with Movie Maker," later in this chapter.

Creating a movie in iMovie

iMovie is a fun, intuitive software package that you can use to edit your YouTube video into a smart, professional-looking presentation, complete with titles and transitions. In this section, we show you the basics of organizing a sequence of clips in the Movie Timeline, previewing clips, setting in and out points, and exporting an optimized file for upload to YouTube. With just a little practice and experimentation, you can use iMovie to create your very own video editing suite in your home office.

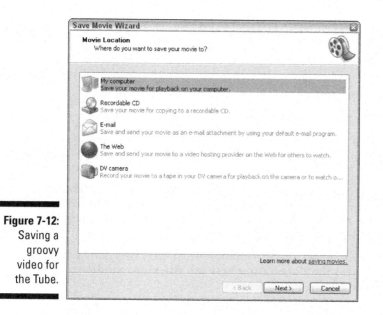

Figure 7-12:
Saving a
groovy
video for
the Tube.

To create a movie in Movie Maker, follow these steps:

1. **Import your clips into the Clips Pane or directly into the Movie Timeline.**

   In Figure 7-13, eight clips have been imported into the Clips Pane.

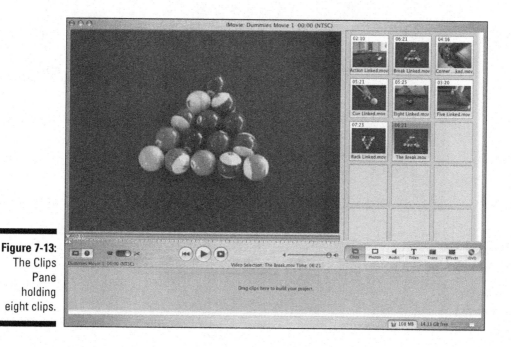

Figure 7-13:
The Clips
Pane
holding
eight clips.

You can specify which field you want iMovie to capture video to — Clips Pane or the Movie Timeline. To do so, click iMovie on the menu bar, click Preferences, and then in the Import section, choose Clips Pane or Movie Timeline.

2. Drag a clip from the Clips Pane into the Movie Timeline.

The clip is added to your movie.

If you want to upload movies that are longer than ten minutes or higher in file size than 10 MB, create a specialty account, such as a Directors or Gurus account. We cover specialty accounts in detail in Chapter 9.

It's a good idea to drag a copy of the clip into the Movie Timeline, thereby leaving the original clip to use again if you like. To drag a copy, press and hold the Option key while you drag the clip from the Clips Pane into the Movie Timeline.

3. Click any clip in the Movie Timeline or in the Clips Pane to select it and then press the Play button beneath the view window to preview the clip. See Figure 7-14.

4. Add additional clips to the timeline to flesh out your movie.

You can add as many clips as you want to the timeline. If you have a normal YouTube account, your video needs to be less than 10MB and no longer than 10 minutes.

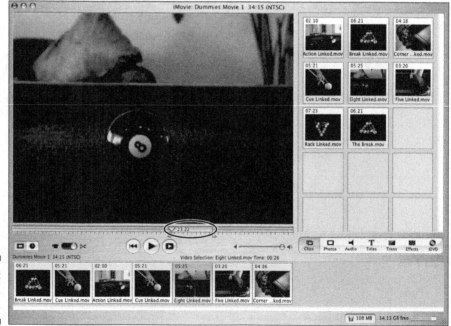

Figure 7-14:
Previewing
a single clip.

5. **Reorganize the sequence of clips in the Movie Timeline simply by dragging them left or right.**

   When you drag a clip left or right in the Movie Timeline, other clips move to make space for the clip you're moving.

6. **Preview your *movie* — the entire sequence of clips — any time by verifying that no clips are selected and pressing the Play button beneath the view window.**

   You can simply press the Spacebar on your keypad to start and stop the playback.

7. **Save your work.**

Optimizing video for the Tube with Movie Maker

We use video in our work and we write books on video; therefore, we feel qualified to show you how to optimize video. The normal course of events when optimizing video is to optimize the video for the intended destination. When you optimize video, the bandwidth of the intended audience is what you factor into the optimizing equation. That logic flies out the window when you optimize for the Tube. The lads at the Tube have their own compression algorithm (the codec and compression setting used to convert your file into the video you see on YouTube). The file you upload to the Tube is converted to a Flash movie, which can be played on the YouTube video player, which is their derivative of the Flash 9 Player. When the file's converted, it's also compressed. Therefore, you get the best possible YouTube video if you compress it just enough to beat the 100MB file size limitation. To optimize a video for the Tube in Movie Maker, follow these steps:

1. **Choose Start⇨Programs⇨Accessories⇨Windows Movie Maker.**

   Windows Movie Maker launches, and you're ready to make some movie magic.

2. **Choose File⇨Create New Project.**

   Alternatively, you can press Ctrl+N.

3. **Capture or import video into the project.**

4. **Preview clips from collections and arrange them on the timeline.**

5. **Preview the project.**

6. **Choose File⇨Save Movie.**

   The Saved part of the Saved Movie File section of the Movie Wizard appears (see Figure 7-15).

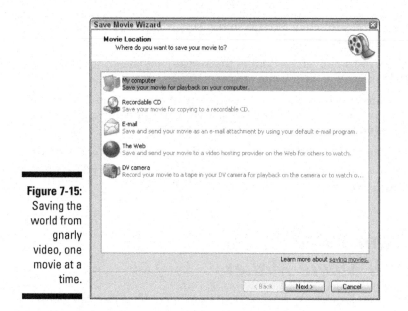

Figure 7-15:
Saving the
world from
gnarly
video, one
movie at a
time.

7. Choose My Computer and then click Next.

The Saved Movie part of the Save Movie Wizard appears (see Figure 7-16).

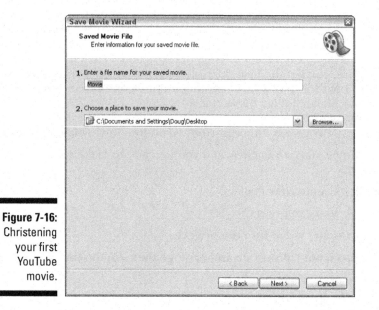

Figure 7-16:
Christening
your first
YouTube
movie.

8. **Type a name for the movie and specify the destination on your computer where you want to store the rendered movie.**

   Type whatever name you like. You can enter a different title when you upload to the Tube.

9. **Click Next.**

   The Movie Settings part of the Save Movie Wizard appears. The default settings produce a file that's the wrong aspect ratio and too large for the Tube.

10. **Click Show More Choices.**

    The Wizard shows more choices. Amazing.

11. **Click Other Settings and then choose Video for Broadband (512 kbps), as in Figure 7-17.**

    If you know digital video, you know the data rate may be too high for some broadband connections. Remember that YouTube applies additional compression to your precious video after you upload it. If you upload good-quality video, you end up with good video. Notice that the Save Movie Wizard also shows you how large the rendered movie is.

12. **Click Next.**

    The Saving Movie part of the wizard appears, along with a nifty progress bar that shows you how long it'll take to render your video. After the video is rendered, the Completing the Save Movie Wizard Section of the Save Movie Wizard appears.

13. **Select the Play Movie when I Finish check box if you want a sneak preview before exiting Movie Maker.**

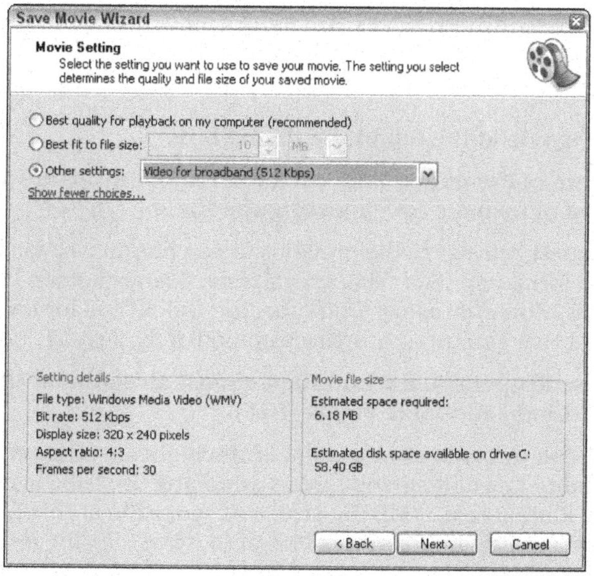

Figure 7-17:
To optimize
or not to
optimize;
that is the
question.

14. Click Finish.

The wizard closes, and you can start your next masterpiece or chill out and watch some video on the Tube.

Optimizing video for the Tube with iMovie

In this section, we go through the steps of exporting your video from iMovie and compressing its file size (often referred to in techie lingo as *optimizing*) for upload to YouTube.

Even though YouTube allows all registered users to upload clips as large as 100MB, many users create and upload dozens of videos to YouTube in as little time as a week. Even if you don't create that many videos, most users don't want 100MB files sitting around on their computers taking up so much hard drive space.

With that in mind, in this chapter, when we discuss optimizing a video clip, we'll do so with the idea that you want to keep your video under 10 minutes in length and under 15MB in file size.

Here's how to optimize your video in iMovie:

1. Be sure to save your project.

2. Click File on the menu bar and then click Export.

3. Click the Export drop-down list and then choose To QuickTime.

4. Click the Formats drop-down list and then choose Expert Settings.

Choosing Expert Settings offers you more choices for optimizing your video.

5. Click Export.

6. Name your movie at the top of the dialog box.

7. At the bottom of the dialog box, click the Export drop-down list to see your choices of formats for exporting the file.

Choosing Expert Settings in the previous dialog box allows you to access this menu of format options. Though you have many choices, when saving a movie from iMovie for use on YouTube, the QuickTime format is an established format that YouTube recognizes immediately. It's your best choice.

8. Click the Use drop-down list and then choose Broadband-High. Your dialog box should resemble Figure 7-18.

We recommend that you always start at the highest setting to achieve the best quality possible. If you have a standard YouTube account and are thereby limited to a 10MB file size, save your file at this high-quality choice. If the resulting file's size is too large, save it again and choose a lower-quality setting.

If you know a lot about digital video and want even more options for exporting your file and choosing a compression algorithm, click the Options button.

9. **Click Save.**

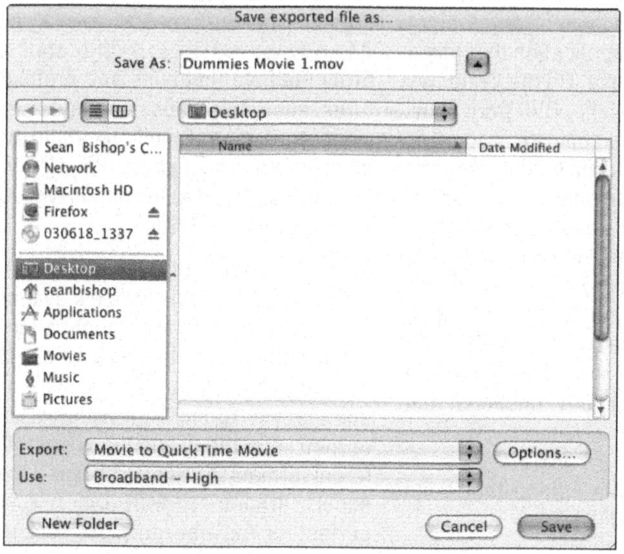

Save exported file as...

Save As: Dummies Movie 1.mov

Desktop

Name	Date Modified

Sean Bishop's C...
Network
Macintosh HD
Firefox
030618_1337
Desktop
seanbishop
Applications
Documents
Movies
Music
Pictures

Export: Movie to QuickTime Movie   Options...
Use: Broadband – High

New Folder   Cancel   Save

Figure 7-18:
Exporting an optimized video in iMovie.

Digital Video 101 For Dummies

If you've done any research on video for the Web, you know that there are *beaucoup* codecs. If you don't have the right codec on your computer, you can't view a video rendered with that codec. The founders of YouTube started the site for that very reason: They couldn't view videos sent by friends and colleagues, so they evened the playing field by choosing the codec most people have on their computers. Another factor is the video frame rate. The frame rate determines whether your video plays smoothly. We dive into both topics in the upcoming sections.

Understanding frame and pixel aspect ratio

Video *frame rate* is the number of frames used to play a second of video. *Broadcast quality video* (you know, the stuff you watch on TV) is 29.970 fps (frames per second), and high definition video is 60 fps. You guessed it, more frames means smoother video. If you're capturing video from a standard camcorder, you get good video for the Tube if you render the video with a frame rate of 30 fps.

Taking your video editing to the next level

Windows Movie Maker and Apple iMovie are great little applications for capturing and editing video. However, if you really want to trick out your video, you can do so by investing a bit of money in a video-editing application that has a few more tricks up its sleeve. On the Windows side, you can use Movie Studio+DVD from Sony. The application features a sophisticated timeline control and drag-and-drop editing. You can mix four video and four audio tracks. The application also features sophisticated transitions. You can render your edited video in numerous formats. You can also create a DVD from your finished work. As of this writing, the application sells for $89.95. The platinum edition of the software is the answer if you shoot high-definition video. You can download a fully functional trial version at www.sonymediasoftware. com/download/step2.asp?did=613. They also offer a platinum edition that edits high-definition video for $119.95.

If you own a Macintosh computer and you want a more sophisticated video-editing application, consider purchasing Final Cut Pro's baby brother, Final Cut Express (www.apple.com/ finalcutexpress). The application features multiple timelines and professional features, such as compositing layers, compelling video transitions, multiple audio tracks, and much more. The application also works with high definition video. As of this writing, Final Cut Express sells for $299.

One of the best-kept video secrets on the planet is Apple's QuickTime Pro. It's available for the PC and Macintosh. The application gives you video-editing capabilities and enables you to add text tracks to videos. The application enables you to import a wide variety of video formats, edit them, and then export them in different formats. Two of QuickTime's most popular export formats are MPEG-4 (.mp4), which is perfect for YouTube, and AAC, which is the proprietary format for iTunes and iPod.

Video that's destined to be broadcast on an NTSC television has rectangular pixels with an aspect ratio of .09091. Video for monitor display has a pixel aspect ratio of 1.0. In other words, video pixels for NTSC television broadcast are rectangular, and video pixels for monitor display are square. Most video-editing applications make the conversion when you choose a preset. However, if you ever have to do it manually, it's good to know the correct choice for aspect ratio.

Choosing the right codec

There are almost as many proprietary video *codecs* (applications or devices that encode digital video when saving and decode it when playing) as there are videos on the Tube. You can't just fling anything at the Tube. They have standards. They also have software that compresses what you fling at them. They don't cater to every codec, just the following ones:

✔ **Window Media Video (WMV):** This is Microsoft's video codec, which can be viewed in the Windows Media Player and several other players. The codec offers clean video at data rates above 340 kbps (kilobytes per second).

✔ **Audio Visual Interleave (AVI):** This is another Windows file format. And just when you thought it was safe to just click AVI as the file format, you have several AVI codecs from which to choose. In our humble opinion, the best AVI video format for the Web is Cinepak Codec by Radius.

✔ **Apple QuickTime Movie (MOV):** This is another file format capable of delivering stunning video provided you have a data rate of 300 kbps or higher.

✔ **Motion Picture Experts Group (MPG):** MPG is the shortened version of MPEG. There are quite a few variations of this file format as well. By far, the best MPEG choice for a video destined for YouTube is .mp4, which is derived from Apple's QuickTime Container format. You get the best results if you optimize MPG video with a data rate of 300 kbps or higher.

Freeware Applications for Optimizing Video

If you're doing video on a shoestring, you'll be happy to know freeware is available, which gives you the power to convert video files to different formats. Don't ask us what prompts people to give away software. Perhaps they get paid sponsors on their Web site. But most moms offer their kids the following sage advice, "For free, take. For buy, waste money."

Super for Windows

If you own a PC and have Windows XP or later, a free application, *Super,* imports video and exports it to different file formats. As of this writing, the application (see Figure 7-19) opens most popular file formats, including AVI, ASF, FLV, MPG, MOV, MP4, and SWF. To import files, you drag and drop them into the file window. You can import multiple files and batch process them. You can export the file in a different format and specify data rate, frame rate, frame size, and so on. The only negative thing we can say about the application is that the current version doesn't give you the option of specifying the folder in which exported files are saved. By default, they're saved to the root folder of your C: drive. You can download Super at `www.erightsoft.net/ SUPER.html`. Scroll to the bottom of the page and then click the link to download Super.

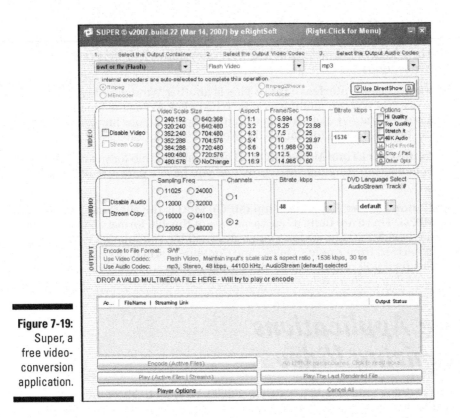

Figure 7-19:
Super, a
free video-
conversion
application.

Creating Instructional Videos

If you sign up for a Gurus account, your primary goal on the Tube is to share information with people. If the information you want to share is about how to master a computer application, you need software capable of capturing still images and video from your computer screen. Combined with your scholarly narration, videos captured from your computer and uploaded to YouTube create an excellent venue for you to inform potential clients and show off your expertise.

Choosing capture software

The easiest way to show someone how to do something with a computer application is to create an instructional video. We know many authors who have used instructional videos to augment their incomes. The videos can be available for download from the author's Web site or in the form of a CD with jam-packed with instructional videos that can be viewed on the student's computer. We highly recommend two applications.

To capture still shots of our computer screens, we use SnagIt8 (see Figure 7-20) by TechSmith. This application gives you the capability of capturing a window, the entire screen, or multiple regions. The captured image can be exported in a wide variety of file formats, including TIFF, PNG, and JPEG. You can create a video by importing the captured screenshots into a video-editing application and then recording a voice-over. A trial version of the Windows-only application can be downloaded from www.techsmith.com/download/snagittrial.asp.

To capture video of an application, we use Camtasia Studio 4 by TechSmith. The suite comes with Camtasia Audio Editor, Camtasia MenuMaker, Camtasia Player, Camtasia Recorder, and Camtasia Theatre. The application we use the most is Camtasia Recorder, which enables us to capture video of every step we perform in an application. Camtasia Recorder is also capable of recording your voice, provided you have a microphone connected to your computer. You can record your captures as just video and do a voice-over after the fact in Camtasia Studio. You can access individual applications from the Windows Programs menu, or launch Camtasia Studio (see Figure 7-21), which enables you to record your computer screen and then perform edits to the captured video, such as adding titles, importing other media, and so on. You can download a trial version of Camtasia Studio 4 from www.techsmith.com/download/camtasiatrial.asp.

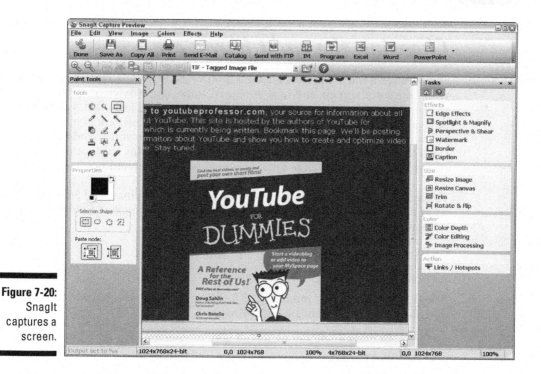

Figure 7-20:
SnagIt
captures a
screen.

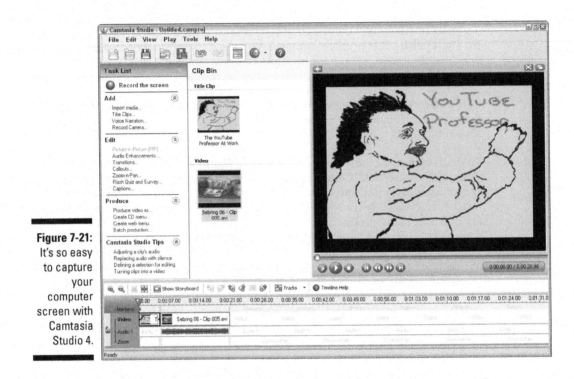

Figure 7-21:
It's so easy
to capture
your
computer
screen with
Camtasia
Studio 4.

Choosing the right hardware

So you have a Guru YouTube account, you've purchased software to capture your computer screen, and now you need some sage advice on what hardware to use. Oh, you hadn't considered hardware? First and foremost, you have to have a computer that has enough resources and is robust enough to capture video. Then you need a microphone that doesn't make you sound like Daffy Duck after inhaling helium or Walter Cronkite addressing the world through a tin can tied to a string. Here are some suggestions for Windows users.

To capture still shots of your computer screen, we recommend SnagIt8. If you want to capture full motion video of your screen, we suggest Camtasia 4. The minimum system requirements for Camtasia are:

- Microsoft Windows 2000, XP, or Vista
- Microsoft DirectX 9 or later version
- 1.0 GHz processor minimum (2.5 GHz is recommended if you use PowerPoint or Webcam recordings)
- 500MB RAM minimum (1.0GB is recommended)
- 60MB of hard-disk space for program installation

These are the minimum requirements. If you're capturing video of applications that require lots of resources, you need more memory and a more powerful processor.

The other side of the video capture equation is audio. If you're capturing video for the Tube in order to drive potential clients to your Web site, the end result must be professional. Therefore, you need the best microphone you can afford. One convenient option is a headset microphone that plugs into your USB port. Plantronics makes computer headsets with noise cancelling microphones that plug into your computer USB port (www.plantronics.com/north_america/en_US/products/cat640035/cat1430032). If you have room, you can get great sound quality by connecting a professional microphone to a USB pre-amp. We use M-Audio's Podcasting Factory, which contains a USB interface, broadcast quality microphone, stand, and software. If you're going to multi-task and create video podcasts as well as YouTube videos, this is the ideal solution. You can find out more about M-Audio's Podcast Factory at www.m-audio.com/products/en_us/PodcastFactory-main.html.

One Giant Step: Uploading Your Video

After you slave over a hot computer and slice and dice your video to pixel perfection, you can upload it to the Tube. Trust us, it's not a big deal. We do it all the time. But there's more than one way to skin an interface. If you prefer the intimacy of a spontaneous recording, you can record a video while you upload it. We show you how to do both in the upcoming sections.

Uploading video from your computer

If your video is ready to rock and roll, you can upload it directly from your computer to the Tube. It's quick and easy, but it takes awhile depending on the size of your video and the speed with which you connect to the Internet. After it uploads, you can watch your video. After you upload it, you have to wait a few minutes before you can notify your friends that your latest and greatest is on the Tube. After all, the boys at YouTube have to convert your video to Flash format. To upload a video from your computer, follow these steps:

1. **Log in to YouTube.**

   Fire up your favorite Web browser, go to www.youtube.com, enter your username and password, and then click Log In.

2. **Click Upload Videos.**

   The Video Upload page appears (see Figure 7-22).

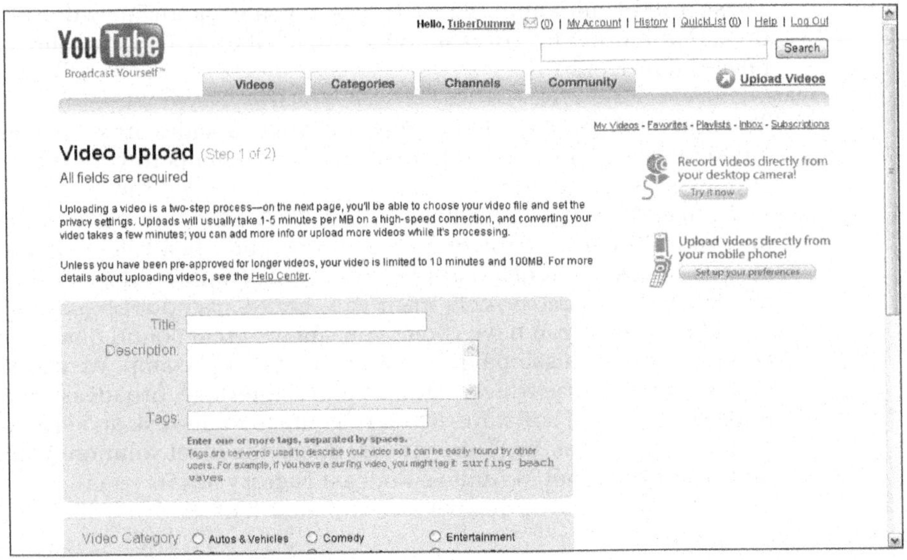

Figure 7-22:
Video going
up to
YouTube.

3. **Enter a title for the video.**

   This is what your fellow Tubers see when they view your video.

4. **Enter a description for the video.**

   Enter a meaningful description because that content is used in a search.

5. **Enter tags for the video.**

   Tags are text information that's used during a search. Tags are important; therefore, we give them a special section in Chapter 8.

6. **Choose a video category.**

   The category in which you place your video is important because some Tubers jump straight to a category to find what they want.

7. **Choose a language from the drop-down list.**

   This is the language spoken by people in your video or used in text overlays. At this point, read the copyright notice. If you don't own the copyright to the video you're uploading, continuing to upload is a breach of the copyright laws and YouTube's regulations.

8. **Click Continue Uploading.**

   The Video Upload (Step 2 of 2) appears (see Figure 7-23).

9. **Click Browse and then navigate to the video you want to upload.**

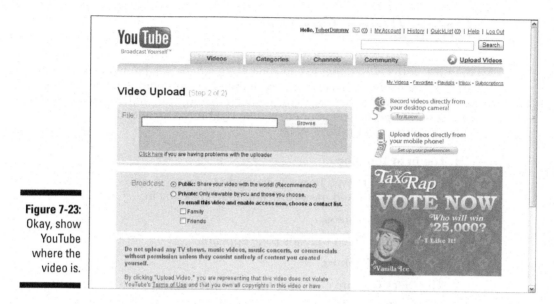

Figure 7-23:
Okay, show
YouTube
where the
video is.

10. **Choose whether your video is public or private.**

    If you click the Public radio button, anyone who logs in to YouTube can view your video. If you click the Private radio button, you can choose whether only your Family list can view the video or people on your Friends list can view the video.

11. **Read the disclaimer about TV shows, music concerts, and so on.**

    You can't legally upload a video clip from a TV show, music concert, or any of the other categories listed unless you created all the content in the video or have been given permission to upload the video.

12. **Click Upload Video.**

    At this point, you see a progress bar and text that shows the size of video. At this point in the process, Chris takes his dog for a walk, and Doug teaches his cat how to make Origami out of the endless barrage of credit card offers that arrive in his mailbox. In other words, the upload takes some time. Unless you're fond of looking at scrolling progress bars, relax and have a cigar, you're gonna go far.

You also have to wait for a few minutes while YouTube converts your video into Flash format. While the conversion is taking place, you can upload other videos or check out the latest-and-greatest videos in your favorite category.

Using Quick Capture

If you like to be in the spotlight and do so spontaneously, you'll love Quick Capture. With *Quick Capture,* you can create videos at a moment's notice as long as you have a video camera connected to your computer. Quick Capture is the perfect way to fire off a quick video response for another Tuber's video or just get something off your chest, like right now. To upload a video using Quick Capture, follow these steps:

1. **Log in to YouTube.**

   In your favorite Web browser, navigate to www.youtube.com, enter your username and password, and then click Log In.

2. **Click Upload Videos.**

   Page 1 of the Video Uploads page appears.

3. **Click Quick Capture.**

   The Quick Capture page appears. (See Figure 7-24).

4. **Enter a title for the video.**

   This is the title that appears on the results page of a search and above your video when it's played.

5. **Enter a description for the video.**

   Descriptions are used in searches, so give an apt description of what your quick capture rant is all about.

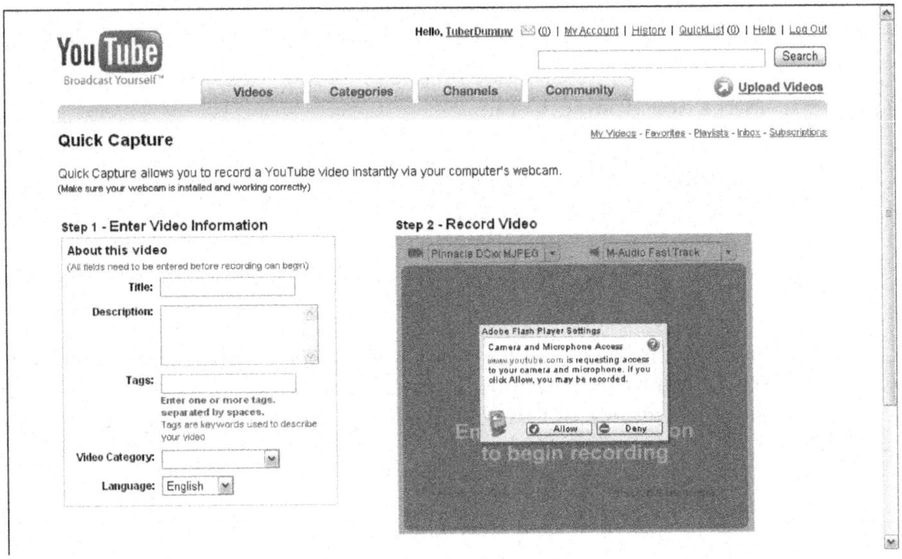

Figure 7-24: Quick, capture my video before I change my mind.

6. **Enter tags for your video.**

   Tags are text separated by spaces. We show you everything you need to know about tags in Chapter 8.

7. **Choose a category from the Category drop-down list.**

   This is the category in which your video rant can be found on the Tube.

8. **Choose a language from the drop-down list.**

   This is your native language. That is of course unless you decide to speak a foreign tongue.

9. **Click Allow.**

   This allows YouTube to connect to your camera. Cool huh? Big brother is watching.

10. **Choose your video and audio device from the drop-down list.**

    YouTube can see the devices on your system. If it doesn't pick the right device, choose it from the drop-down list.

11. **Click Record.**

    Okay, this is it, your 15 minutes of fame. Don't get nervous, and for good-ness sakes, don't break out in a cold sweat or flub your lines. But seri-ously, if you don't like it, you can always delete it later.

12. **Click Finish and Exit.**

    YouTube stops capturing your video, and it's uploaded to the Tube.

Chapter 8

Look at Me! Tips for Getting Your Video Seen

In This Chapter

▶ Trimming and splitting video clips

▶ Adding transitions, titles, and credits

▶ Creating slide shows

▶ Adding soundtracks, titles, and credits to your videos

▶ Adding tags to your videos

▶ Getting your video noticed on the Tube

As you've probably noticed, almost as many videos are on the Tube as sites are on the Web. And like Web sites, many of the videos are bad; some in fact are downright awful. If you don't want to be the laughingstock of YouTube, upload something that's well done. And if you really want to gain notoriety on the Tube, you have to upload videos that are interesting, polished, and as professional as possible. In Chapter 7, we show you the building blocks for capturing quality video, editing it, and then optimizing it for the Tube. In this chapter, we kick it up a notch and show you how to make your video stand out against the competition. First, we show you how to trim unwanted video from your clips — you know, the bits where your subject was pouting, or your dog turned his tail toward the camcorder. We also show you how to make your videos shine by adding professional transitions, titles, and ending credits to your videos. In addition, we show you how to master the fine art of adding tags to your video clips.

Your Video on the Cutting Floor

When you download video to your computer, it's exactly what your camcorder captured when you pressed the record button. Inevitably, you end up with some footage that should never be seen by anybody but yourself. Doug's litmus test for good video is his cat. If she falls asleep while Doug's screening clips, the video's boring. If she bolts and runs away, the video's too scary for the Tube. And if she has a violent physical reaction, the video's revolting. No matter what test you use, you have to have a method of separating the good, the bad, and the ugly. If the whole clip's bad, the obvious solution is the Delete button. But if a clip has some redeeming material, you can trim the bad footage and save the good stuff. In the upcoming sections, we show you how to do this with Movie Maker on the PC and iMovie on the Macintosh.

Trimming a video clip in Movie Maker

Trimming a video clip with a video-editing program is much easier than it is to trim film movies. You don't need sharp instruments to trim footage, and you don't need clear tape and solvent to put it all back together again. In fact, trimming a clip in Movie Maker is downright simple. Here's how you do it:

1. **Create a new project in Movie Maker.**

2. **Capture or import the video clips you want to use in your project.**

   Your clips are added to Collections.

3. **Preview clips from Collections and then add them to the Timeline.**

   We show you how to preview clips and create movies in Chapter 7. If you need a refresher course or if you haven't read the chapter yet, put Mr. Bookmarker to work and come back to this section when you know how to add clips to the Timeline.

4. **Begin playing your movie.**

   You can start playing your movie by clicking the Play Movie button. Alternatively, you can press the spacebar. After you begin playing the movie, the Play Movie button becomes the Pause Movie Button (see Figure 8-1).

5. **When you see a spot where you want to trim some footage, pause the movie.**

   You can pause the movie at the current frame by pressing the spacebar.

   If you're working with short clips, click the Zoom Timeline In button, which looks like a magnifying glass with a plus sign (+).

6. **Click the Split Clip button.**

   Alternatively, you can press Ctrl+L to split the clip in two on the current frame.

7. **Select the portion of the clip you want to delete and then press Delete.**

   The footage is gone from your project but still remains on the original clip.

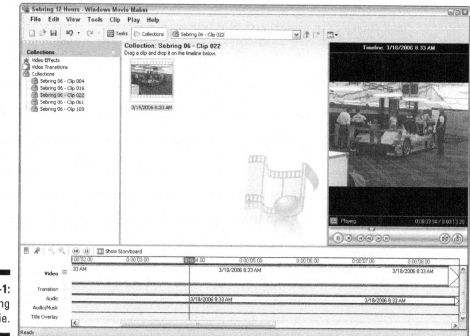

Figure 8-1:
Previewing
your movie.

If you have unwanted footage at the beginning and end of a clip, split the clip into three pieces and then delete the head and tail of the clip.

Trimming a video clip in iMovie

If you've tried to make even a short video — especially one that tells a story — you know that it takes hours of footage to get a few good clips that can be used in the final presentation.

When you're working in iMovie, you often want to use only a segment of a clip as part of your video. In editing lingo, choosing what parts of a clip to discard is *trimming*.

When editing film, you actually have to slice the film with a blade to select discarded material. With iMovie and digital editing, you'll see that it's much easier and you have the freedom to try all kinds of different editing combinations.

To trim a video clip in iMovie, identify the frames that you want to remove and then you remove them. Here's how:

1. **Hold down the Option key and then drag a copy of a clip from the Clips pane into the Movie Timeline.**

   Holding down the Option key when you do this makes a copy of a clip, thus leaving the original clip in the Clips pane for you to use again if you so choose.

2. **With the clip selected in the Timeline, drag the blue triangle at the bottom of the view window back and forth to view the contents of the clip.**

   This is *scrubbing* the clip. The blue triangle is identified in Figure 8-2.

3. **Click to select a crop marker and then drag it to the first frame of the section that you want to remove, as shown in Figure 8-3.**

   As shown in the figure, the crop mark is positioned at a frame that's 17 seconds and 18 frames into the movie. This is the first frame to be removed. (Note that the clip we're working on is titled Start it up.mov, which is selected in the Timeline.)

Figure 8-2:
Drag the blue triangle to scrub the clip.

Figure 8-3:
Positioning
the first crop
marker.

This clip, Start it up.mov, is the first clip in the Timeline (reading from left to right). Therefore, 17 seconds and 18 frames into the movie is also 17 seconds and 18 frames into the clip. However, it's important that you realize that the time code at the bottom of the view window refers to the movie, not to the clip. In this case, they are the same. If you want more clarification on this concept, see the following section, "Cropping a video clip in iMovie."

To move the crop marker frame-by-frame forward and backward, use the right and left arrows on your keypad. To move forward or backward in ten-frame increments, hold down the Shift key while you press the arrow key. You can also use this method to scrub the video.

4. **Position the other crop marker at the last frame that you want removed.**

   As shown in Figure 8-4, the frames between 17:18 and 22:26 are now between the crop markers. You can think of these frames as being *selected* or *targeted*.

5. **Click Edit on the menu bar and then click Clear.**

   The targeted frames are deleted from the clip. As shown in Figure 8-5, the last frame of the clip is at 17:18, and the duration of the selected clip in the Timeline is also noted as 17:18.

Figure 8-4:
Targeting
frames to be
deleted.

Figure 8-5:
Viewing a
trimmed clip.

It's important that you understand that the clip you trim is a *copy* of the clip in the Clips pane. This means that any changes that you make to the clip in the Timeline will not affect the original clip in the Clips pane. For example, note that the original clip in the Clips pane shows 22:27 as its duration: It wasn't trimmed.

You can trim the same clip more than once. Let's say that after trimming the end of the clip, as you do in this exercise, you want to remove footage from the beginning of the clip or from a section in the middle. Repeat the preceding steps, targeting the other sections of the clip that you want to remove.

Cropping a video clip in iMovie

You can think of *cropping* a video clip as the exact opposite of trimming a clip. When you *trim* a clip, you identify a section of a clip that you want to remove and then you delete it. Conversely, when you *crop* a clip, you identify a section of a clip that you want to keep and then you crop it to delete the other areas not identified.

Trimming and cropping are two sides of the same coin, and you'll find it useful to know how to execute both procedures.

To crop a clip in iMovie, follow these steps:

1. **Select the clip in the Timeline that you want to crop, or hold down the Option key and then drag a copy of a clip from the Clips pane into the Movie Timeline.**

   Holding down the Option key when you do this makes a copy of a clip, thus leaving the original clip in the Clips pane for you to use again if you so choose.

2. **Click to select a crop marker and then drag it to the first frame of the section that you want to use, as shown in Figure 8-6.**

   As shown in the figure, the crop marker is positioned at a frame that's 31 seconds and 16 frames into the *movie*. This is the first frame of the section of this clip that remains after being cropped.

   To move the crop marker frame-by-frame forward and backward, use the right and left arrows on your keypad. To move forward or backward in ten-frame increments, hold down the Shift key while you press the arrow key. You can also use this method to scrub the video.

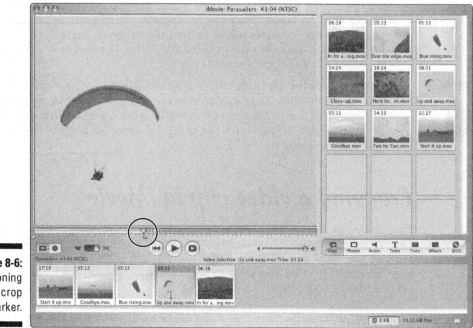

Figure 8-6:
Positioning
a crop
marker.

3. Position the other crop marker at the last frame that you want removed.

As shown in Figure 8-7, the frames between 31:16 and 35:10 are now between the crop markers. You can think of these frames as being *selected* or *targeted*.

4. Click Edit on the menu bar and then click Crop.

The selected frames remain, and all other non-selected frames are removed. As shown in Figure 8-8, the duration of the Up and away.mov clip in the Timeline is now 3:24, whereas its duration was 8:01 before the crop.

Note how efficient cropping a clip is. In the above set of steps, you removed footage at the beginning of the clip *and* at the end of the clip with a single command.

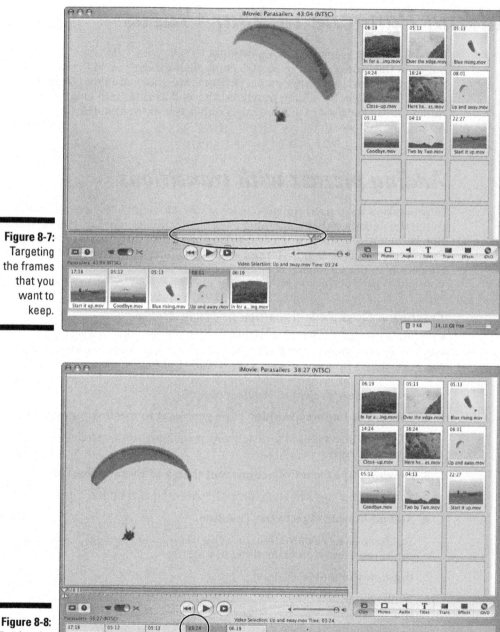

Figure 8-7:
Targeting
the frames
that you
want to
keep.

Figure 8-8:
Viewing the
cropped
clip.

Adding Panache to Your Videos

If you have a message to tell or a product to sell, your video needs to stand out from the crowd. You can easily accomplish this by making your video look professional. In the upcoming sections, we show you how to create compelling videos by adding transitions as well as titles and ending credits. Adding these features to a video takes only a few extra minutes, and the results are well worth it.

Adding pizzazz with transitions

Moviemakers have used transitions for years. Moviemakers use a transition to tell the audience that something important will happen. The classic transition is the *Cross Fade* — when one video clip fades into another. The standard Cross Fade works well, but you can kick it up a notch or two by adding a video transition. In the upcoming sections, we show you how to add transitions to your video productions in Movie Maker and iMovie.

Creating a Cross Fade transition in Movie Maker

Creating a Cross Fade isn't rocket science. You're merely overlapping two clips. When the video's rendered, the tail of one clip fades into the head of the next. Here's how you create a Cross Fade in Movie Maker:

1. **Create a new project in Movie Maker.**

2. **Capture or import the video clips you want to use in your project.**

   A Collection is created for each clip you import or for each videocassette you capture.

3. **Preview clips from Collections and then add them to the Timeline.**

   To add a clip to a Timeline, drop the selected clip on the Timeline.

4. **Add additional clips to the Timeline.**

   You have to have more than one clip to create a transition. After all, you can't transition from something to nothing.

5. **Preview the movie.**

   While you watch the movie, decide where you want to add a Cross Fade transition.

6. **Select the clip that'll be the end of the Cross Fade transition and drag it over the preceding clip.**

   The bottom of the clip you're dragging is signified by a blue bar. A triangle appears where the clip overlaps the preceding clip. This triangle signifies the duration of the Cross Fade (see Figure 8-9).

7. **Release the mouse button when the Cross Fade is the desired duration.**

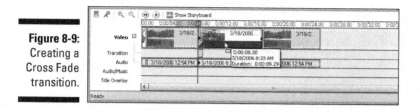

Figure 8-9:
Creating a
Cross Fade
transition.

Creating a Cross Dissolve transition in iMovie

The iMovie approach for adding transitions between clips is simple and straightforward and still offers you a number of options for creating complex and dynamic transition effects. In this set of steps, we'll show you how to insert a simple Cross Dissolve transition. A Cross Dissolve transition — called *Cross Fade* on the PC in Movie Maker — is a standard transition in which one frame "fades" into another.

1. **Create a new project, import clips, and then drag a few clips into the Timeline.**

2. **Click the Transitions icon to display the Transitions pane, as shown in Figure 8-10.**

   The Transitions pane lists all the transition effects that come standard with iMovie:

   - **Circle Closing:** The first frame is cropped to a circle that gets smaller and smaller, revealing the second frame.

   - **Circle Opening:** The second frame appears in a circle in the center of the frame and gets larger until it replaces the first frame.

   - **Cross Dissolve:** The first frame fades gradually to reveal the second frame.

   - **Fade In:** A black frame gradually reveals the image.

   - **Fade Out:** The image gradually fades to black.

   - **Overlap:** The two frames overlap for the duration of the transition.

   - **Push:** The second frame moves in from top, bottom, right, or left and "pushes" the first frame off the screen.

   - **Radial:** Like the hands of a clock, a line clockwise or counterclockwise rotates to reveal the second frame behind the first.

   - **Scale Down:** The first frame gets smaller and smaller until the second frame is revealed.

   - **Twirl:** The first frame twirls rapidly and scales down until it disappears into a black background, then the second frame appears small and twirling in the center of the frame and scales up to full frame size.

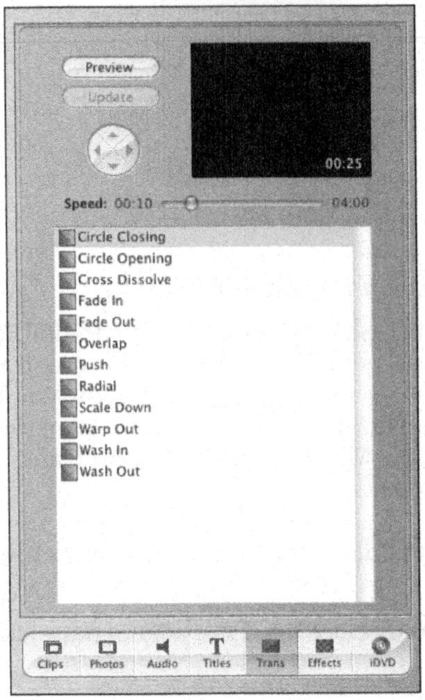

Figure 8-10:
The
Transitions
pane holds
some
very cool
transition
effects.

- **Warp Out:** A hole appears at the center of the first frame and gets larger to reveal the second. As the hole gets larger, the first image distorts or warps.

- **Wash In:** The image fades in gradually from a white background.

- **Wash Out:** The image fades out gradually to a white background.

3. **Click each transition in the Transition pane to see a preview in the Preview window.**

4. **Click the Cross Dissolve transition and then drag the Speed slider to 2:00, as shown in Figure 8-11.**

   While you drag the slider, the settings are displayed in the lower corner of the Preview window.

5. **Identify two clips in the Timeline where you want to insert a transition and then drag the Cross Dissolve transition to the Timeline and place it between them.**

   As shown in Figure 8-12, the transition icon appears between the two clips and is selected automatically in the Timeline.

   In iMovie, the transition icon is the same for all different types of transitions.

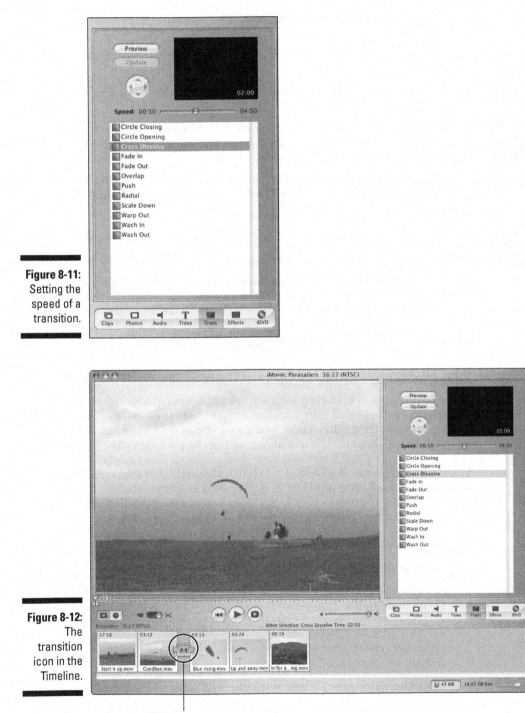

Figure 8-11:
Setting the
speed of a
transition.

Figure 8-12:
The
transition
icon in the
Timeline.

Transition icon

6. **Drag the blue triangle beneath the view window to preview the transition.**

The end of the first clip overlaps the beginning of the next clip by two seconds.

To preview a transition, select the transition in the Timeline just as you would any other clip.

Some transitions affect the duration of your movie. With a two-second Cross Dissolve transition, for example, the length of the movie is reduced by two seconds because two clips now overlap by that amount of time.

7. **With the Cross Dissolve transition icon still selected in the Timeline, drag the Speed slider to 3:00 and then click the Update button.**

The duration of the transition is now 3:00.

Double-click a transition icon in the Timeline to see its duration.

8. **Click the Cross Dissolve transition and then drag the Speed slider to 1:00.**

9. **Identify two clips in the Timeline where you want to insert a second transition and then drag the Cross Dissolve transition to the Timeline and place it between them.**

A second transition — with a duration of 1:00 — is added to the Timeline. The duration of the first transition you added isn't affected.

Adding video transitions in Movie Maker

Movie Maker comes standard with a number of video transitions. *Video transitions* are those that add a motion transition to your movie. For example, a circle may appear at the center of the movie and get larger and larger to reveal the next clip, simultaneously replacing the previous clip.

Video transitions range from the sublime to the wild. For example, you can have one clip push into another (this is known as a *wipe transition*), or you can add a video transition that looks like a key opening the next clip. To add video transitions to a video in Movie Maker, follow these steps:

1. **Create a new project in Movie Maker.**

2. **Add the desired clips to the Timeline.**

For those of you that need a refresher course, you drop clips from Collections to the Timeline.

3. **Press the spacebar to begin previewing the movie.**

While you watch the movie, decide where you want to add video transitions.

4. **Click the Show Storyboard button.**

The Timeline disappears, and the thumbnails designate each of the clips in your movie. (See Figure 8-13.)

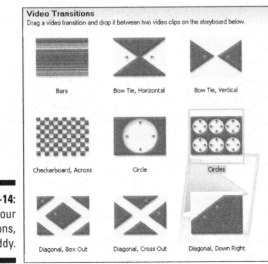

Figure 8-13:
Switching to
Storyboard
mode.

5. **Click View Video Transitions from the Edit Movie menu.**

   The workspace displays the available video transitions (see Figure 8-14).

Figure 8-14:
I got your
transitions,
buddy.

6. Click a transition to select it and then click the Play button in the Preview window.

Movie Maker displays the transition over stock footage. Figure 8-15 shows the Pixelate video transition being previewed.

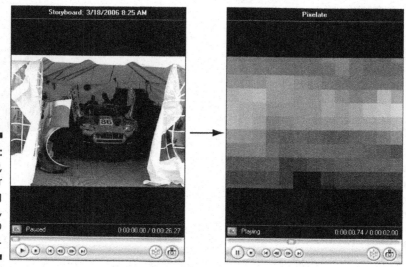

Figure 8-15:
And now, pixelated for your viewing pleasure, a video transition.

7. Drag the desired transition to the space between two clips.

A thumbnail appears in the slot that designates the type of transition you've applied.

The default duration is 1.25 seconds in duration, which isn't very long. To change the duration of video transitions, choose Tools➪Options and then click the Advanced tab. In the Default Durations section, enter the desired value in the Transition Duration text box. Alternatively, you can click the spinner button to increase or decrease transition duration.

8. Add additional transitions as desired.

Don't use multiple video transitions in a video, especially a short one. When you use more than one video transition, it looks unprofessional and detracts from the focus of your video.

To delete a transition, right-click it and choose Delete from the shortcut menu.

Adding video transitions in iMovie

The default transitions that come standard with iMovie include a number of video transitions. Video transitions are those that add a motion transition to your movie. For example, a circle may appear at the center of the movie and get larger and larger to reveal the next clip, simultaneously replacing the previous clip.

In this section, we add a Radial Wipe video transition to a movie. With a Radial Wipe transition, one frame transitions to another through a circular motion, as though the hands of a clock were moving to show you the first frame and then the second. It's a classic transition, and here's how to do it:

1. **Create a new project, import clips, and then drag a few clips into the Timeline.**

2. **Click the Transitions icon to display the Transitions pane.**

   The Transitions pane lists all the transition effects that come standard with iMovie.

3. **Click each transition in the Transition pane to see a preview in the Preview window.**

4. **Click the Radial transition and then drag the Speed slider to 3:00.**

5. **Identify two clips in the Timeline where you want to insert a transition and then drag the Cross Dissolve transition to the Timeline and place it between them.**

   The Transition icon appears between the two clips and is selected automatically in the Timeline.

   The duration of any two clips must be longer than the duration of the transition that you want to place between them. For example, a four-second Cross Dissolve transition couldn't play between two two-second clips — neither has the four seconds required for the transition to play out.

6. **Drag the blue triangle beneath the view window to preview the transition.**

   As shown in Figure 8-16, a Clockwise Radial Wipe transitions the first clip to the next.

Figure 8-16:
Viewing the radial transition.

Adding video effects in Movie Maker

Windows Movie Maker has yet another tool for adding compelling effects to your movie: video effects. A plethora of video effects are with the program; with them you can fade to black, create an aged film look, and add film grain. Want your video to look like it was shot on film in the mid-'80s? No problem. You can do that and more with video effects. Here's how:

1. **Create a new project in Movie Maker.**
2. **Add the desired clips to the Timeline.**

   For those of you that need a refresher course, you drop clips from Collections to the Timeline.
3. **Press the spacebar to begin previewing the movie.**
4. **Click the Show Storyboard button.**

   The video clips are displayed in Storyboard mode.
5. **Click View Video Effects from the Edit Movie menu.**

   The workspace displays all video effects (see Figure 8-17).

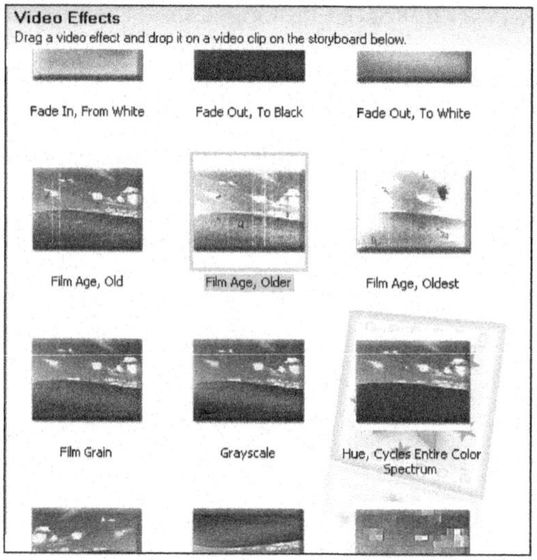

Figure 8-17: Now that's a lot of video effects.

6. **Click a video effect to select it and then click the Play button in the Preview window.**
7. **Drop the desired video effect on the gray star in the lower-left corner of a video thumbnail on the Storyboard.**

   The star changes to blue to signify a video effect has been applied. Figure 8-18 shows a clip to which one of the old film effects has been applied.

Figure 8-18:
Applying a video effect to a clip.

Adding video effects in iMovie

By now, most people have seen the amazing things that can be done to a digital image in applications, like Photoshop. Warps, distortions, filter effects, color effects — no problem. If you consider that a video on your computer is simply a series of still images, you understand that the same types of effects can be applied to your video with many of the same concepts. In fact, you'll find effects in iMovie that are identical to effects that can be applied to a still image in Photoshop.

In this section, we work with iMovie's built-in effects to adjust the color of one clip, convert another clip to black and white, and apply a special effect to the entire movie. Just follow these steps:

1. **Create a new project, import clips, and then drag a few clips into the Timeline.**

2. **Click the Effects icon to display the Effects pane.**

   The Effects pane lists all the effects that come standard with iMovie. See Figure 8-19.

   Don't think of effects as only "special effects" that add something eye-popping to your video, like a thunderbolt or a motion blur. Many of the effects in the Effects pane are important for practical purposes, such as adjusting color, brightness, or contrast.

3. **Press and hold the Shift key to select multiple clips in the Timeline that you want to apply effects to.**

   In many cases, you want to apply an effect — such as a color adjustment or a grain effect — to all the clips in the movie.

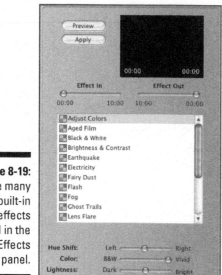

Figure 8-19:
The many
built-in
effects
listed in the
Effects
panel.

To select all the clips in the Timeline, click Select All under the Edit menu or use the quick key.

4. **Click Adjust Colors in the Effects pane and then drag the Hue Shift slider all the way to the right.**

The Preview window displays the effect.

You can drag the Effect In and Effect Out sliders to determine at what points in the clip you want the effect to begin and end.

5. **Click the Apply button.**

The hue shift is applied and the clip in the Timeline now displays the Effects icon, alerting you that an effect's been applied.

6. **Select a single clip, click the Black & White effect in the Effects pane, and then click Apply.**

The clip now appears in black and white.

7. **Select all the clips in the Timeline, click the Aged Film effect, set the Exposure, Jitter, and Scratches sliders to your liking, and then click Apply.**

Figure 8-20 shows the effect applied; note how well the Aged Film effect works in conjunction with the Black & White effect to make the clip appear like old newsreel footage.

The number 2 appears beside the Effects icons in the first and third clip in the Timeline, indicating that two effects have been applied to these clips.

Figure 8-20:
Applying the
Aged Film
effect to
the entire
movie.

Adding titles and credits in Movie Maker

Every good movie deserves a title, and for that matter, ending credits. Movie Maker offers a wide variety of very cool titles and an equally impressive assortment of ending credits. Adding a title and ending credit to your movies gives them a sense of flair and professionalism. To add titles or ending credits to your movies, follow these steps:

1. **Create a new project in Movie Maker.**

2. **Add the desired clips to the Timeline.**

   Drag clips from Collections to the Timeline.

3. **Click Make Titles or Credits.**

   The Where Do You Want to Add a Title Page dialog box appears (see Figure 8-21).

4. **Choose the desired option for title placement.**

   You can choose whether to create a title or ending credit as well as the placement. After choosing an option, the Enter Text for Title dialog box appears.

5. **Type the desired text.**

   After typing the title text for your movie, the default title appears in the Preview Window, which, quite frankly, is boring. If you like what you see, click Done, Add Title to Movie. However, if you don't, Movie Maker has more tricks up its sleeve. Before adding the title to the movie, you can change the font face and color by following the next step.

6. **Click Change the Font Size and Color.**

   Movie Maker displays the Select Title Font and Color dialog box.

7. **Select a font face from the Font drop-down list.**

   The menu displays all fonts installed on your system with the exception of Adobe Professional fonts, which can be used only with Adobe applications.

8. **Select a font style.**

You can boldface, italicize, and/or underline title text. When you change any text attribute, the changes are displayed in the Preview window.

9. **Change the font and/or background colors.**

To change the font color, click the A in the Color section. To change the background color, click the color swatch to the right of the A. This opens the system color picker from which you can select a font and background color.

10. **Change the text transparency.**

To lower the opacity of title text, drag the Transparency slider left. This allows more of the background color to bleed through the text.

11. **Change the size of the title text.**

To increase text size, click the A with the up-pointing arrow. To decrease text size, click the A with the down-pointing arrow.

12. **Change the alignment of the title text.**

You can align the text to the left, center, or right by clicking the associated icon.

13. **If you're satisfied with the title, click Done, Add Title to Movie. But if you're adventurous like us, click Change Title Animation.**

After you click Change Title Animation, the Choose the Title Animation dialog box appears (see Figure 8-22).

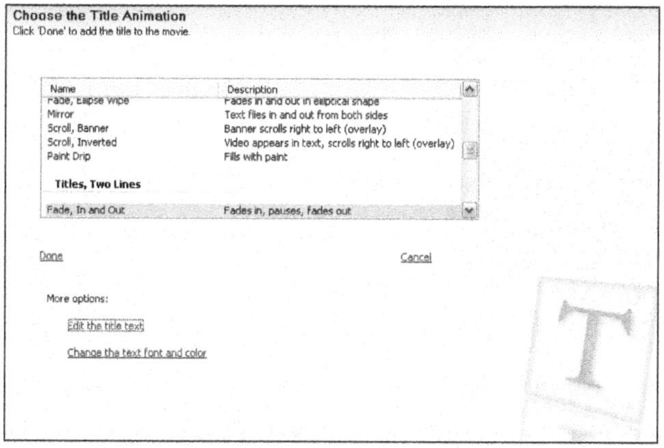

Choose the Title Animation
Click 'Done' to add the title to the movie.

Name	Description	
Fade, Ellipse Wipe	Fades in and out in elliptical shape	
Mirror	Text flies in and out from both sides	
Scroll, Banner	Banner scrolls right to left (overlay)	
Scroll, Inverted	Video appears in text, scrolls right to left (overlay)	
Paint Drip	Fills with paint	
Titles, Two Lines		
Fade, In and Out	Fades in, pauses, fades out	

Done   Cancel

More options:

Edit the title text

Change the text font and color

Figure 8-22:
Changing
the title
animation.

14. **Choose the desired title animation.**

You can choose from three categories: Titles, One Line; Titles, Two Lines; or if you're creating ending credits, Credits. When you choose a different title animation, the animation is applied to your title text and is displayed in the Preview window.

15. **Click Done, Add Title to Movie.**

Note that some title animations, such as Newspaper and Sports Scoreboard, are designed to display over the first clip in your movie. Therefore, you have to specify that the title should appear over the first clip in your movie. If you've specified already that the title should appear before the first clip and then switch to one of the animations that's designed to appear over the first clip, simply drag the title animation clip to the text overlay track and it appears over the first clip. Figure 8-23 shows the Newspaper title animation, as displayed in the Preview window. We have to admit, that's a way-cool title for a free application.

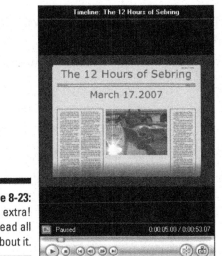

Figure 8-23:
Extra, extra!
Read all
about it.

Ending credits are created in the same manner. Choose where the credit's displayed, create the text, modify the text to suit your tastes, and then choose an animation from the Credits section. Figure 8-24 shows ending credits, as displayed in the Preview window.

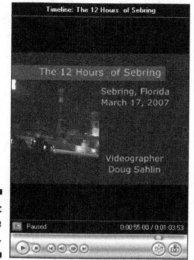

The 12 Hours of Sebring

Sebring, Florida
March 17, 2007

Videographer
Doug Sahlin

Paused   0:00 55.00 / 0:01 03.53

Figure 8-24:
This is the
end....

Don't use rolling credits if you apply high levels of compression to your movies.

Adding titles and credits in iMovie

Text can be a very big part of your video, and not only for practical components, like beginning and ending credits. Many video artists use text as an artistic element in their movies.

When you add text to a video, the text is referred to as a *title card,* or simply as a *title.* iMovie offers a number of options for integrating titles into your movie in ways that are dynamic and visually interesting. In addition to a full font list and a full color palette to choose from, iMovie also offers a number of really cool animation modules that really bump up the energy of your title presentations. Here's how you use them:

1. **Create a new project, import clips, and then drag a few clips into the Timeline.**

2. **Click the Titles icon to display the Titles pane.**

   The Titles panel lists the many title effects that come standard with iMovie.

3. **Click Centered Title.**

   Centered Title is the most basic title card, which offers you two lines of text.

4. **In the text boxes below the list of Titles, type a title for your movie in the top box and then type a byline or a subhead in the box beneath.**

Your screen resembles Figure 8-25.

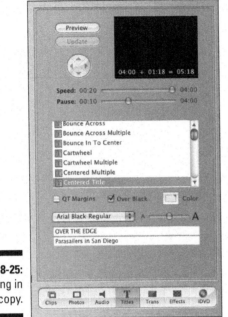

Figure 8-25:
Typing in
title copy.

5. **Click the Font menu, select a font, and then drag the Size slider all the way to the right.**

iMovie doesn't let you choose a specific font size. Instead, when you drag the Size slider all the way to the right, iMovie creates your titles at the largest size they can be and still fit on the card.

6. **Activate the On Black option.**

When you choose this option, the text appears over a black background.

7. **Click the Color button and then click anywhere in the rainbow radial to select a color for your text.**

Your screen resembles Figure 8-26.

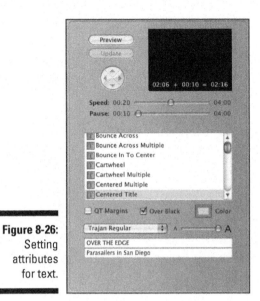

Figure 8-26:
Setting
attributes
for text.

8. **Drag the Speed slider all the way to the right and then drag the Pause slider all the way to the left.**

   The Centered Title title is set up to fade in and then fade out. Together, the Speed and Pause settings determine the duration of the title, with the Speed slider determining the fade-in and fade-out duration. At 4:00, the title fades in for two seconds and then fades out for two seconds. The Pause slider determines how long the title stays on-screen after fading in and before fading out. In other words, it's a *pause* between the fades. At the minimum setting, the title pauses for only ten frames. Thus, the total duration of the title would be four seconds and ten frames.

9. **Drag the Pause slider to 1:00.**

   The Speed and Pause values are specified at the bottom of the Preview window — Speed plus Pause equals the total duration of the title card. The title card's duration is now five seconds: two seconds of fade-in, one second pause, and two seconds of fade-out. See Figure 8-27.

10. **Click and drag the Centered Title icon from the Titles list and drop it into the Timeline where you want the clip to play.**

   In Figure 8-28, we dragged the icon to the left of all the clips in the Timeline to make the title card appear at the very beginning of our movie.

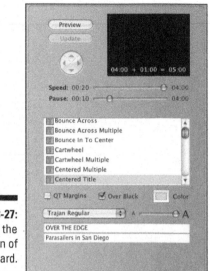

Figure 8-27:
Setting the
duration of
the title card.

11. **Click Rolling Credits in the Titles list.**

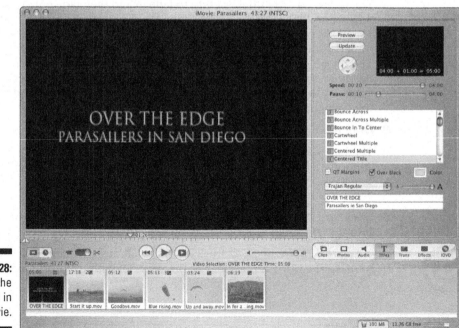

Figure 8-28:
Viewing the
title card in
the movie.

12. **Activate the Over Black option.**

13. **Click the Color button, click the center of the rainbow radial, and drag the slider on the right all the way to the top to set a white color.**

14. **In the first set of text boxes, type** Directed by **in the top box and** Blake O'Malley **in the bottom box.**

15. **In the second set, type** Written by **in the top box and type** Twiggy Cooley **in the bottom box.**

16. **In the third set, type** Starring **in the top box and type** Ben Bishop **in the bottom box.**

17. **In the fourth set, type** Co-Starring **in the top box and type** Rex Rosen **in the bottom box.**

    Your screen resembles Figure 8-29.

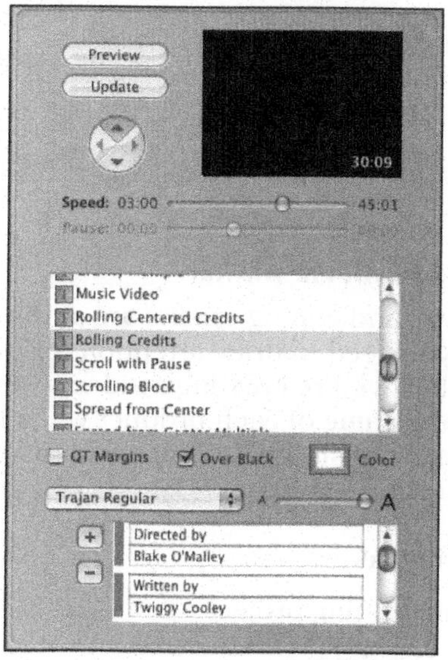

Figure 8-29:
Entering text
for rolling
credits.

By default, the Rolling Credits animation moves the titles up from the bottom of the page. You can change the direction of the animation by clicking an arrow on the compass above the list of titles.

18. **Click and drag the Rolling Credits icon from the Titles list and drop it to the right of all the clips in the Timeline.**

19. **Preview the clip to view the animation.**

    As shown in Figure 8-30, iMovie formats the credits, placing them side by side and entering dots to connect them for easier readability.

Figure 8-30:
Viewing
the Rolling
Credit title
card.

Adding a text overlay to a video in Movie Maker

Title clips are at the start of a movie, and ending credits are at the end of a movie. But what do you do when you need to draw attention to something in the middle of a movie? For example, if you're creating a video to announce a product line, you need to display the name of each product when it appears in the video. The easiest way to accomplish this is with a text overlay. To add a text overlay to your movie, follow these steps:

1. **Create a new project in Movie Maker.**

   Alternatively, you can open an existing project.

2. **Add the desired clips to the Timeline.**

   Drag clips from Collections to the Timeline.

3. **Select the clip to which you want to add a text overlay.**

4. **Click Make Titles or Credits.**

5. **Click Add Title on the Selected Clip.**

   The Enter Text for Title dialog box appears.

6. **Type the desired text.**

   Movie Maker displays the text with the default animation in the Preview window. We find that the default animation is distracting when adding a text overlay to announce a product. We prefer that the text is static at the bottom of the video, which we accomplish in the next step.

7. **Click Change the Title Animation.**

   The Choose the Title Animation dialog box appears.

8. **Choose Subtitle.**

   This option causes the text to appear at the bottom of the frame (see Figure 8-31). Another viable option is Basic Title, which causes static text to appear in the middle of the frame.

9. **(Optional) Click the Change the Text Font and Color link.**

   This displays the Select the Title Font and Color dialog box. This dialog box enables you to change the font face, color, and size. You can also change the text opacity, stylize the text, and change the text alignment.

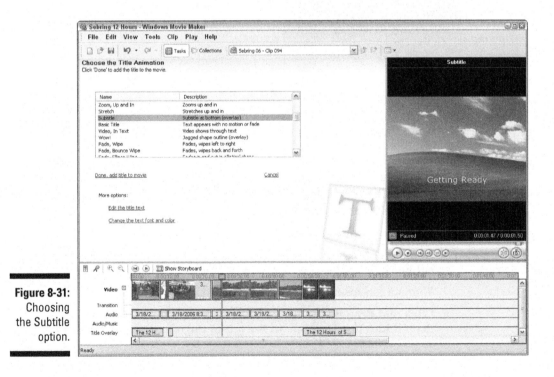

Figure 8-31:
Choosing
the Subtitle
option.

10. **Click the Done, Add Title to Movie link.**

This operation applies the text overlay to the selected clip. Figure 8-32 shows a text overlay applied by using the Subtitle animation option.

Figure 8-32:
Adding a
text overlay
to a clip.

Adding a text overlay to a video in iMovie

You create a *text overlay* when you superimpose text over your video footage. In iMovie, you create a text overlay in very much the same manner that you create a title card over a black background; the only difference is that you turn off the black background (Over Black) option. Here's how you do it:

1. **Click Centered Title again in the Titles list.**

2. **Deselect the Over Black option.**

3. **Click the Color button and then select a bright red.**

4. **In the text boxes below the list of Titles, type a headline and a subhead.**

Your screen resembles Figure 8-33.

5. **Click and drag the Centered Title icon from the Titles list and drop it into the Timeline to the left of the clip that you want it to superimpose.**

As shown in Figure 8-34, the title is superimposed over the clip.

Figure 8-33:
Entering text
for the title
overlay.

Figure 8-34:
Viewing the
title overlay.

Adding a soundtrack to a video in Movie Maker

If the video for your movie contains an audio track, you're off to the races. However, you can augment the video audio by adding a soundtrack in Movie Maker. If you have a microphone attached to your computer, you can also add a voice-over in Movie Maker. To add a soundtrack to your production, follow these steps:

1. **Create a new project in Movie Maker.**

   Alternatively, you can open an existing project.

2. **Add the desired clips to the Timeline.**

   Drag clips from Collections to the Timeline.

3. **Click Import Audio or Music.**

   The Import File dialog box appears. You can import any of the following sound formats: `.aif`, `.aiff`, `.aifc`, `.snd`, `.mp3`, `.au`, `.mpa`, `.mp2`, `.wma`, or `.asf`.

4. **Navigate to the desired file, select it, and then click Import.**

   The file is added to a collection.

   To comply with YouTube regulations and copyright laws, you must use a soundtrack to which you own the license, or the soundtrack must be royalty-free.

5. **Drop the sound file on the Audio/Music track.**

   The title of the soundtrack is displayed on the Audio/Music track. The soundtrack may be too long for your movie, as shown in Figure 8-35. In that case, you have to do some trimming.

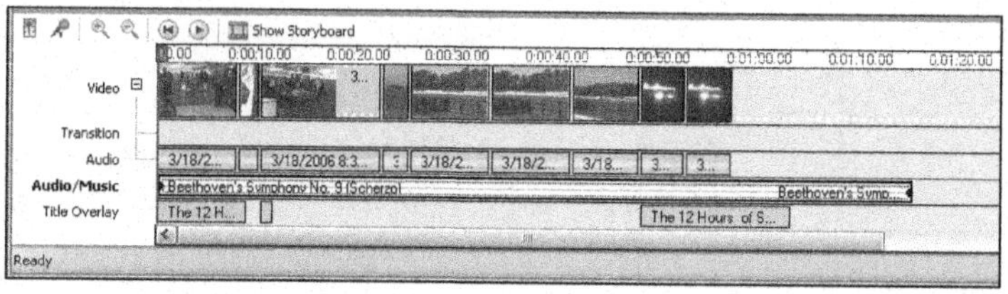

Figure 8-35:
Roll over
Beethoven
and tell
Tchaikovsky
the news.

6. **Position your cursor over the tail of the soundtrack.**

   Your cursor becomes a red line with an arrow at each end.

7. **Drag to the left to trim the clip to size.**

   The clip snaps to the end of your last track. When this happens, release the mouse button to complete the operation. When the sound clip is the desired length, you have to make sure it fades out at the end of your movie. Otherwise, you have *endus abruptus*.

8. **Right-click the Audio/Music track.**

   The shortcut menu appears.

9. **Choose Fade Out.**

   Note that you can also cause the soundtrack to fade in and control the volume of the soundtrack. The volume option is handy if your video also has a soundtrack. You can choose the proper volume so that both tracks are audible, and the resulting soundtrack isn't over-modulated.

You can also adjust the volume of audio tracks attached to video clips. Select the sound track from the Audio track, right-click, and then choose Volume from the shortcut menu to open the Audio Clip Volume dialog box. Drag the slider left to decrease volume or right to increase volume. Click OK to apply the change. Repeat for other audio clips as needed.

To add a voice-over to your production

1. **Position your cursor where you want the voice-over to begin.**

2. **Click the Narrate Timeline icon that looks like a microphone.**

   This opens the Narrate Timeline dialog box.

3. **Click the Show More Options link.**

   This displays all options for recording an audio track (see Figure 8-36).

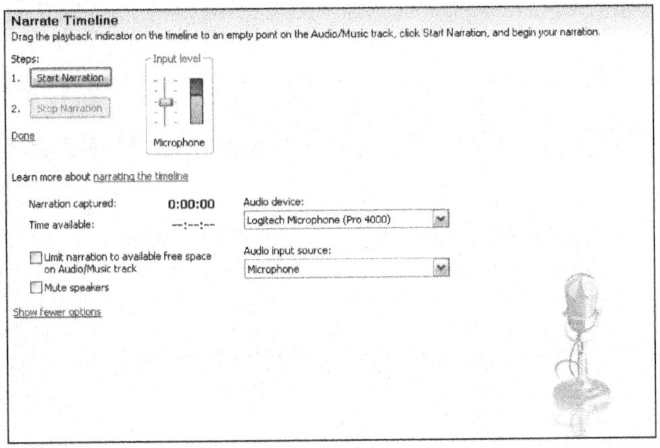

Figure 8-36:
Say a few
syllables for
the folks.

4. **Choose the proper device from the Audio Device drop-down list.**

5. **Choose the proper source from the Input Source drop-down list.**

6. **Speak in to your microphone.**

   While you speak, the Input Level meter moves.

7. **Drag the Input Level slider while speaking.**

   Your goal is to adjust the input volume so that the loudest passage peaks in the yellow zone and not in the red.

8. **Press Start Narration and begin talking.**

   While you talk, the movie plays.

   Click the Mute Speakers check box. Otherwise, you record any audio clips already in your project. You can also click the Limit Narration to Available Space on Audio Track, and the narration doesn't exceed the length of your movie.

9. **Press Stop Narration.**

   The Save Media File dialog box appears.

10. **Type a name for the file and then press Save.**

    The file is saved to your computer and added to the Audio/Music track of your Movie Maker project.

Adding a soundtrack to a video in iMovie

Chances are that your video camera also records sound; that sound is imported with the clip when you begin your project. In addition, you might want to add additional sounds to your movie: music, voice-overs, sound effects, and so on. You'll be happy to know that iMovie offers some robust controls for working with sound, and it also automatically links up with your iTunes software, giving you easy access to the music already on your computer.

Creating custom soundtracks for your movies

When you add a soundtrack to a video, you must be in compliance with YouTube regulations. And you have to steer clear of the Copyright Police. Therefore, you must be licensed to use any soundtrack you add to a movie or you must own the copyright to the soundtrack. That's easy if you're uploading a video with audio you've captured. However, when you add music as a soundtrack, the record company, the performer, and the person who wrote the music are potential problems when it comes to copyright. However, if you have a good ear for music, you can create your own soundtrack with a music sampling application, like Sony Acid Music Studio (Windows) or Apple's GarageBand (Macintosh).

Both applications ship with royalty-free music loops from a specific genre, which you arrange on a Timeline. For example, you can mix a drum track, rhythm track, and guitar track to create a royalty-free soundtrack. Your imagination and taste in music enable you to create a unique soundtrack to suit the video to which you're adding it. You can download a trial version of Acid Music Studio, which as of this writing sells for $69.95 from www.sonycreativesoftware. com/download/step2.asp?DID=621. GarageBand is part of iLife 06, which as of this writing sells for $79.00. For more information on GarageBand visit www.apple.com/ilife/ garageband.

To access your iTunes library, click the Audio button and all the songs in your iTunes library are listed. How cool is that?

At the bottom of the Audio pane is the iMovie microphone. If your computer has a built-in microphone or if you've connected a microphone to your computer, click the red record button to the right, speak into the microphone, and iMovie records the audio directly into the Timeline.

To import sound from a CD or from a file on your computer that's not in iTunes, follow these steps:

1. **Click File on the menu bar and then click Import.**

2. **Navigate to the sound file that you want to work with and then click Open.**

   As shown in Figure 8-37, iMovie automatically imports audio clips directly into the Timeline. The Timeline changes automatically to accommodate the audio clip.

Figure 8-37: Viewing an audio clip in the Timeline.

3. **Move the sound clip in the Timeline to align it with the clips that you want it to play over.**

4. **Activate the Edit Volume option.**

   When you activate the Edit Volume option, black lines appear over the audio clip, as shown in Figure 8-38. These are volume controllers that you use to manipulate the volume of a clip.

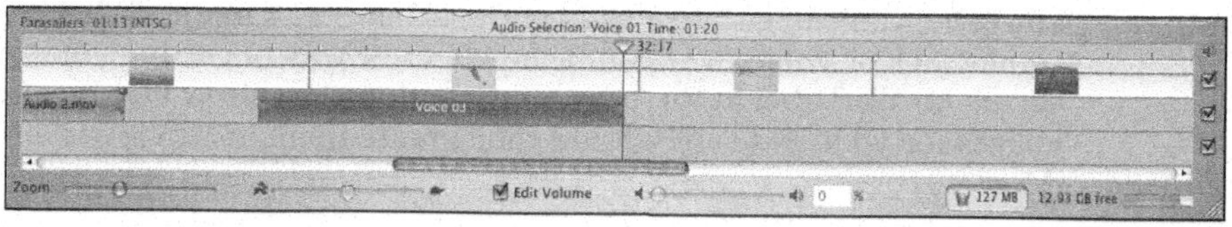

Figure 8-38: The Edit Volume option offers you controls for manipulating the volume of an audio clip.

5. **Click the horizontal line in the audio clip to add a handle and then experiment with changing the audio curve for the clip.**

    In Figure 8-39, the volume of the clip is turned off for the first two-thirds of its duration and then it increases dramatically toward the end of the clip.

Figure 8-39:
Manipu-
lating the
volume of an
audio clip.

6. **Import a second sound file.**

7. **If necessary, activate the second audio track in the Timeline by clicking its check mark and then dragging the second sound clip down into the second audio track.**

    Your screen resembles Figure 8-40. The two clips play simultaneously.

Figure 8-40:
Positioning
the second
audio clip.

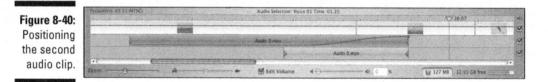

If you're on a tight budget, and still want to add cool sound to your movies, check out Acid Xpress (www.sonycreativesoftware.com/download/step2.asp?DID=551). It's free.

Creating Image Slideshows

If you don't have a snazzy camcorder and you still want to post clips on YouTube, you can create a slide show of images. A static slide show with a soundtrack or voice-over can be an effective way of getting your message across on YouTube. In the upcoming sections, we show you how to optimize images for your slide shows and then create them in Movie Maker and iMovie.

Optimizing images for slide shows

You can optimize images for a slide show in any image-editing application. Most point-and-shoot digital cameras process images in the JPEG file format. Therefore, all you need to do is size them and add them to a video-editing application, like Movie Maker or iMovie. Here are a few recommended settings for saving images you use in a slide show:

✔ **File Format:** Use JPEG. JPEG is an acronym for Joint Photograph Experts Group is a lossy file format, which means that color data is lost when the file is compressed. It's the format most digital cameras use.

✔ **Image Quality:** Save the images with the highest quality. In Photoshop Elements, the setting is JPEG: High Quality. You'd think the way to go would be to optimize the image for Web viewing. However, YouTube compresses any video you send. Therefore, it's best to start out with images of the highest quality.

✔ **Image Size:** Size your images to the default size of a YouTube movie, 320 x 240 pixels.

If your image-editing application has a batch-processing option, select the files for your slide show and then apply batch processing to convert them to the recommended settings.

Creating a slide show in Movie Maker

Creating a slide show in Movie Maker is easy. The hardest decision is selecting which images to use. After you figure out which images to use, you can create a compelling slide show by following these steps:

1. **Optimize the images for your slide show and save them in a folder.**

   If you skipped straight to this section, check out the preceding section, "Optimizing images for slide shows."

2. **Create a new project in Movie Maker.**

3. **Click Import Pictures from the Movie Tasks menu.**

   The Import File dialog box appears.

4. **Navigate to the folder in which you stored your slide show images and then select them all.**

5. **Click Import.**

   Movie Maker organizes the images in a Collection (see Figure 8-41).

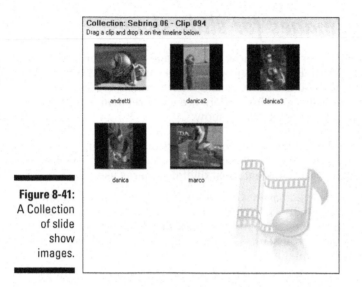

Figure 8-41:
A Collection
of slide
show
images.

6. **Click the Show Storyboard button.**

The Timeline disappears and slots appear, which is where you add the slides for your show.

7. **Drop a slide from the Collection into the first slot on the Storyboard.**

Congratulations, you've taken the first step in creating a slide show.

8. **Continue adding slides to your show.**

If you have a lot of slides in your show, you have to use the bottom scrollbar to see them all. Figure 8-42 shows a show being created.

9. **(Optional) Click the Tasks button and then click Show Video Transitions.**

Transitions are a nice way of spicing up a slide show. If you do add transitions, we suggest you go with something subtle, like the Fade transition.

10. **(Optional) Add Transitions.**

To add a transition between slides, select the transition and then drop it in the slot between two slides.

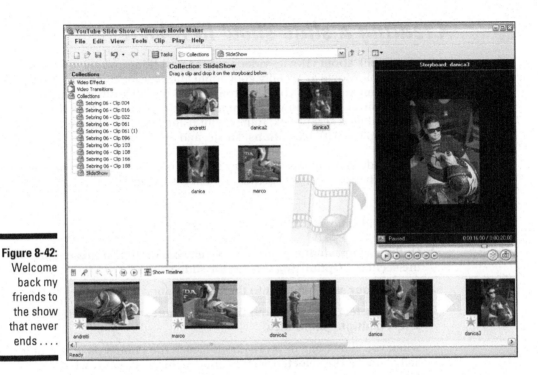

Figure 8-42:
Welcome
back my
friends to
the show
that never
ends . . . .

11. **(Optional) Add a soundtrack or voice-over.**

    If you don't know how to add a soundtrack or voice-over to a Movie Maker project, check out the section, "Adding a soundtrack to a video in Movie Maker," earlier in this chapter.

12. **Add a title and ending credit.**

    If you don't know how to add a title or ending credit to a Movie Maker project, check out the section, "Adding titles and credits in Movie Maker," earlier in this chapter.

13. **Save the project.**

14. **Choose File⇨Save Movie File.**

    This opens the Save Movie Wizard, which enables you to save the project as a movie that you can upload to the Tube. If you haven't saved a movie in Movie Maker yet, we show you how in Chapter 7.

Creating a slide show in iMovie

When you think about iMovie, videos are the first thing you think of, but don't overlook iMovie as a really cool application for making slide shows. If you're like most people, you have tons of still photos from your digital camera just sitting there on your computer. Rather than just toss them into a folder or a digital scrapbook, think about using iMovie to create a slide show — complete with transitions, music, and even voice-overs.

Creating a slide show in iMovie is very similar to creating a video presentation, except that you string together still images in the Timeline rather than video clips.

To create a slide show in iMovie, follow these steps:

1. **Optimize your digital photos, as we discuss earlier in this chapter in the section, "Optimizing images for slide shows."**

2. **Import your still images into the Photos pane.**

3. **Click to select a single photo file in the Photos pane or Shift-click to select multiple photo files.**

   When you select one or more photo files in the Photos pane, a thumbnail of one of the selected photos appears in the Preview window.

4. **Drag the Duration slider to set the duration for the selected clips.**

   The duration value that you set determines the length of time that each image appears on-screen in your slide show.

   Think about pace when you choose the duration for the slides in your show. If your presentation contains lots of images, you might want to progress relatively quickly; a duration of three seconds per image keeps things moving. On the other hand, if the images in your show are the types of images that warrant spending time with — if you're showing stunning photography from the Grand Canyon, for example, or if your slide show is a tour through the rooms of a house you're selling — consider giving each image more time on-screen.

5. **(Optional) If you select a single clip, use the Zoom slider to move in more tightly on the image.**

   The *Ken Burns Effect,* which you activate above the Preview window, is a built-in animation feature named after the famous documentarian. You use the Zoom slider to set the appearance of the first frame and then set a different appearance for the last frame. When you play the slide show, the Ken Burns Effect pans the slide, either zooming in slowly or zooming out slowly, depending on your settings. It's a subtle but very effective way to make your presentation more visually interesting.

6. **Click the Apply button.**

   When you click the Apply button, the duration that you set is applied to all the selected image files, which are all moved into the Timeline, as shown in Figure 8-43.

   In most cases, you want every slide in your presentation to have the same duration. Therefore, selecting all the images that you want to work with and setting the duration for them all at one time is often a smart idea.

7. **Drag the photo files left and right in the Timeline to determine the order you want them to play.**

8. **Add transitions between each clip for a presentation that's more visually interesting and polished.**

   To learn more about transitions, see the section "Creating a Cross Dissolve transition in iMovie," earlier in this chapter.

9. **Click the Audio button to access any music files that you have in your iTunes library and then drag a music file into the Timeline to play along with your slide show.**

   For instructions and options for working with audio files, see the section "Adding a soundtrack to a video in iMovie," earlier in this chapter.

10. **Click the Play button — or press the spacebar to preview your slide show.**

Figure 8-43:
Create your slide show with image files in the Timeline pane.

Getting Noticed on YouTube

Getting seen on YouTube is a big deal for many users, but it's not the only game in town. Millions of users utilize YouTube as a simple, practical video-sharing site, a way to share videos — usually family videos — with friends and relatives across the miles. They're not looking to get famous, and they're not hoping to get their videos seen by millions of viewers. In fact, many tubers upload their videos as private videos, able to be seen only by those with an invitation.

So, getting seen on the Tube isn't necessarily for everyone, but for some Tubers, it's all that matters. They upload their videos for one reason only: to attract an audience. Not to get famous, necessarily, but to get their videos seen.

In Chapter 9, we talk at length about getting famous on YouTube and how many talented people are using the Tube to launch showbiz careers for themselves. This section isn't about getting famous, but it is about getting your videos seen. We look at a number of strategies that you can use to find an audience — and maybe even a fan base — to check out your videos. If you happen to get famous in the process, well, maybe it's time to find an agent.

Tag, my video's It

The essential machinery on YouTube is search-and-find: Type in a search element and then look through the search results to find the video clip you're looking for. If you upload a video titled, "My Beautiful '57 Chevy," and I search for "Chevy," YouTube lists your video as one of the results of my search.

The YouTube search-and-find machinery is more complex than a simple title search, however. In the above example, if I search with the word "Chevrolet," does "My Beautiful '57 Chevy" still show up in the search results? If searching was limited only to title matches, the answer is No because "Chevrolet" and "Chevy" aren't the same words, even though they describe the same thing.

Tags are a fundamental search component that YouTube uses to search and find videos. Think of tags as keywords that describe what's in a video. Whenever you upload a video, you have the opportunity to enter tags that help other users find your videos. In the preceding example for your "My Beautiful '57 Chevy" video, you'd be smart to enter some or all of the following tags:

✔ Chevrolet

✔ Classic

✔ Cars

✔ Automobile

✔ Antique

✔ Fifties

✔ 50s

✔ 1957

If you like puzzles — especially word puzzles — you can see from the above list that tags can be a word-association challenge. You need to think about what's in your video — its *content* — and then you need to anticipate the various keywords that users might search for to find that content. It's an interesting puzzle: Making smart choices for tags can have a big effect on how many people watch your video. Looking at the preceding list, can you think of any important tags that we overlooked?

Adding tags to your video

Adding tags to your video — or *tagging* your video — is something that you do first as part of the upload procedure.

The Video Upload page, as shown in Figure 8-44, is the first page you encounter when uploading a video, and you enter the tags for your video on this page. Type directly into the Tags text box. Separate each tag with a space; you don't need to use commas.

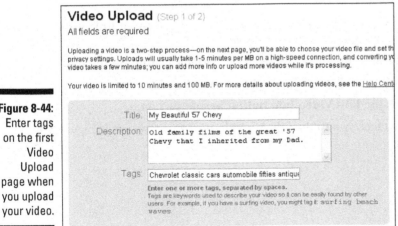

Figure 8-44: Enter tags on the first Video Upload page when you upload your video.

As you can see, entering tags is simple. Thinking up smart tags that get you found is the real trick.

The tags that you enter are listed with your video, as shown in Figure 8-45. An interesting thing about tags is that they also function as search inquiries. Click any tag listed with any video, and YouTube executes a new search based on that tag. This can be very useful for finding other videos that are related in content to a video you've found already.

Figure 8-45:
Tags are listed with a video and are links for additional searches.

Editing tags after you upload a video

After you upload your video, you can always edit the tags you applied when you uploaded. Here's how:

1. **From any page on YouTube, click the My Account link at the top of the page to go to your account page.**

2. **Click My Uploaded Videos in the Videos section on the left.**

3. **Scroll to find the video that you want to edit.**

4. **Click the Edit Video Info button beside its name.**

    This takes you to the Edit My Videos page, as shown in Figure 8-46.

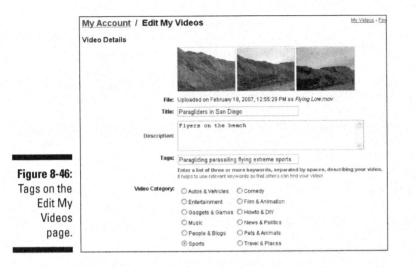

Figure 8-46:
Tags on the
Edit My
Videos
page.

5. **In the Tags field, delete the tags that you want to remove and then type in the tags you want to add.**

6. **After you're satisfied with your changes, click the Update Video Info at the bottom of the page.**

Smart strategies for tagging your video

As we said earlier, if you like puzzles, you'll enjoy brainstorming to find the best tags for your videos — tags that get them seen. As you might imagine, more than a few crafty Tubers have come up with some smart (and some sneaky) strategies for tagging. Here's an unofficial list of some tagging techniques you might want to think about when uploading that video that will make you famous — if only it gets seen:

- **Spell it right:** There's not much chance that all those people searching the word "Chevy" will find your video if your tag reads "Chevvy."

- **Spell it wrong:** You can't count on the fact that all those people doing searches know how to spell, so include tags that are reasonable misspellings of your key tags. If one of your tags is "Chevy," include another called "Chevvy."

- **Your title is a tag:** The words in your title are all tags and are found in a search. Don't duplicate a word in your video title as a tag.

✔ **Tag your username:** This is a smart and sneaky tip. Your username is searchable. If I type your username into the Search field, your videos are listed in the results. Many Tubers think that this is a good reason to not bother to include your username as a tag, especially because every one of your videos features your username as a link to your channel page. Here's the tip: If you use your username as a tag, it functions differently from the default link that links to your Channel page. If your username is there as a tag, your username links to your other videos, *not* your channel page. This is a smart way to get Tubers to keep seeking out your videos — an alternative to sending them to your channel page.

✔ **Include alternates:** What do you call that metal ring that holds your keys? A keychain, a key ring, or a keyring? Fact is, there are a lot of different ways to say (and spell) the same thing, and you're smart to think of alternate terms for your main tags. If your video's about parasailing, include `paragliding`, `hang gliding`, *and* `hanggliding` as alternate tags. If your video is about the 1950s, use `50s`, `50's`, and `fifties` as alternate tags. Remember, two alternate tags could mean the difference of thousands of hits.

✔ **Think global:** Use very specific tags to attract people doing a narrow search, but also include more global terms to attract a broader audience. If your video's about a classic car, include the tags `retro` and `antique` even though those two terms don't usually apply to cars: A good percentage of people searching the word "retro" are interested in your classic car. If your video is about parasailing, include the terms `parachuting` and `sky diving`. Granted, parasailing and sky diving are two different things, but many people who search for skydiving videos on the Tube are probably also interested in a sweet video with some cool parasailing footage.

✔ **Follow the leader:** Get tag ideas by searching for videos that are similar to yours and then use those tags. Kick it up a notch and search out similar videos that are also some of the most-viewed videos for that subject matter. If it worked for them, it might work for you, too.

✔ **Don't mislead:** One of the oldest tricks in the book is to tag your video with words, like sex and porn, and with names of popular Tubers, like lonelygirl15 and Mia Rose. Here's the problem with that: The viewers you get will be disappointed and resentful and may flag you. Here's a good tip though: "sexy" is different than "sex." Nothing is misleading about tagging your parasailing footage as `hot` and `sexy` extreme sport footage, and those two words alone might bring a few thousand more viewers to your video.

A tale of two categories

The importance of categories for getting your video seen can't be under-stated. Categories are the first and most fundamental method that YouTube uses to filter the millions of videos on the site, and millions of users follow suit. In fact, many users use categories as their primary filter for finding videos, and many others search *only* specific categories.

Choosing which category your video fits best plays a big part in how many people see it, and making that choice isn't always as easy as it seems. If you have a video of you meeting Muhammad Ali at a sports convention, what cat-egory do you list it under? Sports? People & Blogs? Entertainment?

Here's the rub: YouTube allows you to choose only one category when you upload a video. Here's a simple way around that: Upload the same video twice. When you do so, choose a title that's slightly different and then choose a different category than you did the first time you uploaded it. Now, you're covering two bases.

Always look for new categories! YouTube is rapidly evolving, and new fea-tures show up on the site quite often. For example, in April 2007, YouTube added the Howto & DYI (do it yourself) category. Whenever you see a new category, list your video in that category if it's reasonably appropriate. Why? Because a new category has fewer submissions, and that means less competi-tion. If your video gets popular, it doesn't take hundreds of thousands of views to make it to the top of the most-viewed or most-favorited lists. As with many other things in life, it's good to get in early.

After you upload your video, you might come to the realization that it would've been better suited in another category. No problem: You can always change a video's assigned category. Here's how:

1. **From any page on YouTube, click the My Account link at the top of the page to go to your account page.**

2. **Click My Uploaded Videos in the Videos section on the left.**

3. **Scroll to find the video that you want to edit.**

4. **Click the Edit Video Info button beside its name.**

   This takes you to the Edit My Videos page.

5. **In the Video Category section, choose the category that you want to switch to.**

6. **Click the Update Video Info at the bottom of the page.**

Promoting your YouTube videos

After your video is tagged, categorized, and uploaded, what more can you do to get it seen?

If being seen on the Tube is one of your goals, promoting your videos needs to become one of your passions. The idea that you'll upload a video, go to bed, and wake up in the morning to realize that a million people have watched your video is a fantasy. In the early days of YouTube, when there were thousands — as opposed to multi-millions — of members, it was easier to become a YouTube star. Today, it takes smarts, strategy, and a good dose of luck. But most of all, it takes work.

Promoting your video through the YouTube community

Sometimes it's easy to forget just how many people are surfing this site, but don't make that mistake when you're devising a strategy to promote your videos; the YouTube community is enormous and very powerful.

One great thing about messaging other Tubers is that you create a network of friends that you can alert when you upload a new video. Of course, if your video is boring, poorly produced, or just plain dumb, no amount of networking will make it popular. But if you have a video that most people will like, a network of YouTube friends can have an enormous impact on how many views your video gets.

Never underestimate the concept of *viral video*. If you send your video to me, and I send it to two friends, and they send it two more friends, and they send it to two additional friends, that's already 15 people who see your video. When that scenario progresses, it's not too hard to imagine thousands and then hundreds of thousands of people passing around your video. So don't underestimate the power of the 25 friends you've made on YouTube — they could deliver you an audience of thousands.

Networking with friends in high YouTube places

Another scenario in which the YouTube network can deliver you a huge audience happens when a very popular Tuber likes your video enough to list it as a favorite or to subscribe to your channel. For example, if lonelygirl15 lists you as one of her subscriptions on her channel page and her channel page gets hundreds of thousands of views every day, expect the view statistics for your channel page to go through the roof!

So how do you get lonelygirl15 to check out your channel? Send her a message! She's a Tuber, just like you.

Promoting your video through personal contacts

Your greatest promotional asset is probably sitting right in front of you on your computer: your e-mail Address Book. If you're like most people, your e-mail application probably contains hundreds if not thousands of e-mail addresses — friends, family, strangers, co-workers, ex-wives, Mr. Wrongs — you get the idea.

No matter what the size of your e-mail Address Book, these are great resources for getting your movie seen. You can send out an e-mail with a text link to your video on YouTube and ask your friends to take a look. Even better, you can embed your YouTube video in the e-mail itself, which makes it much more tantalizing and much more likely that the vast majority of those who receive the e-mail will actually look at it.

It's all about getting *viral,* so don't rely only on your own Address Book — access your friends' Address Books, too! When you send out your video, ask (beg, plead) that they take the time to look at it, but also ask (beg, plead more) that they *forward* the link to their Address Book. The potential is there to reach thousands of people.

This discussion emphasizes the importance of maintaining a contact list — whether it's your personal e-mail Address Book or your list of contacts on YouTube. If you're serious about getting your videos seen, your list of contacts is by far your greatest asset.

Creating a Vlog

Do you blog? Blogging has taken the nation — and for that matter, the world — by storm. A *blog* (short for Weblog) is an ongoing diary, a way to speak your piece. But YouTube is all about video, so it only makes sense that you'd have the option to add a video log *(vlog)* to your channel. Your vlog can be any playlist or a video you've actually recorded with your Webcam or camcorder. A vlog is prominently displayed on your channel. You can create a vlog from any of your playlists. However, if you want to create a personal vlog of your own, follow these steps:

1. **Create a video with your Webcam or camcorder.**

2. **Optimize the video.**

3. **Log in to the Tube and upload your video. (See Chapter 7 for full coverage of this.)**

4. **Click the My: Playlists link.**

   YouTube displays your first playlist.

5. **Click Create Playlist.**

   The Create/Edit Playlist page appears.

6. **Enter a name for the playlist, description, and tags.**

7. **Click the Video Log check box.**

   This tells YouTube that this playlist is the vlog in your channel. Figure 8-47 shows a playlist that's the vlog for TuberDummy's channel.

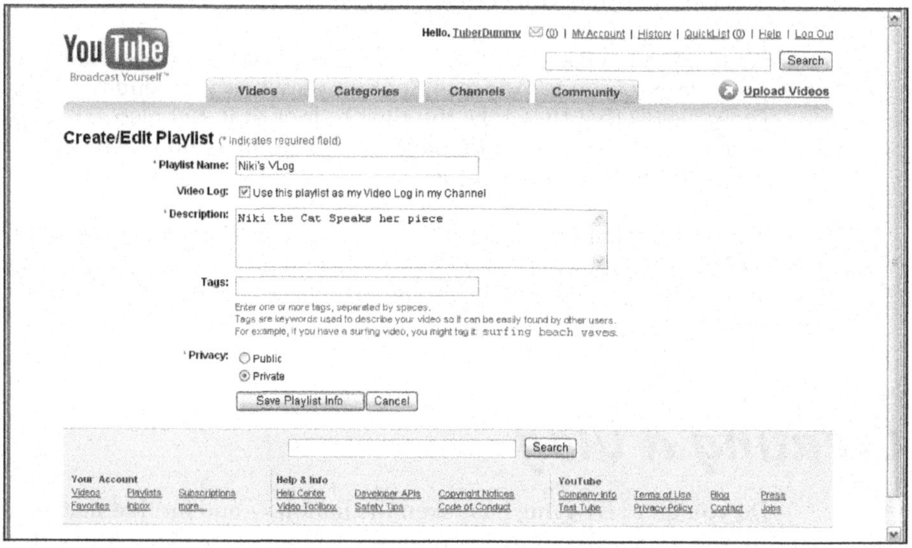

Figure 8-47:
Soon to be a vlog on a YouTube Channel.

8. **Click the My Videos link.**

   YouTube displays an icon for each of your uploaded videos.

9. **Click the icon for the video you want displayed on your channel as a vlog.**

   The video plays.

10. **Click the Save to Favorites link.**

    The Save to Favorites dialog appears.

11. **Choose the vlog playlist you created to store your video log.**

12. **Click OK.**

    The video log appears on your channel (see Figure 8-48).

If you update your vlog on a regular basis and provide interesting content, your subscribers will continue to return to see what you have to say. If the vlog is really interesting, you'll pick up new subscribers as well.

Figure 8-48:
Let the world know how you feel with a vlog.

Chapter 9

Getting Famous on YouTube

In This Chapter

▶ Creating YouTube specialty accounts

▶ Finding performers on YouTube

▶ Accepting an award from the YouTube Academy

Sudden fame is a very strange and interesting phenomenon of the Internet age. You don't necessarily need to be beautiful or talented, and you don't need to move to Hollywood, either. Suddenly, you can get famous from the comfort of your own home — famous just for being you.

At the 2007 Academy Awards, Jennifer Hudson took one very giant leap from former *American Idol* contestant to Oscar winner, and in that one moment, it was reality TV that really took home the award. With so many videos and so many viewers, it's only a matter of time until YouTube makes someone famous — very famous.

YouTube fame is already a reality. Many Tubers have used their videos and channels as a portfolio to score record deals, television appearances, acting roles, and comedy gigs. At the end of 2006 — the year young YouTube came of age — YouTube's breakout star Lonelygirl15 was featured on many "Top 10" lists in newspapers and magazines throughout the country. She was even interviewed by none other than the "gray lady" herself — *The New York Times.* That's validation.

In this chapter, we look at YouTube from the perspective of fame. We show you how to create a specialty account and get yourself listed as a director, a comedian, a musician, and yes, a guru. We also look at video clips of various players — teachers, musicians, comics, filmmakers, and so on — and check out some of the smart ways that these people are using the Tube to get themselves on fame and fortune's radar screen.

Creating Specialty Accounts

A basic YouTube account is called a *YouTuber* account. When we refer to it as basic, we mean really that it's generic — it's identified only as an account, no different from the millions of other accounts.

But many users want to kick it up a notch and have their accounts identified in very specific terms. Singers want to create accounts that can be identified in a YouTube search as a singer's account, and comedians want their channels identified as comedy channels. Thus, the evolution of the YouTube specialty account.

The first specialty account was Directors, and it's still a very popular account on the Tube. In the early days of the Tube, basic YouTuber accounts were limited in terms of file size and length of video. The original concept for a Directors account is that it allowed filmmakers more room to upload substantial videos — videos of longer length and with less compression and therefore with better quality and greater file size. As you see, the Directors channel evolved in many different directions beyond that original concept.

YouTube is always rapidly evolving, and one big change was to do away with the length and file size constraints on basic YouTuber accounts. Now, all accounts allow a user to upload a video with a file size as large as 100MB.

That's a big change, and just as YouTube keeps evolving, the concept of the specialty account itself has evolved. Tubers realized that they needed more than just extra time and space; they needed to be *identified*. Let's say you're a violin virtuoso, and you've uploaded all your performances to promote your talent. It only makes sense that you want YouTube to provide users a way to search and find musicians.

Thus, the evolution of the specialty account as a means of identification. YouTube now offers specialty accounts for Directors, Comedians, Musicians, and the new one — Gurus. All specialty accounts are listed as special sections at the top of the Channels page, as shown in Figure 9-1.

 YouTube defines the new Gurus account/channel as a place for "experts who show others how to cook, bartend, create better videos, or (almost) any other skill you can pass on."

Another great benefit of a specialty account is that it offers you increased options for customizing your channel page:

✓ **Director:** Allows you to add your personal logo artwork to your channel page.

✓ **Musician:** Allows you to add personal logo artwork, genre, tour date information, and CD purchase links to your channel page.

✓ **Comedian:** Allows you to add personal logo artwork, style, show date information, and CD purchase links to your channel page.

Regardless of what type of account you create, anyone who registers gets a channel on YouTube; your channel name is your username. But if you're a musician, you want users to find you in a search for musicians, which is why you register your channel as a Musicians channel.

In this section, we show you how to create specialty accounts when you first sign up, and we show you how to convert an already-existing account to a specialty account. We also tell you about some of the bonuses that come with different types of accounts.

For step-by-step instructions for registering a standard YouTube account, see Chapter 2.

Specialty accounts

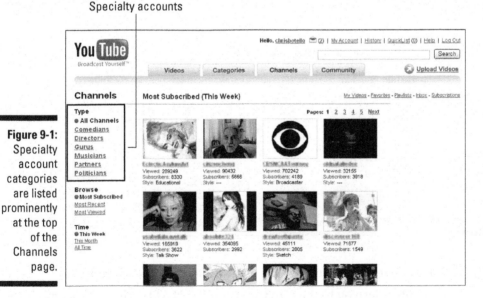

Figure 9-1:
Specialty
account
categories
are listed
prominently
at the top
of the
Channels
page.

Creating a specialty account when you first register

You can register a brand-new account as a specialty account when you first sign up. Choose which type of specialty account best fits your YouTube plans, but don't feel trapped: You can always switch your account to another type of specialty account.

To register a new account as a specialty account, follow the following steps:

1. **From the YouTube home page, click the Sign Up link at the top of the page.**

   This takes you to the Join YouTube page.

2. **Click the Account Type menu arrow and then choose which type of account you want to register.**

   Figure 9-2 shows the start of a Musicians account.

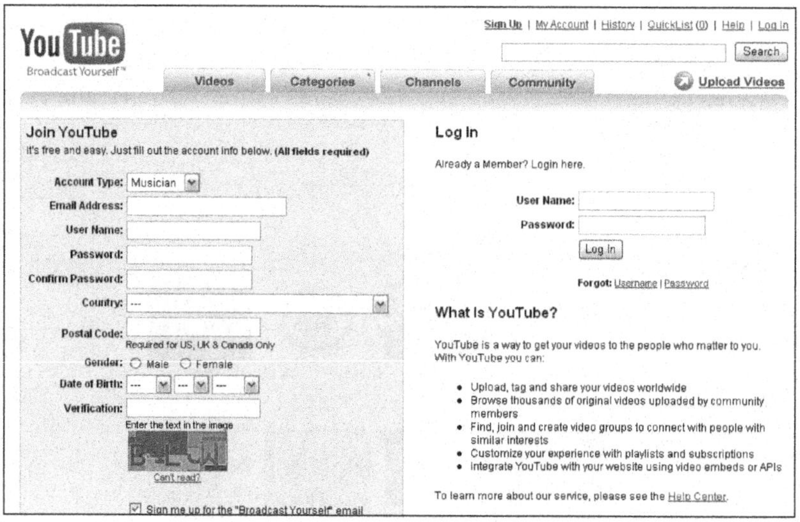

Figure 9-2:
Creating a
Musicians
account.

3. **Fill out the rest of the information and then click Sign Up.**

   This takes you to the Sign Up/Please Select a Style page, as shown in Figure 9-3.

Musician Signup

It's free and easy. Just fill out the account info below. (All fields required)

> Musician Channels are for bands, singers, songwriters, labels and others involved in making music and music videos.
>
> Uploading videos or music that you do not own is a violation of the artist's copyrights and against the law. If you upload material you do not own, your account will be deleted.

Account Type:	Musician
Email Address:	
YouTube Username:	[ ] check
	Your username can only contain letters A-Z or numbers 0-9
Password:	
Confirm Password:	
Country:	United States
Postal Code:	
	Required for US, UK & Canada Only
Style:	---
Record Label:	
Label Type:	---

Figure 9-3: The Musicians Sign Up page. Note the Style drop-down menu.

Whatever type of specialty account you choose, you go to the Sign Up/ Please Select a Style page. Each offers you the warning in the red box — tweaked slightly for each type of account — and each wants you to further define your account by specifying a style. The style that you choose is listed beneath your clips when they appear on a search results page. For example, a Musicians account offers you more than 60 style choices, everything from Folk and Country to Christian Rap, Glam, and something called Psychobilly.

4. **Choose a style from the list, verify that all other fields are filled out, and then click Sign Up.**

If you're creating a Musicians account, you have the option of entering the label that you record for (if you do indeed record for a label) and you can also specify the type of label, such as independent or major.

Switching your account to a specialty account

If you're registered already on YouTube and you didn't choose a specialty account, did you know that your account type is officially called YouTuber? It is, and if you do indeed have a YouTuber account and want to switch it to a Directors, Musicians, or any other type of specialty account, you can do so quickly and easily. If you register your account as a specialty account and want to switch it to another type of specialty account, you can do that, too. Here's how:

1. **From any YouTube page, click the My Account link at the top of the page.**

2. **Scroll down and then click the Channel Info link in the Channel Settings section.**

3. **Click the Change Channel link.**

   The New Channel Type list appears below the link, as shown in Figure 9-4.

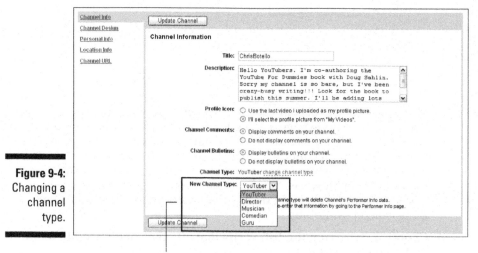

Figure 9-4:
Changing a
channel
type.

The New Channel Type list

4. **Choose the type of channel you want to switch to and then click the Update Channel button.**

Finding Performers on the Tube

If we wanted to get cute about it, we would've saved the fame discussion for Chapter 14 because all talk of fame and YouTube inevitably leads to someone quoting Andy Warhol's famous line that someday everybody will be famous for 15 minutes. That someday has arrived. Andy Warhol would've *loved* YouTube as the great equalizer, the venue through which *anybody* can get famous for *anything* — good or bad.

Just as Andy took everyday objects — like soup can labels — and presented them as art, YouTube is taking everyday people — Lonelygirl15, for example — and presenting them as stars. Do you think that by putting the 15 at the end of her username, she was making a sly reference to Andy's 15 minutes of fame?

Probably not. In fact, the very awkwardness of that username (who are Lonely girls 1–14?) suggests that Lonelygirl15 probably had no idea that she'd ever get so popular and so famous. And that's the other edge of the YouTube sword: You never know just how big it all might get.

YouTube for singers and musicians

Talk about a marriage made in heaven: YouTube is a perfect vehicle for the musically talented among us to perform for the masses. Do you ever sing into the mirror with a hairbrush as a microphone? C'mon — we know you do. Throw a video camera into the scenario, upload it to YouTube, and just like that, you have an audience. And if you have a little thing called *talent* to add to that equation, you just might find yourself suddenly famous.

We're reminded of a great line from the great Mike Nichols' movie *Working Girl:* Joan Cusack says to Melanie Griffith, "Sometimes I sing and dance around the bedroom in my underwear. Doesn't make me Madonna. Never will." In the age of YouTube and video sharing, never say never, Joan.

You might be surprised to find out that many users choose YouTube as one of their major sources for music. When they find a clip that they like, they save it to their favorites or to a playlist and then "listen" to YouTube all day long. The people at YouTube are of course aware of this enormous audience, and they make finding music and musicians on YouTube very easy. When you want to find them, just follow these steps:

1. **From any YouTube page, click the Channels tab.**

   This takes you to the Channels home page, as shown in Figure 9-5. Note the Type section on the left, which lists six types of channels.

   Channels are like opinions: Everybody's got one. When you register an account with YouTube, you automatically get a channel. You don't need to be a performer to have a channel, but YouTube uses channels to help you find performers.

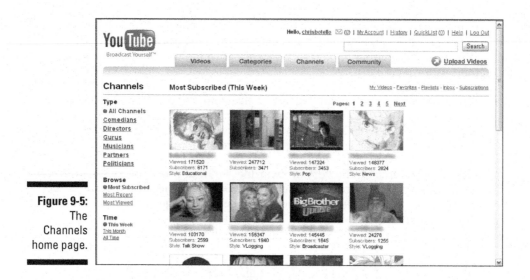

Figure 9-5:
The
Channels
home page.

2. **In the list on the left side of the page, click Musicians.**

This takes you to the Musicians channel home page, as shown in Figure 9-6.

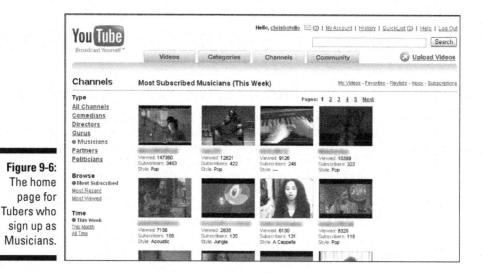

Figure 9-6:
The home
page for
Tubers who
sign up as
Musicians.

To have your video listed on the Musicians channel home page, you need to register a specialty account as a musician. To do so, see the section, "Creating Specialty Accounts," earlier in this chapter.

All the videos you see on this page are uploaded by Tubers who created a Musicians specialty account. The total number of subscribers for each channel is listed under the thumbnail, so you can see at a glance who really has generated a following. It's not a guarantee, but it's a good bet that if some singer, guitar player, or pianist has thousands of subscribers to her channel, something interesting is probably happening there.

Another important listing under each clip is Style. This tells you the type of music that the clip contains: rock, acoustic, R&B, and so on.

By default, when you first click the Musicians link, the videos on the Musicians channel home page are sorted by Most Subscribed/This Week.

3. **In the Time section on the left, click All Time.**

This gives you a list of YouTube's most-subscribed-to Musicians channels of all time.

On the day we did this search, the results are shown in Figure 9-7. We weren't surprised to see that miaarose was at the top of the list of most-subscribed-to musicians — with 50,000 subscribers to her channel. Note that on that day, her channel had been viewed over five million times! Now that's what we call an audience.

Miarose is a YouTube phenomenon, one of the first singers to get very popular on the Tube. She's featured in various music venues and publications, including *Rolling Stone* magazine. In various online blogs and vlogs, she discusses offers that have come her way from managers, promoters, and labels.

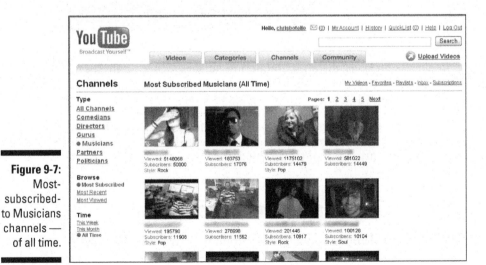

Figure 9-7: Most-subscribed-to Musicians channels — of all time.

She's even become a bit controversial — is she a "legit" talent, or "just" a YouTube fad? Is it the artist who's hot, or is it just the venue? These are reasonable questions, but one of the great things about YouTube is that you can always check out things and decide for yourself.

YouTube fame is a two-way street. Yes, YouTube is chock-full of performers who want to get noticed, but it's also a venue for smart young artists who've already scored contracts with major labels to build an audience. Ashley Tisdale and Terra Naomi are two artists who have gained significant popularity on the Tube. Both have recording deals — Ashley with Warner Bros. and Terra with Island Records — and each is using her channel on YouTube for online promotion. Both keep their channels updated frequently with messages and vlogs, and both use their channels as springboards with links to their official Web sites and to online merchants where Tubers can purchase their CDs. Ashley Tisdale's channel is shown in Figure 9-8.

Figure 9-8:
Ashley
Tisdale's
channel is
a smart
promotional
vehicle.

Musicians on YouTube aren't limited to singers — not at all. On the Tube, you find any and all types of musicians: from piano players to oboists, flautists to harpists, guitar players, and tuba players — any instrument you can think of and any style of music you like is represented. Speaking of guitarists, check out my co-author Doug Sahlin's nephew's video, as shown in Figure 9-9. Please don't confuse my referral as nepotism: First, he's not *my* nephew, and second, this guy can *really* play the guitar.

Becoming an online music star

Music on YouTube is breaking new ground: Many singers and musicians are creating big names for themselves — and attracting large audiences — without ever going to a recording studios. For many, the setup is a simple microphone and a video camera. Some singers use a karaoke machine. Others mix and edit their music on their desktops. The concept of the "home-grown" rock star is the real deal.

Colin Hughes-Guitar Virtuoso

00:08 / 03:53

Figure 9-9:
Colin
Hughes
works the
strings.

If you're serious about trying to be a professional singer or musician, the Internet offers you some amazing new options for parlaying your YouTube success to a bigger and brighter future. In fact, Internet music is evolving so rapidly that you can create an entire release campaign just by working with various Web sites.

Are you making music and getting good feedback from your YouTube exposure? Then consider some of the following services as potential next steps. We're listing them not as recommendations but as information for you to see how *real* the online music business is becoming and how many opportunities are really out there for the home-grown musician.

- ✔ **Distribution and Marketing**: TheOrchard.com and InGrooves.com offer digital distribution of your music in exchange for a flat percentage of your sales. The Orchard, for example, claims to be the leading digital distributor for independent record labels. Their Web site says that they supply music to such big online outlets as iTunes, MSN, eMusic, and Napster. Both sites tout their marketing expertise: InGrooves boasts promotional relationships with AOL Music, Yahoo!, and Sony PSP.

- ✔ **Sales**: iTunes ain't the only venue in town. If you have a recording that you think will sell, check out CDbaby.com. (Their no-flash old-school home page is shown in Figure 9-10.) CDbaby.com appears to be one of those cool Internet "grassroots" stories: They say they're "a little online record store" run by "just a few people in a cool Portland, Oregon warehouse." They claim that they listen to *every* CD before they sell it, and that they work only with *independent* musicians, who they define as someone who hasn't "sold one's life, career, and creative works over to a corporation." They say that musicians get a great deal with them — a bigger cut on the sale than is standard — and they boast that they are the largest seller of independent CDs on the Web.

Figure 9-10:
CDbaby,
wants to
sell your
music...
baby.

✔ **Studio Time:** Sellaband.com has a unique concept that is either brilliantly original or just plain unrealistic. You put up a profile on their site advertising you and your music. Then you get people to "invest" in you by giving Sellaband.com $50,000 (yep, that's 50-grand). This happens on the site, where users — friends or strangers — pledge money toward helping you make it. You can get 50 investors at $1,000 per, or 5,000 investors at $10 per, whatever gets you to the goal. When you do, Sellaband gets you into a professional recording studio and then promotes and sells your CD. Everybody — you, Sellaband, and your investors — all get a cut of the sales. That's the theory. Figure 9-11 shows their site's home page, which celebrates the few artists who have *paid* $50k but none who have *made* $50k in record sales. It doesn't appear that Sellaband has produced any big success stories just yet, but their Experts page suggests that they have some great contacts in the industry, and you have to give them kudos for a cool concept.

Figure 9-11:
Sellaband.
com wants
to sell your
band . . . for
a price.

✔ **Promotion:** Companies, like Musictoday.com, are like supermalls for all types of promotion. They create and host an "online fan club" for you, which you can use as a platform to promote yourself and sell your merchandise. Musictoday offers CD replication services, and their Digital Download service enables artists to sell audio and video merchandise directly through the Musictoday official Web store. For the most part, although they work with new and unsigned talent, they're affiliated with already-successful acts. Their About Us page lists such performers as John Mayer, Christina Aguilera, and the Rolling Stones (no less!) as clients.

✔ **Licensing:** If you want to diversify from trying to get a recording contract or selling your music online, companies like Rumblefish.com and PumpAudio.com can introduce you to the world of licensing. They're agencies that work with musicians the way a stock photography house works with photographers. If they like your music and think they can sell it, they put you into their catalogue, which they promote to businesses, like advertising agencies and film and television production companies, who they consult with for music identity branding. They take a percentage of the licensing fee, and you keep the rest. So maybe your new song or jingle becomes the music for the new Coke or Pepsi commercial (that's the dream, anyway). This could be a smart alternative to the competitive and arbitrary become-a-rock-star path and has the potential to be very lucrative.

YouTube for comedians

It's funny how Web sites evolve. eBay, when first launched, was some sort of online garage sale, a place to sell old knick-knacks and board games. Who could've guessed that in a very short time, people would be selling cars there?

When YouTube launched as a video sharing site — a place for people to share their home movies — do you think the founders had any idea that the site would evolve into a platform for people who want to get famous? An online performance space?

Well, that's exactly what did happen, and the Comedians channel has become one of the most visited areas of the site. From an audience point of view, the Comedians channel is a great place to see performances from some of the country's hottest and upcoming comics. Add them to your playlist, put on a set of headphones, and you can laugh your way through the work day.

From the comic's point of view, YouTube is a great place to try out new material and get some feedback from a very large audience. For them, YouTube has created an entirely new venue, a new place to be seen, and a new place to build a fan base. YouTube isn't just about TV and the comedy clubs anymore.

An interview with singer ysabellabrave

It's not hard to find ysabellabrave on the Tube; in fact, it's hard to *not* find her. It seems that any tab you click, there she is. Even in a thumbnail photo, with that face, and those eyes — she's instantly recognizable.

Ysabellabrave ("Isabella Brave") is, in every sense, a YouTube star. A singing star. She's attracted an enormous fan-base for her remarkable renditions of jazz and pop standards. Two of her many statistical achievements:

- ✔ Number 15 on the list of Most-Viewed channels in a single day
- ✔ Number 26 on the list of Most-Viewed channels of all time

Ysabellabrave's enormous presence on YouTube is based on a number of factors. She's a talented singer with a unique voice — and she's got more different looks than Madonna. Her production values are simple and good. Her voice is clear. And she never hits a bad note. In this age of bubblegum pop, she chooses to sing classic standard songs from the American Songbook, songs like "Night and Day," "Why Don't You Do Right," and "Blue Bayou." One can surmise that her videos are perhaps the first time that her younger fans are hearing these classics.

If you're looking for YouTube fame, you can discover a lot from ysabellabrave; she's clearly a smart young lady with a talent for marketing herself. Nearly all her videos are shot in front of the same black background, which makes her the sole center of attention and has evolved as some simple sort of branding: Her clips have a look that you recognize instantly. Check out some of her early videos and you'll be amazed at how her look has changed and evolved. She's even parlayed her popularity into a vlog advice column, which get *tens* of thousands of views!

If you haven't guessed yet, we are big fans and were thrilled when she agreed to be interviewed for the book.

You have such a unique look and that name — ysabellabrave — only adds to the allure. We always think of you as a singer from some exotic locale, like Rio or Buenos Aires. Where are you from, really?

I live in northern California — not too exotic. However, my mother is Apsaalooke (Crow Indian), and my father is from the Azores (Portuguese islands). My father came up with ysabellabrave as a screen name for me in a moment's notice — ages ago. My middle name is Ysabel, after his mother Isabel, and he thinks me a brave lady. I hope I can live up to that for him.

Before uploading your YouTube videos, were you a professional singer? What were your singing experiences before your YouTube exposure?

I've been singing for roughly a year and a half. Before that, as far as I was concerned, I couldn't hold a note — I'd mumble or mouth "Happy Birthday" if I had to! One day, I was suddenly able to sing, and I began making videos.

When did you put up your first YouTube video?

I put up my first videos around August 2006. I recall finding it odd that people I knew were "spreading the word" about me to people they knew, and then to people *they* knew, and so on, and so on.

Tell us about your video production. Is this a high-tech operation you have going?

Not quite. I use a karaoke machine for the music. For the video, I use a Kodak Easyshare z760. This isn't some high-end video camera; basically, it's a simple digital camera, which also records video, and the microphone is inside the camera. For lighting, I use a (broken) desk lamp with a 60 watt bulb in it. That's it! Actually, the fact that it's such a simple operation is what's allowed me to produce so many videos.

What would you say that your goals were when you first uploaded your videos?

I uploaded my initial videos with the idea that they'd be a great way to sing for my friends and family who live too far away. After a few months, everything just burst open and I found that a huge number of people were watching my videos on YouTube.

I was very surprised — not only was it never my intention to achieve any fame from these videos, I would've laughed if I'd been told that'd happen. You must remember: The only reason I knew I could sing was because of what I heard from my friends. So any moment I was expecting to be on *Candid Camera,* not to hear it confirmed by thousands of strangers.

What types of things happened that made you realize that you were becoming very popular on YouTube?

When people started sending me fan mail saying that everyone they told about me had already heard about me, I was impressed. Reading and responding to the messages I received began to take up a great deal of my time.

Why do you upload your videos as a Directors account and not a Musicians account?

Because when I first started uploading videos, there was no such thing as a Musicians account. Director accounts were the newest thing, and could send out unlimited messages, which was great because I could respond to fans.

(continued)

(continued)

Tell us about some of the great feedback and experiences that you've had interacting with other YouTube members.

I've been told that people have played my video songs at funerals, weddings, all day at work, in firehouses — even in hospitals to sick people or to newborn babies.

I've heard just about everything you can imagine. People tell me that my music has healing properties (one man claimed to have his near-blindness cured!), breaks language barriers, brings memories, and inspires hope. Most of these people tell me they've become members of YouTube simply to interact with my videos.

At a recent YouTube meet-and-greet, I met some of the other quite popular YouTube members and was *amazed* to hear them tell me they were fans of mine, some saying they were too in awe to speak much. It's flattering, of course, but I found this *very* bizarre.

Were there any bad or negative experiences that you've had with YouTube members?

An occasional heckler is in the crowd — even on YouTube — but your beefy security guard is at your fingertips with the Delete button.

Have you received any attention from the media other than YouTube?

Oh, yes. I was on MSNBC, was in *The New York Times* twice, and was written about in hundreds of blogs. I've also been contacted for work by several big record companies and the like, all who have seen me on YouTube.

It's very odd to be famous on YouTube — many people flip out if I comment on their videos, and I'm often asked, "Can you even go outside anymore without people bothering you?" That one makes me laugh because no one in my entire city, I believe, knows anything about this, and I've *never* been recognized in public.

Like many young girls, I always secretly dreamed of becoming famous as an actress or something similar, but I gave up the dream mainly when I realized how difficult the whole process of being discovered is. I come from a small town, I don't have any money, I have no industry contacts, and so forth. I never guessed that with a few simple, unedited videos — intended for nothing more than communicating with friends — that I could create a situation in which people are knocking down my door.

Comedy is a tough sport, a take-no-prisoners game. Even the lingo is violent: When a comic does well, she "kills." When she gets no laughs, she not only "bombs," she "dies." Seems like either way, someone's torch is snuffed out. One can imagine that the YouTube Comedians channel has had a big impact on would-be or wannabe standups entering this arena.

It sure takes guts to get up on a stage as an actor, singer, or juggler, but nothing takes more guts than standing up as a comedian in front of a live audience just daring you to make them laugh. YouTube puts a new spin on that. With the Comedians channel, a wet-behind-the-ears comic can perform by video — without having to step out onto the stage. Just as it is for a professional comic, YouTube is a great place for a new comic to try out some material, get some feedback, and get some idea if he can make *anybody* laugh. Just the act of making a video gives you some performance experience — even if you do it with no audience.

Of course, a video on a Web site is no substitute for the experience that a comic gets on a stage, but comedy isn't only about performing. Comedy is also about writing, and you can be sure there are plenty of showbiz types surfing through YouTube to find great comics — and great comedy writers. So even if your performance is bad, if your material is good, doors might open for you.

One thing about registering a specialty account as a Comedian: You don't have to be a comedian to do so. In other words, not everybody on the Comedians channel is a professional stand-up comedian, nor are all the performance videos of comics onstage. Instead, the Comedians channel is also occupied by regular old Tubers who *think* they're funny, and experience tells us that people who tell you that they're funny usually aren't. Trust us, you won't have any trouble finding some unfunny clips on the Comedians channel. But for all the good reasons — all the talented comics and standups — the Comedians channel is a YouTube hot spot, and very easy to find. Here's how you do it:

1. **From any YouTube page, click the Channels tab.**

   This takes you to the Channels home page. Note the Type section on the left, which lists six types of channels.

2. **In the list on the left side of the page, click Comedians.**

   This takes you to the Comedians channel home page. By default, when you first click the Comedians link, the videos are sorted by Most Subscribed/This Week.

3. **In the Time section on the left, click All Time.**

   This gives you a list of the most subscribed-to Comedians channels of all time on YouTube. Figure 9-12 shows the results of our search.

   To have your video listed on the Comedians channel home page, register a specialty account as a comedian. See the section, "Creating Specialty Accounts," earlier in this chapter.

All the videos you see in the Comedians channel are uploaded by Tubers who created a Comedians specialty account. The total number of subscribers for each channel is listed under the thumbnail, so you can see at a glance who's really created a fan base. It's less a guarantee here than in any other specialty section, but it's a good bet that if a registered comedian has thousands of subscribers to her channel, something funny is going on there.

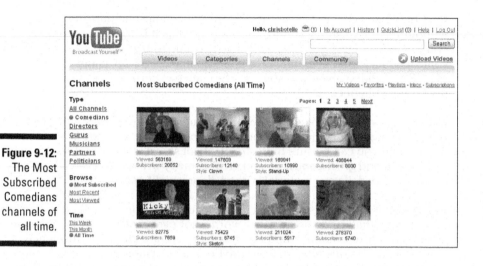

Figure 9-12:
The Most
Subscribed
Comedians
channels of
all time.

One last thing about YouTube fame and the Comedians channel: Videos that are funny are the videos that get passed around most — more than cute babies, more than scary airplane landings, and even more than great singers. People love to share the funny stuff. And though most people seem to think of singers or filmmakers when they think about fame on YouTube, we suspect that the first person to get *really* famous off of the Tube just might come from the Comedians channel.

YouTube for directors and filmmakers

Earlier in this chapter, we talk about how Web sites evolve in unexpected ways. One interesting area of YouTube is its Directors channel, which was the first specialty channel that YouTube created. Here's how you can find it:

1. **From any YouTube page, click the Channels tab.**

   This takes you to the Channels home page. Note the Type section on the left, which lists six types of channels.

2. **In the list on the left side of the page, click Directors.**

   This takes you to the Directors channel home page. By default, when you first click the Directors link, the videos are sorted by Most Subscribed/This Week.

3. **In the Time section on the left, click All Time.**

   This gives you a list of the most subscribed-to Directors channels of all time on YouTube. Figure 9-13 shows the results of our search.

A profile of comedian Frank Caliendo

At the top of all the Most Viewed and Most Subscribed comedy charts, you find a comic named Frank Caliendo. Frank is one of those comics that, if you heard him on the radio, you'd say, "He's a funny guy," but after you see him perform, you'd say "You have to see him onstage." A big component of his appeal is visual — he does killer impressions, especially of Clinton and Bush — which makes YouTube a perfect venue for his many talents.

We were very eager to interview Frank because the timing of the interview is perfect: He's not yet a household name but he's already a _big_ name on YouTube. We met his manager Terry Caliendo (he doubles as Frank's brother) and got way more than we bargained for. Turns out, Frank and Terry's YouTube story is a primer on how to make it on YouTube and a peek behind the scenes into the go-for-it world of getting your guy seen.

Terry's in charge of Frank's promotional efforts, and he was feeling guilty that he missed the MySpace wave. His determination to take YouTube for everything it has to offer is impressive — and somehow funny in a great way. This guy was on a mission to get his brother seen on the Tube. And even after a major screw-up by YouTube, he wasn't taking No for an answer.

How did the Frank Caliendo team first hear about YouTube?

I vividly remember Frank calling me and asking me, "Have you heard about this YouTube thing? Someone said my Letterman set is on it." Being the technology guy, I should have known about it first. But the site was just starting to take off, and I hadn't stumbled upon it yet. Apparently word of mouth travels faster. I asked Frank, "What is YouTube?" And he said, "It's some sort of video site. Look into it. . . ."

So I did. I went to the site and was amazed that not only did somebody finally make a site where you could upload video, but that it was _free_ and easy for non-tech savvy people to use. I knew it'd

(continued)

(continued)

be a huge site: People don't read as much as they watch TV, so you could pretty much forecast that You Tube video would be just as big, if not bigger, than blogs and MySpace.

Before YouTube, was Frank using the Internet as part of his promotion/publicity strategy?

I missed out on the early MySpace growth in promoting Frank and figured this could be my redemption. Here's a great story in comedy circles about a very popular comedian who used MySpace to explode his career. The story goes that, while other comedians were out partying and drinking after shows, this comedian would go straight back to his hotel room to chat online and try to get as many friends as he could on his MySpace profile. If you don't know who I'm talking about, make 50 random friends on MySpace and it's almost a sure thing that one of them is friends with this pioneer and marketing genius.

When did Frank Caliendo make his YouTube debut?

The first — and most successful — video we put on You Tube was *Frank Caliendo — Impressions*. From past experiences, I knew that it had to be good — "HOLY WOW!!" type good. So rather than just put a single, short clip or a series of short clips, I chose to put up eight minutes of Frank's *best* stuff, especially the visual stuff — the *impressions* — that don't have as big an effect on the radio or on CDs.

According to the video's page, I uploaded it on March 6, 2006. A year later, it's been viewed an astounding 4.9 million times, and it currently averages 8,000 views per day — that's 240,000 views per month!

Are you always conscious of making sure that your YouTube presence doesn't compete too much with your other areas of promotion?

That's definitely a consideration. In the *Frank Caliendo — Impressions* video, I make sure to show only *parts* of each individual bit so that people see Frank's talent but still want to visit our Web site or go to a live show to get more of him. Also, I know that people can download the video, possibly chop it up, and post it wherever they want. So to make sure Frank got credit, I embedded his name and Web site at the bottom throughout the *entire* video. I figured out this lesson from a comedian whose audio clip was passed around the world in an e-mail. It was a funny clip — everybody was listening to it. But it did nothing for the comedian because his name wasn't on it or mentioned anywhere in the audio. So, I made sure that when people put the video on their blogs or did whatever they wanted with it, that Frank's name is guaranteed to be there.

It's one thing to upload a video to YouTube, it's another to make it one of the most videos ever seen. What types of things did you do to make that happen?

From the moment that I uploaded Frank's first video clip, my goal was to get it to the top of each of the YouTube Most Viewed sections because I knew that these sections are where people go to find the best clips. I spent the first day doing everything I could to get onto the Most Viewed — Today page. I sent out e-mails to our Web site's fan mail list. I went to chat rooms and told people to watch the video. I posted the link to the video on forums, and I put a link to the video on Frank's Web site. Back then, you needed only a couple thousand hits to get Most Viewed — Today status. Now it takes about 10 to 20 times that many hits, so getting on YouTube in the early days *really* helped.

After we got on the Most Viewed — Today page, the video went up the "charts" faster than I thought it would. After that, achieving the other Most Viewed lists required just some daily reminders to the fan mail list and some postings on Frank's Web site. I also did some forum posts and chat room sessions, and Frank promoted the YouTube clip when he did radio appearances. Frank's talent really played a role here: I could've worked my brains out to get hits for his video, but if it wasn't funny, it wouldn't have become nearly as "viral" as it did.

Sounds like it took on a life of its own.

Definitely. Another help was that lots of people favorited Frank's video. So we get hits from the Most Viewed lists, Most Discussed lists, Highest Rated lists, Most Favorited lists, and now from people's favorites on their individual pages. In other words, when users visit other user's channel pages, Frank's video is often there under the favorites listing. Currently, Frank's video has been favorited by 10,589 users so that alone probably gets us a good percentage of our average daily 8,000 hits.

Another major benefit was that people did just what I thought they'd do: They took the video and posted it on other sites. Because I had Frank's name plastered in the video, they were doing my work for me and I didn't have to worry about Frank not getting credit. I was going to upload Frank's video to every site I could find, but most of the sites I found already had Frank's video posted on them!

Have you had any negative experiences on YouTube?

About five months after we uploaded our first video, a small but major tragedy struck: YouTube pulled our video due to a copyright violation. After freaking out and sobbing like a child, I responded to the instructions on the automated e-mail that informed me that our video was pulled. I responded that this was our video, we owned the rights, and we demanded they reinstate the video immediately! Within a couple days, our video was taken out of its violation status, and YouTube replied they were sorry for the mix-up.

But that didn't solve the problem completely. When YouTube removes your video, you lose every YouTube link that's attached to that video. So, in other words, for the time we were in violation, people couldn't view our video, and when they reinstated us, we lost *everyone* who had listed us on their channels as a favorite. Our favorites statistic went from somewhere around 5,000 to 0. To this day, I think we would be in the Top 5 if we hadn't lost all the people that originally favorited Frank's video.

Have you found that YouTube is useful for *networking* — for getting the word out to lots of people?

In my experience, YouTube hasn't evolved into as powerful of a social networking Web site as MySpace. On YouTube, it seems to me that *average users* — people who aren't trying to promote something — don't network and communicate with other users as much as they do on MySpace. This is why I'm always working to increase Frank's friend list on *both* YouTube and MySpace so that I can send out bulletins with news about his performances and upcoming events.

I have, however, found that I can continue to post Frank's tour schedule in the comments section below his YouTube video. That's very powerful: A good percentage of our average 8,000 daily viewers scroll down to see the comments.

(continued)

(continued)

You said in the beginning of the interview that you had missed out on the early days of MySpace and wanted to redeem yourself with YouTube. With all that's happened, do you feel you've achieved that redemption?

Let me answer that by sharing some of the results of our online promotions: In the summer of '06, not only did Frank's tour dates sell out, Frank needed to start *adding* shows to keep up with the demand. During the summer, comedy clubs slow down and shows don't sell out as easily, but Frank was adding shows at times that don't usually sell at all, like at midnight.

Sales of Frank's CDs and DVDs on FrankCaliendo.com have increased significantly as well, and we are now getting orders from all over the world. People now come up to Frank and tell him, "Hey, I watch you all the time on YouTube." They say it like they're watching TV. It's pretty amazing. Frank has also told me that a few producers have approached him about doing some work in movies — just because they saw his promotional clip on You Tube.

Frank has been on TV for seven years (MADtv, FOX NFL Pregame, and others) and it seems like he's *always* doing something on some radio station somewhere. YouTube wasn't the sole cause of his growth in popularity, but it's definitely been a significant help, and it's introduced him to a new and more global audience.

To have your video listed on the Directors channel home page, register a specialty account as a director. See the section, "Creating Specialty Accounts," earlier in this chapter.

All the videos you see in the Directors channel are uploaded by Tubers who create a Directors specialty account.

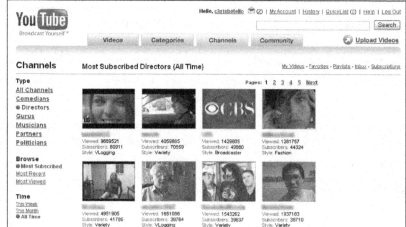

Figure 9-13:
The Most Subscribed Directors channels of all time.

The term *Directors* is a really big hint of what the YouTube team had in mind when they created this specialty account. It was only logical: Because YouTube is a site that contains lots of homemade video clips, it's just a matter of time before video artists want to upload longer "short films" to the site. YouTube would become a platform for new directors, a place where a young filmmaker could make his or her mark. Thus the title: Directors account.

But as we say earlier, you really can't predict how Web sites will evolve. The YouTube team probably never could have predicted that comedians would become so involved with the Tube that they'd need to create a Comedians channel, just as they probably never guessed that the Directors channel wouldn't evolve to be primarily about directors.

TIP

If you register a Directors account and you're a filmmaker or a video artist and want to be identified as such, choose the Art style.

That's not to say that no young filmmakers have embraced YouTube, but if you click around the Directors channel, you might be surprised to find that Art clips in the style category are few and far in between. In fact, those types of clips are seldom at the top of the Most Viewed list for the Directors channel. If you're interested in viewing the clips that are there, look for clips labeled Art or Acting in the style category.

On the other hand, the Directors channel has become a huge success in its own right, as a melting pot for all types of "variety" clips. No less a YouTube star than LonelyGirl15 is at the top of the Most Subscribed Directors (All Time) channel. She lists her clips as *vlogging*. Following suit, so many other Tubers are using the Directors channel to post their vlogs that vlogging has become the most popular category in the Directors channel.

Perhaps YouTube hasn't emerged as a venue for conventional filmmaking, but you can certainly find lots of creative and sometimes experimental video projects labeled Variety in the Directors channel. As its name implies, this is a catch-all category; you never know what you're going to find when you click one of these clips. Check out Smosh (as shown in Figure 9-14) for a fine example of the Variety category. This is some strange hybrid of low-budget filmmaking, absurdist comedy, and post-slacker sitcom. Love it or hate it, it was the second most-visited Directors channel of all time on the day that we visited.

YouTube for gurus

Here's a sentence the YouTube founders probably never thought they'd hear when they created the site: "YouTube is a great place to discover how to play piano." Of course, in hindsight, it only makes sense that people would upload how-to videos, but in terms of YouTube's evolution, it's a great new direction for the site.

Smosh - Three Wishes

Figure 9-14:
Smosh
on the
Directors
channel —
call it what
you will, it's
found a
following.

Tubers have been uploading how-to videos for a long time, but the thing that makes it all seem so new is that early in 2007, YouTube added the Gurus specialty account for "experts who show others how to cook, bartend, create better videos, or (almost) any other skill you can pass on." Figure 9-15 shows search results for the Most Subscribed Gurus clips of all time.

Now there's a wide-open definition, and sure enough, in a very short time the Gurus channel has become something of a free-for-all for jacks- (and jills-) of-all-trades. But the proverbial cream does rise to the top, and the Gurus channel has emerged as one of the most practical and valuable channels on YouTube — a place where people share the best of what they have to offer and where Tubers can go to be taught something valuable.

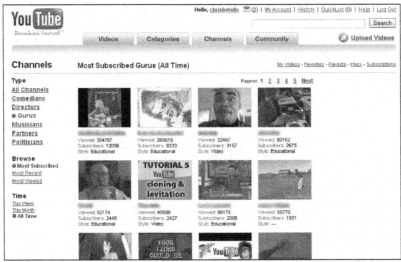

Figure 9-15:
The gurus
with the
most sub-
scriptions.

An interview with piano teacher Shawn Cheek

Imagine by John Lennon

On YouTube, Texas teacher Shawn Cheek is known as Shawncheekeasy, and his videos are high on the list of Most Subscribed Gurus.

Shawn is a piano teacher, and his story has some really neat angles. His rise to the heights of the YouTube Gurus channel is that much more impressive when you discover that he's been teaching piano on YouTube for a very short time — less than two months when we interviewed him.

If the terms *piano* and *computer* don't quite go together in your imagination, think of it this way: No, Shawn's students probably aren't dragging the piano upstairs to the home office to watch Shawn teach on the computer, but yes, the idea of a laptop computer sitting on top of the piano and playing Shawn's videos is easy to imagine.

When you talk to Shawn or watch his videos, his energy and enthusiasm are contagious. This guy loves the piano, and he loves teaching. Another interesting thing about Shawn is that he has his own very unique method of teaching the piano, one that he shares with a few thousand students on YouTube.

Tell us a bit about you, Shawn.

I am a native Texan and live near Dallas. I've been playing the piano since I was 8 years old (I'm now 33). I've been making my living as a professional musician and teacher since I was 12 years old. I now teach private lessons full-time and am a stay-at-home dad with two toddlers.

What first got you to upload videos to YouTube, and what were some of your early experiences?

I heard about YouTube from one of my students and decided to post some lessons to see what would happen, just for fun. What's going to surprise you is that I've only been on YouTube for about a month and a half. I posted my first video, and within hours, I started getting e-mails and YouTube

(continued)

(continued)

messages about it. People were sending me videos of what they'd been taught from my lessons and requesting more songs.

It's amazing that you're so high-ranked on the Gurus channel, given that you've been on YouTube for such a relatively short time.

Within a few days, I was number 9 on the Most Subscribed This Week, and I was getting about 300 e-mails a day. To beef up my subscriptions, I sent messages with a lesson attached to other YouTubers who were subscribed to *other* piano lesson channels. Half of them subscribed to my channel. Then I decided to do a Student of the Week feature. I pick one of the videos that are sent to me and use it as My Featured Video on my channel. That really got everyone involved. My second featured student of the week received 10,000 views in one week!

The other thing you have to remember is that when I signed up, the Gurus channel was a new feature on YouTube. So it's not like gurus had been logging two years' worth of page views. With the momentum I had going, it didn't take me long to rise to the top. The timing was just right.

Speaking of gurus, tell us a bit about being a part of this new feature.

I realized that being on one of the Channel pages was the best way to get subscribers. That's why I switched to being a Guru two days ago instead of a musician. Like I said, there wasn't as much competition. As a Musician, I was on the 4th page of Most Subscribed of All Time. But as a Guru, I'm on the first page.

Did you ever think you'd get this popular, this fast?

I had no idea I'd receive so much attention. No idea.

You've been teaching nearly all your life. Has the YouTube experience affected you as a teacher?

As a teacher, I find nothing more gratifying than knowing that someone understood how to play something because of me. On YouTube, I can teach a lesson one time, and thousands discover how to play. That's awesome! I get messages every day from people who took traditional piano lessons for years and couldn't do it. I even get messages from people who have never touched a piano, and they can be taught. What I'm doing is so simple, and I can't believe that no one else has tried to teach this way.

Maybe you're a YouTube prodigy. Do you have any insights or advice that you can share from your experience?

To be successful on YouTube you have do two things: Provide something that people want and do it in a way that no one else is doing it. There are tons of piano lessons to be had on YouTube, but no one uses the method that I use, at least not yet! One other thing: I read every response that I get and try to provide lessons that most people ask for. When people hear back from you, when they know that you're there, that's when you really build a following.

You'd never guess some of the things people teach on the Gurus channel. One of our favorite surprises is *Ellaskins*, the fourth most-subscribed guru of all time when we visited. He's a seemingly very nice guy from Wales who's garnered a huge following by teaching skills for becoming a deejay. His channel is full of responses from Tubers thanking him for the great info — many comment that he's a "huge help" — and debating with him over various musical philosophies and interpretations. His video, "Let's Look at Electro from the 80s," generated a slew of responses that are fun to read.

The list of what is available to find out on the Gurus channel is just endless; if you can think of it, someone's probably there teaching it. Videos are on cooking, gardening, drawing and painting, golf, tennis, and yoga. You meet magicians, spiritualists, fitness instructors, and mechanics. Want to fix your carburetor? Lift up the hood and surf the Gurus channel.

Part IV
Famous Final Scene: YouTube for Fun and Profit

The 5th Wave   By Rich Tennant

"Try putting a person in the video with the product you're trying to sell. We generated a lot of interest in our YouTube channel once Leo started modeling my hats and scarves."

In this part . . .

In Chapter 10, we show you how to promote products and ideas on YouTube. Chapter 11 shows you how to surf the Tube safely and how to stay within the YouTube guidelines. In Chapter 12, we show you how to upload video from your mobile phone, embed a YouTube video in your Web site, and more.

Chapter 10

Thinking outside the YouTube Box

. . . .

. . . .

*W*hen YouTube first became the most popular video sharing Web site on the net, most users surfed the Tube looking for entertaining videos. Then YouTube became a Google company, and things started changing. Many companies realized the value of YouTube: It has an audience of millions looking for interesting and informative videos. Major networks such as CBS and Fox became YouTube partners. Aspiring entertainers and comedians posted videos on the Tube. And they were noticed.

So where do you fit into the Tube? If you're just in it to view entertaining videos and to share your own videos with friends and fellow Tubers, we suggest that you skip this chapter and surf the Tube. However, if you're an educator or a businessman, or if you sell stuff on eBay, this chapter is just what your marketing guru ordered. With an audience of millions, the Tube is a portal that you can use to promote yourself, your products, or your services.

Promoting Products and Services on YouTube

A plethora of Tubers promote products and services on the Tube. As registered YouTube users, they have their own channels. Savvy businessmen also know the value of having crosslinks to their Web sites and list the URL in their channel and on their videos.

Many commercial channels are on the Web. Most of them are set up as Director or Guru accounts, which enable the user to upload longer videos. Apparently, YouTube isn't that picky about who signs up for what type of account. We've seen Director accounts that have content unrelated to actors, videographers, or film directors. If enough users flagged an account as inappropriate, YouTube would probably get the drift and do something about it. If you're posting legitimate videos of value to the YouTube community, though, you don't have a thing to worry about.

Using YouTube to promote services and products is still in its infancy. We've surfed the Tube extensively and found quite a few channels that do a good job promoting a service. For example, the National Association of Photoshop Professionals (NAPP) mirrors its Photoshop TV Web site and podcast (audio and video presentations that can be played on iPods and similar devices) content on YouTube. Their shows are almost 30 minutes long; therefore, NAPP set up a Directors account with YouTube. The channel is shown in Figure 10-1.

In the following sections, we list some ways that we think the Tube can be used to promote products and services. It is our humble opinion that companies and entrepreneurs have just scratched the tip of the iceberg when it comes to using YouTube as a marketing tool.

Figure 10-1:
And now, previously recorded in living color, Photoshop TV.

Infomercials on YouTube

Do you have a service that can be handled over the phone or over the Web? Do you sell material such as Web-based video tutorials, or sell CD tutorials from your Web site? If so, get your microphone and camcorder ready and create an infomercial to promote your product. If you don't have a camcorder, consider creating an intro using a photo of yourself or your logo with a voiceover and then follow up with a narrated slide show that demonstrates the features, functions, and benefits of your product or service.

A good infomercial begins with a high-energy intro followed by the presentation. To see examples of good intros for infomercials, download a copy of iTunes — it's free at www.apple.com/itunes/download — and subscribe to a couple of video podcasts. The best video podcasts usually have a dynamic intro that sets the pace and tone — or the *hook*, if you will — for the show. The intro is designed to grab the viewer by the lapels and glue him to the monitor until the presenter utters her final words of wisdom.

A good infomercial ends with a bang as well. This is the part of the infomercial where the presenter thanks her audience, which is immediately followed by ending credits that display the company name and URL to her Web site. Podcasts are also a good source of ideas for the end of an infomercial. The best ones end with the same music used on the intro. If you have access to animation software, you can animate the intro and the end of your infomercial. You can also create an effective end for your infomercial by using ending credits created in an application such as Windows Movie Maker or iMovie.

The meat and potatoes of your infomercial are sandwiched between the intro and ending credits. This part of the infomercial needs to be informative. If all you're creating is an advertisement, you'll lose your audience. The crux of your presentation should be compelling and informative plus give viewers a reason to go to your Web site to find out more about your services. Your infomercials should show viewers how your product or service can solve a problem.

If you're a solo entrepreneur who decided to leverage your business by selling information such as eBooks or CDs from your Web site, an infomercial is an excellent way to draw visitors to your Web site. The answer is to create a video that shows Tubers what they can expect to learn from the products you sell on your Web site. There's no need to reinvent the wheel. Sandwich highlights of one of your existing tutorials between effective intro and ending credits. Figure 10-2 shows a YouTube video created by a company that sells memberships to an information portal with tutorials about Adobe Acrobat, Adobe Dreamweaver, Adobe Fireworks, and Adobe Photoshop.

Figure 10-2:
Watch,
listen, and
learn while
you surf
the Tube.

When you set up a YouTube account to promote a business or service, you need to choose the right category. If you're informing Tubers how to do something such as use a computer application, the obvious choice is a Guru account. If you are an acupuncturist or a hypnotist informing people about the benefits of your service, you might consider setting up a Director account. Another thing to consider is that you're competing with the truck-loads of videos that are uploaded every day. In this regard, you need to be a frequent contributor to the Tube. When Tubers know you post new content on a regular basis, they will subscribe to your channel. And if you've created effective infomercials, they'll eventually meander to your Web site.

The possibilities for promoting a service with a YouTube video are endless. The following list is by no means exhaustive, but it gives you an idea of the type of businesses that can benefit by creating compelling videos and upload-ing them to the Tube:

✔ **Business coach:** A business coach can benefit by posting information that entrepreneurs can use to build their business, attract new clients, manage employees, market the business, and so on.

✔ **Hypnotist:** A hypnotist who sells self-help and self-hypnosis CDs from his Web site can draw traffic to the site with an effective YouTube infomercial.

✔ **Instructor:** A person who instructs people how to use a computer appli-cation and sells instructional videos from her Web site can draw poten-tial customers to her Web site by setting up an effective YouTube channel. The instructor's infomercials should stress that the videos available from her site are larger and better quality.

- **Photographer:** A photographer who sells stock art from his Web site can draw visitors by creating an effective slide show with background music of his best images. The ending credits show Tubers that stock photos can be purchased from the Web site.

- **Public Speaker:** A public speaker who is available nationwide can draw visitors to his Web site by creating a video on a topic that will appeal to a wide audience. If the video is an excerpt from a recent speaking engagement, it effectively demonstrates his style and how he interacts with the audience. The ending credits include information about the speaker's Web site, speaking schedule, and availability.

If you're looking for a job, consider creating a video resume and posting it on the Tube. You can e-mail the link to prospective employers anywhere in the world.

Selling products on YouTube

We haven't seen a lot of companies selling products on the Tube, but that doesn't mean it can't be done. Now there is material that appeals to audiences of all ages, the age of the average Tuber is increasing, and all those Tubers have got to buy their stuff somewhere. If you have a product that's interesting or unique, a well-crafted video can draw attention to your product. You've seen the infomercials that crowd the television airwaves on Saturday mornings (or, if you're a night owl like us, in the wee hours of the morning). There's no reason you can't create something similar. Here are a few tips:

- **Your video should be crafted just like an infomercial.** If someone in your company is photogenic and has a pleasant voice, she can be the spokesperson for the product.

- **When your spokesperson demonstrates your product, she needs to show viewers how they will benefit by purchasing the product.** Savvy salesmen will tell you that when you mention a product feature, demonstrate how the feature functions and then make clear how the feature benefits the potential client.

- **The ending credits of your video need to include a call to action.** For example, the spokesperson can say something like, "To find out more about our fabulous Acme Widget, please visit our Web site at `www.AcmeWidgets.biz`." When you edit the video, add a text overlay with the URL of your Web site at the point in the presentation when your spokesperson gives the call to action. For more information on adding text overlays to a video, see Chapter 8.

Creating a Professional Presentation

When you create videos to promote a product or service, you're portraying your company. Get it right the first time. You don't want to foul your reputation by posting a pixilated video that looks like it was created with a Blue-Light Special Webcam. Use the best equipment you can afford. The video should be the highest quality you are capable of creating. You can purchase a camcorder capable of creating good video for a few hundred dollars. If you're creating talking-head videos, don't trust the camera microphone. Invest in a good-quality, lavaliere microphone. If you're recording video of your computer screen, purchase a high-quality USB (Universal Serial Bus) microphone/headset. For even higher quality sound, purchase a dynamic microphone with a USB preamplifier. M-Audio creates a good package with a dynamic broadcast quality microphone, sound editing software, and RSS (really simple syndication) software called Podcast Factory. The package (see Figure 10-3) retails for $179.95.

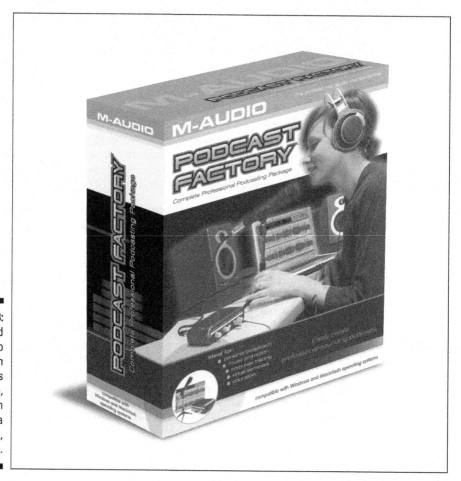

Figure 10-3:
A good video presentation requires good audio, which means a good mike, Mike.

After you purchase your equipment, you're ready to create videos to promote your product or service. Chapters 7 and 8 delve into the nuts and bolts of capturing and editing video. The following list presents a few things you should consider when creating videos of a product or service.

- **Purchase a pop filter for your microphone.** A *pop filter* looks like a sponge that fits over the end of the microphone. If you have a professional, broadcast-quality microphone, the pop filter is a circular frame surrounding fabric or steel mesh. The pop filter prevents the popping sound when you say a word with a plosive letter like *B* or *P*.

- **Record your video at the highest quality and optimize the original for each intended destination.** For example, you can render one version for a podcast, another for YouTube, and a high-quality version for CD.

- **Manually focus your camera on your subject, especially if you record outdoors.** Unless you focus manually, the camera can often be fooled into changing focus when another object appears in the scene.

- **Set the exposure manually, especially if you record on location.** If you don't set the exposure manually, the camera may change the exposure when you pan to a darker area, which can lead to a video with over-exposed frames.

- **Make sure that your audio level is set properly.** If you record audio at a low level and then increase the volume in a video or sound editing application, low-level noise and background hum will be amplified to undesirable levels. If you record on your computer, change the audio input level through your operating system's control panel. If your audio recording software has peak meters, make sure the volume doesn't peak above −3 dB.

- **Rehearse your presentation ahead of time so you'll be more relaxed and have a good idea of what you want to say.** Rehearsing also makes you more familiar with the material. Even though you've rehearsed, the fact that you're relaxed makes your message sound spontaneous and more honest.

- **Imagine that you're telling your story to a best friend.** Your tone will be more conversational and friendlier. There's nothing worse than trying to listen to a presentation in which the speaker's voice is monotone, which you may note is part of the word *monotonous*.

- **Start with a bang and maintain enthusiasm throughout your presentation.** If your presentation sounds like a bad phone solicitor reading a script, it will receive a similar response from your listening audience. In other words, your audience will never listen to the entire presentation. If you're excited about the product or service you sell, your viewers will sense your enthusiasm and be more likely to listen to the entire presentation and visit your Web site.

> ✔ **Make sure that every word that appears on screen is spelled correctly.** Misspelled words are the hallmark of a true amateur.
>
> ✔ **If you make a mistake while recording your video, stop for a few seconds and begin the segment again.** You can fix your mistakes by cutting the offending frames using your video editing application.

Adding a Video to an eBay Auction

eBay is the greatest place in the world to sell just about anything. Think about it: eBay is the virtual equivalent of the world's largest flea market. If you don't need something anymore, dust it off and put it up for auction on eBay. When you buy the latest and greatest digital camera right after it's released, put your old one up for auction on eBay while it's still reasonably new technology. Somebody will pay you what it's worth (and maybe more).

What makes one auction stand out above the others? Well, in most cases, a sharp, properly exposed picture of the object will draw more bids than one that has a dark, out-of-focus image. And, of course, there are horror stories — like the man who photographed a silver chalice and captured a perfect reflection of his overweight nude body. If you really want to stand out from the crowd, create a video of the object you're putting up for auction. Show the object from all sides and add an enthusiastic narration that tells bidders all about your object and why they should buy it. Upload the video to YouTube and then embed the video in your auction.

If you ever tried to create an eBay auction online, you know what a challenge it can be. Fortunately, eBay created the Turbo Lister software that enables you to create an eBay auction on your desktop and then upload it to eBay. And the good news is that you can embed a YouTube video in the auction. To add video to an eBay auction, follow these steps:

1. **Download the latest edition of eBay's Turbo Lister to your desktop.**

   eBay's Turbo Lister is free but is only available for the Windows operating system. You can download it here:

   ```
   http://pages.ebay.com/turbo_lister
   ```

2. **Install Turbo Lister.**

   The installation is fairly straightforward. Double-click the EXE file you downloaded to your desktop and follow the prompts.

3. **Create the video for your listing.**

   When you create a video for an eBay listing, you engage another of the auction viewer's senses: hearing. Therefore your speech should be clear, yet at the same time enthusiastic and upbeat. Give the viewers a pitch they can't refuse. Remember to end the video with a call to action such as, "Add your bid to this great auction now." For more information on creating video for YouTube, see Chapters 7 and 8.

If you use eBay's Buy It Now option, your call to action can include the option to Buy It Now.

4. **Upload the video to YouTube.**

At this stage, you probably want to do something else like train your cat to make useful items from hairballs that you can auction off on eBay. Face it; as usual, it's going to take a while for YouTube to convert the video into their format (which, by the way, is a Flash SWF movie).

Be sure to include the URL to your auction in the description. You can get this information after uploading the auction to eBay and then edit the description of your YouTube video to include the URL to the auction. You never know, you might entice a Tuber to bid on your auction.

5. **Launch Turbo Lister and choose File⇨New.**

The Create New Item dialog box appears (see Figure 10-4).

6. **Enter a title for the auction, enter a subtitle, and then choose a category.**

If you're new to eBay, check out current auctions of similar items (or the same item) to see what terms the sellers used in the title and subtitle fields. These auctions will also tell you the category in which you should list your item. All eBay categories can be accessed by clicking the Select button, as shown in Figure 10-4.

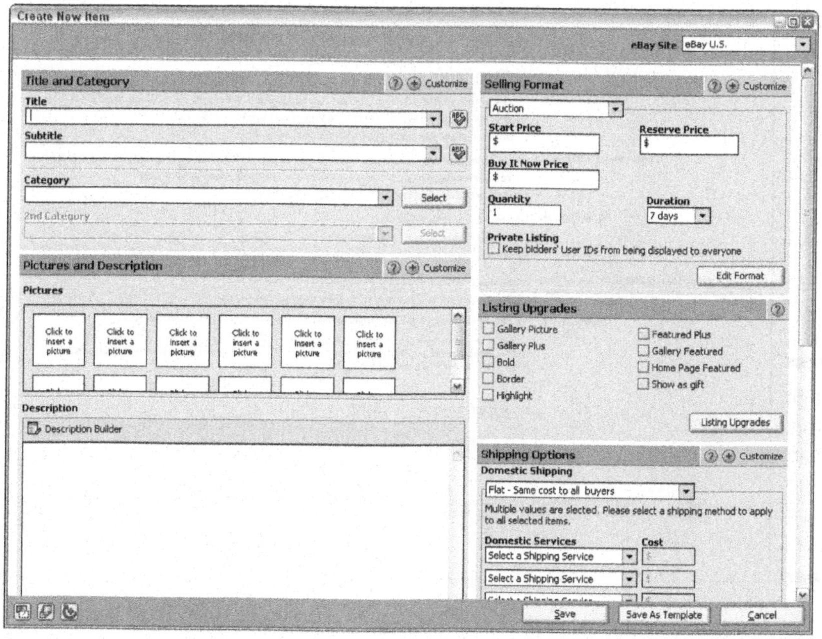

Figure 10-4:
We're gonna sell this on eBay.

![Create New Item dialog box screenshot showing fields for Title and Category, Selling Format, Pictures and Description, Listing Upgrades, and Shipping Options]

7. **Log in to YouTube.**

   You know the drill by now. If not, we tell you how in many other places in this book.

8. **Click the My:Videos link, select the video you uploaded for the auction, and then click the Edit Video Info button.**

   The My Account/Edit My Videos page appears. This page lists all the information about your video, including the description, tags, and the information needed to embed the video in another Web page.

9. **Scroll to the bottom of the page.**

   The information you're after is in the Embed HTML section of the page (see Figure 10-5).

10. **Select the HTML code in the Embed HTML field and then press Ctrl+C.**

    This copies the code to your Windows Clipboard.

11. **Position your cursor in the Description Builder section of the eBay Turbo Lister Create New Item dialog box and then press Ctrl+V.**

    This pastes the code into your auction.

12. **Add any other information you feel is necessary to describe your item.**

    You may want to add a note telling viewers to click the Play button in the YouTube video window. Currently, there are few auctions with embedded videos. The added note will avoid any confusion.

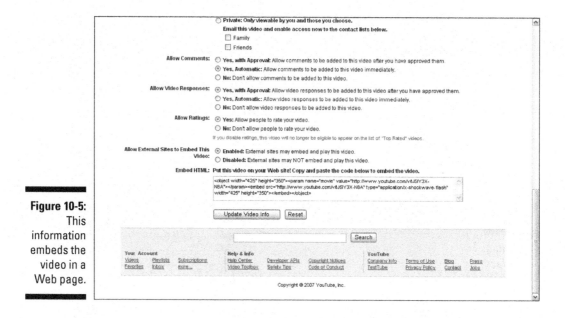

Figure 10-5:
This information embeds the video in a Web page.

13. **Fill out the rest of the items in the Create New Item dialog box.**

    You know, add the important stuff, such as starting price, freight, and so on. Figure 10-6 shows an auction in the making, complete with the HTML to embed a YouTube video describing the auction.

    Don't choose any of the eBay Gallery options as you'll be prompted to add images to the gallery. The YouTube video is worth a thousand pictures, right?

14. **Click Save.**

    The item is added to the Your Items section of Turbo Lister.

15. **Select the item, right-click it, and then choose Preview from the shortcut menu.**

    Turbo Lister displays the listing in a new window.

16. **Click the Play button in the YouTube player to preview the video of your auction item.**

    You likely figured out that you've got to be online to do this. Figure 10-7 shows an eBay auction being previewed in Turbo Lister.

    After preparing the listing, you're ready to upload it to eBay. Turbo Lister does this for you as well. A complete tutorial on Turbo Lister is beyond the scope of this book. However, the software is fairly intuitive and easy to use.

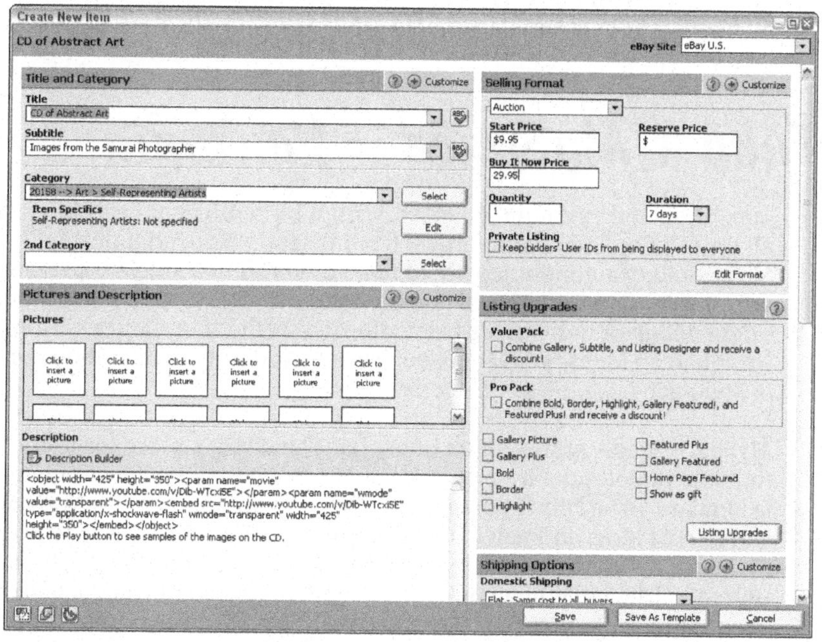

Figure 10-6:
The completed listing.

Figure 10-7:
Preview the
auction in
Turbo Lister.

Savvy auctioneers know that it's imperative to upload the auction at the proper time. If you'd like to find out the best time to upload an auction and more tips on how to maximize your presence on eBay, check out *eBay For Dummies, 5th Edition* by Marsha Collier, or *eBay Listings That Sell For Dummies* by Marsha Collier and Patti Louise Ruby (both published by Wiley).

YouTube + MySpace = YouTopia

Lots of online communities exist. With a bit of diligent searching, you can find all types of online communities, forums, and so on, ad infinitum, ad nauseam. Many online communities are forums devoted to a single topic, such as how to primp your poodle for his next dog show. Other online communities are a hodgepodge of individuals from all walks of life that have a serious need to establish an identity on the Web. The granddaddy of all online communities is MySpace (www.myspace.com).

MySpace boldly states on its home page that it is a place for friends, and you'll find lots of potential friends at MySpace. It's a huge online community, which is similar to YouTube in many ways. When you sign up with MySpace, you get a MySpace blog, and you can communicate with your MySpace friends via the MySpace messaging service and browse the MySpace profiles looking for potential friends. When you find a profile of someone you'd like to become acquainted with, you can ask to be her friend. If she accepts, her profile image is displayed on your MySpace page, and your profile image appears on hers.

Your MySpace page can be customized just like a YouTube channel. However, to customize a MySpace page, you should either know something about HTML or you should visit any of a number of Web sites that help customize your page. In these sites, you can specify the URL for the background image, or specify the background color for the page, text, links and so on. Then with a simple click of the button, the site generates the HTML code needed to trick out a MySpace page and tells you where to paste it when editing your profile. Most of these sites come with strings attached in the form of links or graphics that tell visitors to your MySpace page where they can go to trick out their page. Oh, well. It's better than doing it wrong and having your text and background the same color, which renders a MySpace page illegible.

To create a cool MySpace page, type *custom MySpace layouts* in your favorite search engine and peruse the sites that pop up in the results page 'til you find something that suits your fancy.

Paste the code generated by a page that offers custom MySpace layouts into your favorite word processor, delete the code that points to the site that generated it, and then paste it into your MySpace page. *Voilà!* No advertisements!

After you join the MySpace community and log in, the home page shows your main image — or *mug shot*, if you will — and gives you several options for managing your account. (See Figure 10-8.) As you can see, you also have the option to upload videos. Keeping videos in two online portals, though, is like storing some of your socks in a dresser drawer and the rest in your garage. When it comes to video, we prefer to keep our eggs in one basket, which (of course) is YouTube. After all, if we uploaded most of our videos to YouTube and a few to MySpace, some of our videos might end up being lost.

Figure 10-8:
MySpace
and
YouTube:
twin sons of
different
mothers.

We could tell you more about the MySpace community and its MySpace cadets, but this is a book on YouTube. In upcoming sections, we show you what's acceptable on MySpace as well as how to use your YouTube videos in a MySpace profile.

If you'd like to make MySpace your space, you can find out more by reading *MySpace For Dummies* by Ryan Hupfer, Mitch Maxson, and Ryan Williams (Wiley).

What's acceptable on MySpace

Like every online community, MySpace has rules and regulations that govern what you can and cannot post. If you follow the rules and regulations, you get along just fine with the MySpace high council. But if you screw up, we're sure they send your profile into deep space, never to be seen again. The following are some of the rules that you must abide by when you decide to become a MySpace cadet:

- ✔ **Your MySpace profile cannot include a phone number, street address, or your last name.** This is a good thing. After all, a lot of weirdos are on the Net, and you wouldn't want one showing up on your doorstep because they found your address online.

- ✔ **Your MySpace profile cannot include any photos that contain nudity, or depict lewd, violent, or sexually explicit behavior.** Like YouTube, the MySpace lads want you to keep it clean.

MySpace warns in its terms of agreement that other MySpace profiles may contain inaccurate information in the profile and may in fact contain lewd, suggestive, or sexually explicit material. After that caveat, they tell you how to report objectionable material to the MySpace high council. We're not sure what the punishment is for being reported as lewd, crude, and socially unacceptable. Perhaps the cadet gets banned from MySpace, and his profile is beamed to an isolated planet in the Xectar nebula.

- ✔ **MySpace requests that you provide truthful and accurate information and that you will maintain the accuracy of your information.**

- ✔ **You must be at least 14 years old to set up a MySpace profile.** MySpace states they will give you the boot to Deep Space Nine if they think you're younger than 14 years of age.

- ✔ **Your use of MySpace cannot violate any applicable law or regulation.**

- ✔ **You cannot collect usernames or e-mail addresses from the MySpace community to send unsolicited messages.** Can you say *spam?* We knew you could.

✔ **You cannot add a commercial advertisement to your MySpace profile, post an affiliate link, or post any form of solicitation for a service.** In other words, if it's commercial, MySpace won't let you put it on your profile and reserves the right to remove it without notice.

Adding video to our MySpace page

We spoke our piece about our online video service of choice earlier in this chapter. But in case you didn't read that section and jumped here, we'll state it again:

YouTube rocks, and that's where we prefer to upload our videos.

Having stated that, we'll also say that MySpace is a cool online community: a community in which we commune for the sake of a better word. When we feel the need to add a video to either of our MySpace profiles, we do so by embedding a YouTube video. To embed a video in your MySpace profile

1. **Log in to YouTube.**

2. **Click the My:Videos link.**

   The My Account/Videos page appears.

3. **Click the Edit Video Info button for the video you want to embed in your MySpace profile.**

   The My Account/Edit My Videos page appears.

4. **Scroll to the Embed HTML section of the page.**

   It's at the southernmost perimeter of the page (see Figure 10-9).

5. **Select the code in the Embed HTML text field and press Ctrl+C (Windows) or ⌘+C (Mac).**

   The code is copied to your operating system clipboard.

6. **Log in to MySpace.**

   You enter the right e-mail and password, and you're logged in.

7. **Click the Home link.**

   Your profile image appears on the home page. From this page, you can edit your profile, which is what you do to embed a video.

8. **Click the Edit Profile link.**

   The Profile Edit-Interests and Personality page appears.

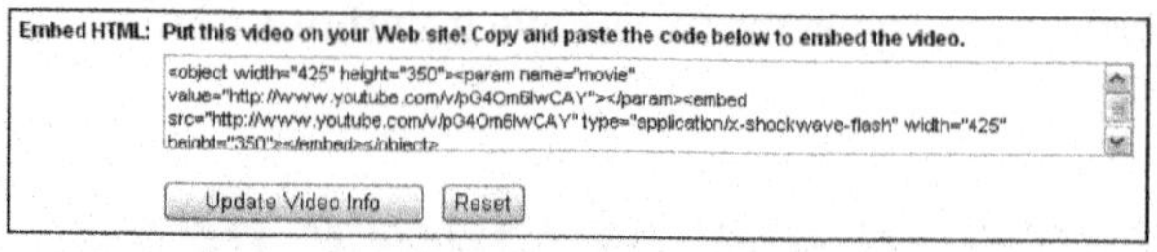

Figure 10-9:
Use this
code to
embed
a video
in your
MySpace
profile.

Embed HTML: Put this video on your Web site! Copy and paste the code below to embed the video.

```
<object width="425" height="350"><param name="movie"
value="http://www.youtube.com/v/pG4Om6IwCAY"></param><embed
src="http://www.youtube.com/v/pG4Om6IwCAY" type="application/x-shockwave-flash" width="425"
height="350"></embed></object>
```

[Update Video Info]   [Reset]

9. **Position your cursor in the About Me field where you want the YouTube video to appear.**

   If the field has any HTML code to change the way your profile looks, make sure you embed your YouTube video after the `</style>` tag.

10. **Press Ctrl+V (Windows) or ⌘+V (Mac).**

   The code to embed your YouTube video is pasted into the section. (See Figure 10-10.)

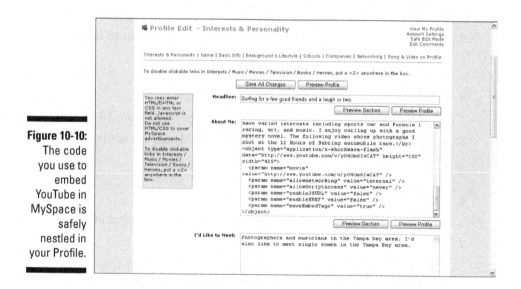

Figure 10-10:
The code
you use to
embed
YouTube in
MySpace is
safely
nestled in
your Profile.

11. **Click Save All Changes.**

   Your profile is updated.

12. **Click View Profile.**

Your profile page with embedded YouTube video is displayed. (See Figure 10-11.)

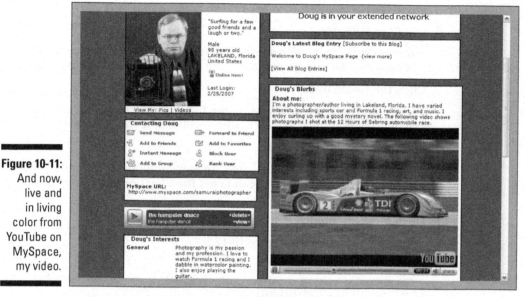

Figure 10-11:
And now, live and in living color from YouTube on MySpace, my video.

Adding a video to your MySpace blog

You're unique. You have opinions, a right to which every individual is entitled. In most parts of the world, you're free to express your opinions. One ideal vehicle for expressing your opinions to the world is an online blog. On YouTube, you can add a video log (known in Tuber-speak as a *vlog*) to your channel. On MySpace, you can have a true multimedia blog with words, photos, and (with a bid of HTML wizardry) a YouTube video. Talk about having your cake and eating it, too! To add a video to your MySpace blog, follow these steps:

1. **Log in to YouTube.**

2. **Click the My:Videos link.**

The My Account/Videos page is displayed in your browser window.

3. **Click the Edit Video Info button for the video you want to embed in your MySpace profile.**

The My Account/Edit My Videos page appears.

4. **Scroll to the Embed HTML section of the page.**

   It's way down near the bottom of the page.

5. **Select the code in the Embed HTML text field and press Ctrl+C (Windows) or ⌘+C (Mac).**

   The code is copied to your operating system Clipboard.

6. **Log in to MySpace.**

   After you enter the right e-mail and password, MySpace recognizes you as a MySpace cadet in good standing, and the Klingon High Council retreats.

7. **Click the Home link.**

   Your profile mug shot appears on the home page. From this page you can manage your blog, which is where you'll add your video.

8. **Click the Manage Blog link.**

   After the Blog Control Center page appears, you hear a whooping siren and then, "Scotty to Bridge. I canna get the Blog Control Center past Warp Factor 6."

9. **Click View My Blog.**

   Your blog appears. (See Figure 10-12.)

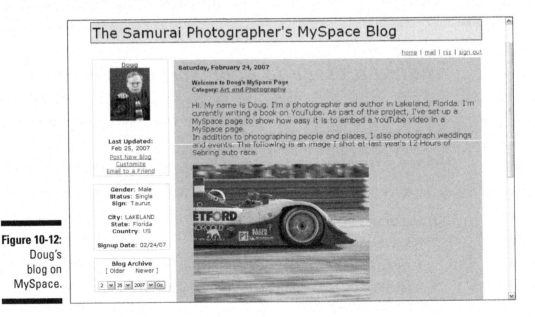

Figure 10-12: Doug's blog on MySpace.

The brave new world of video logging

Blogs are everywhere. Performers use blogs to keep in touch with their fans, businessmen use blogs to inform their customers, and families use blogs to stay in touch with distant family members. A conventional blog combines images and the written word to get a message out. With YouTube, video blogging is very much a reality. You can easily embed a YouTube video in a blog to create a true multimedia experience for blog viewers. The video blog can be something as simple as a slide show that flaunts a photographer's work, a home video showing a child's first birthday, or a video of a marketing specialist discussing the merits of a new product. The possibilities are limited only by your imagination. The figure here shows a video embedded in a WordPress blog.

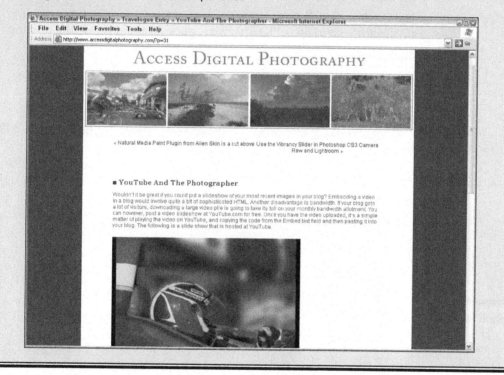

10. **Click Post New Blog.**

   The Post Blog entry page appears.

11. **Enter the desired information in the Subject field and then choose a category from the Category drop-down menu.**

MySpace blogs are segregated by categories, which makes it easy for MySpace cadets to find blogs of interest to them.

12. Enter the desired information in the Body section.

You can also format the text by choosing options from the Style, Font, and Size drop-down menus.

13. Position your cursor where you want the YouTube video to appear and then press Ctrl+V (Windows) or ⌘+V (Mac).

The code needed to display the video in your blog is inserted. (See Figure 10-13.)

14. Click Preview and Post.

The Confirm Blog Posting page appears. If the blog posting is to your satisfaction, go to Step 15. Otherwise, click Edit and revise the posting.

15. Click Post.

Your words of wisdom and YouTube video are posted for the MySpace cadets to review. (See Figure 10-14.)

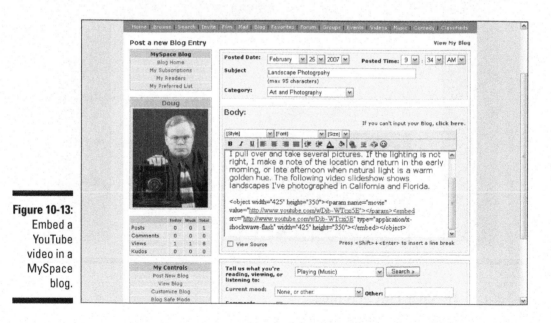

Figure 10-13: Embed a YouTube video in a MySpace blog.

Figure 10-14:
Doug's
YouTube
video on his
MySpace
blog. Now
how cool
is that?

YouTube and Other Online Communities

YouTube and MySpace are probably the biggest online communities. There are other ways, though, that you can connect with people and express your opinion on the Web. Friendster and Blogger are two very active Web portals. Friendster is an online community like MySpace. Blogger is a service that enables you to create a blog for free. The good news is that you can use your YouTube videos as part of a Friendster profile and blog. You can also include YouTube videos in your Blogger posts. We show you how in the upcoming sections.

Adding a YouTube video to Friendster

Friendster is an online community with over 36 million members. After you join Friendster, you'll be able to groove with youngster Friendsters, spinster Friendsters, and every age group in between. Friendster has rules and regulations just like MySpace and YouTube. In fact, they're almost identical with the exception that you must be at least 16 years of age to be a Friendster. After you create a Friendster account, you can add a YouTube video as part of your profile by following these steps:

1. **Log in to YouTube.**

2. **Click the My:Videos link.**

   Your My Account/Videos page appears.

3. **Click the Edit Video Info button for the video you want to embed in your Friendster profile.**

   YouTube displays the My Account/Edit My Videos page.

4. **Scroll to the Embed HTML section of the page.**

   You'll find it at the bottom of the page.

5. **Select the code in the Embed HTML text field and press Ctrl+C (Windows) or ⌘+C (Mac).**

   The code is copied to your operating system Clipboard.

6. **Go to Friendster (`www.friendster.com`) and sign in, please.**

   The song remains the same. Enter the right e-mail and password so that Friendster knows you're a *bona fide* Friendster in good standing.

7. **Click Edit Profile.**

   The My Profile page appears in full-edit mode. This is where you can change information about yourself, list your occupation, your likes and dislikes, and so on. Remember that honesty is the best policy. It's okay to fabricate, but an outright lie may catch up to you sooner or later.

8. **Scroll to the About Me section of the page.**

   This is where you can add HTML to your profile. In this case, you're going to add the HTML that will embed a YouTube video in the About Me section of your Friendster profile.

9. **Position your cursor where you want the YouTube video to appear and then press Ctrl+V (Windows) or ⌘+V (Mac).**

   The YouTube source code is pasted at the point you specify. (See Figure 10-15.)

10. **Click Save**

    Friendster updates your profile. Figure 10-16 shows a Friendster profile with an embedded YouTube video.

You can add a video to a Friendster, Live Journal, WordPress.com, or Piczo blog by going to your My Account page, and then clicking the Video Posting Settings link in the Account Settings section. Follow the prompts and you'll be able to add any video you're watching to the applicable blog by clicking the Post Video link.

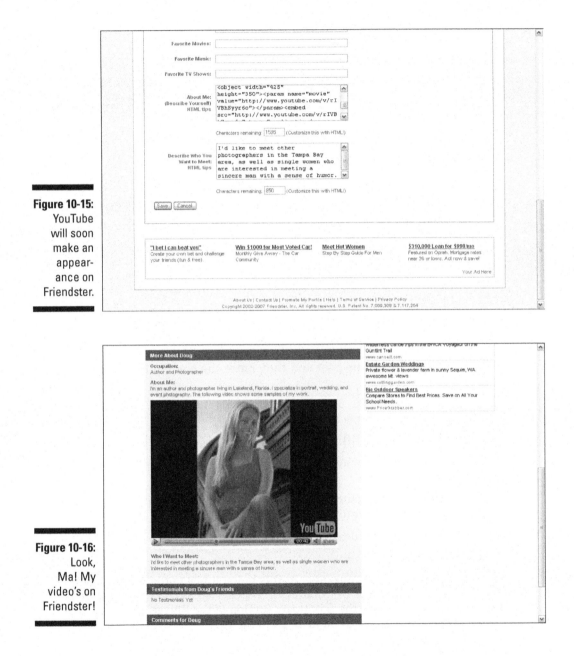

Figure 10-15: YouTube will soon make an appearance on Friendster.

Figure 10-16: Look, Ma! My video's on Friendster!

Using YouTube video on a Blogger page

If you don't have your own Web site, you can still create a blog by using a free blogging service. One of the better-known free blogs is Blogger, which (like YouTube) is a Google company. After you have an account set up, you can use a YouTube video in a Blogger posting as follows:

1. **Log in to YouTube.**

2. **Click the My:Videos link.**

   The My Account/Videos page is displayed in your browser window.

3. **Click the Edit Video Info button for the video you want to embed in your blog.**

   The My Account/Edit My Videos page appears.

4. **Scroll to the Embed HTML section of the page.**

   It's way down at the bottom of the page.

5. **Select the code in the Embed HTML text field and press Ctrl+C (Windows) or ⌘+C (Mac).**

   The code is copied to your operating system Clipboard.

6. **Log in to Blogger.**

   Again, it's the magic combination of the right e-mail address mated to the right password.

7. **Click New Post.**

   The Create New Post page appears.

8. **Enter a title for the post and then enter the content in the body section.**

   You can format the body text by choosing the desired font type and size from the drop-down menus.

9. **Click the Edit HTML tab.**

   This is the section in which you'll paste the code to embed your YouTube movie.

10. **Position your cursor where you want the video to appear, and then press Ctrl+V (Windows) or ⌘+V (Mac).**

    The code is embedded in your blog. (See Figure 10-17.)

11. **Click the Preview link.**

    Blogger displays your blog. At this point, it has not been published. If you find any typos or other errors, click Save as Draft. You can then edit the post by using the Edit Posts section of the Blogger Dashboard. If the blog post is ready to publish, go to Step 12.

12. **Click Publish.**

    Blogger publishes your post.

13. **Click View Blog.**

    Your published post is available for the world to review. (See Figure 10-18.)

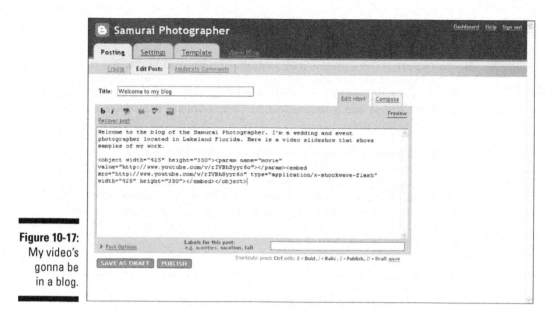

Figure 10-17:
My video's
gonna be
in a blog.

Figure 10-18:
Doug's
video is live
on Blogger.

Advertising on YouTube

If you've surfed the Tube for any amount of time, you know that there are ads. And then there are ads and more ads. Some of the ads are quite annoying, but they pay the bills. If it were not for the ads you see on most pages, you couldn't post and watch videos for free. Some of the ads are probably for services you can use.

If you're an aspiring businessman who has an online presence, perhaps you're interested in advertising on the Tube. The site is definitely high profile and attracts gobs of visitors who may be potential customers. If you think that your product or service is a good match for the YouTube community — and you have a budget of $25,000 or more that you're willing to commit to a YouTube campaign — go to www.youtube.com/advertise and fill out the questionnaire shown in Figure 10-19.

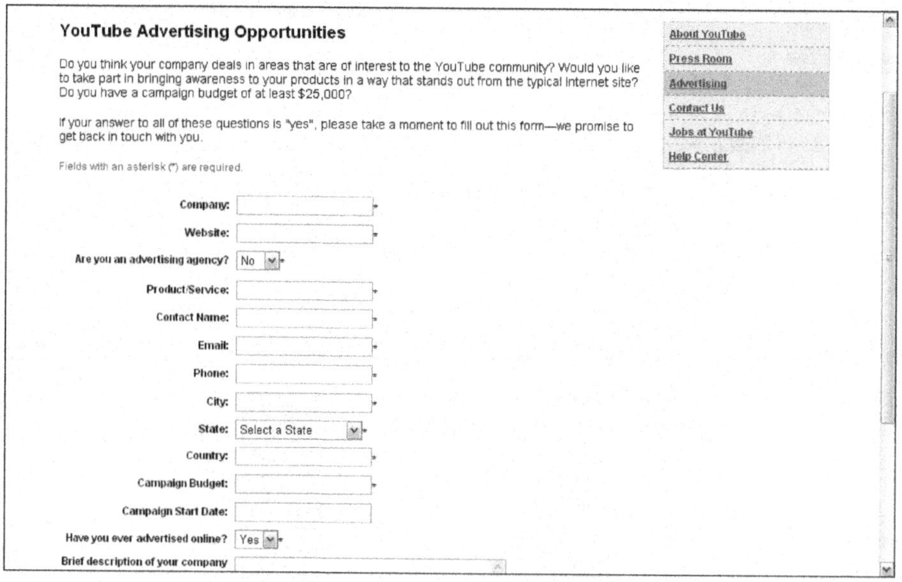

Figure 10-19: Advertising on the Tube.

Safe surf

If you surf the Net without virus protection, you're asking for trouble. Most savvy Web surfers already know this. When you go to Web sites like YouTube, MySpace, Friendster, and so on, you're confronted with a plethora of banner ads. Some of those banner ads generate pop-up ads. And some of those banner and pop up-ads download a cookie to your computer. Accepting cookies and pop-up ads is part of the price of admission to many Web sites and communities.

Most of the cookies that are deposited on your hard drive are absolutely harmless. However, you may also have spyware downloaded to your computer from a banner or pop-up ad created by a less-than-reputable designer. This spyware runs in the background and records the Web sites you visit. This is not a good thing. We recommend that you practice safe surf. Never surf the Net without an antivirus program running. We also recommend that once weekly, you run an application that scans your computer for spyware. If the application finds spyware, you have the option of removing or quarantining the spyware. The spyware problem is more prevalent on PCs than on Macintosh computers. To protect your computer and privacy, you can purchase spyware detection applications. You can also find freeware applications that will perform the same service. If you're on a PC, we recommend using Spybot Search & Destroy (www.spybot.info) and then Ad-Aware SE Personal (www.lavasoft.com), both of which are available for free.

Chapter 11

Playing It Smart, Playing It Safe

. . . .

In This Chapter

▶ Understanding the YouTube Community Guidelines

▶ Protecting yourself and your family

▶ Dealing with copyrights and other legal issues

. . . .

Welcome to Chapter 11: Everything you ever wanted to know about anything and everything that can go wrong and will go wrong by allowing the curse that is YouTube into your home and into your life.

That's right, folks. We're here to cause you sleepless nights. We're here to teach you to worry: Worry about someone coming after you for copyright infringement, worry that you're going to libel someone, and worry that every creepo, skeevo, and nasty character straight out of a Stephen King book is going to find you through the Tube.

Well, maybe not quite that bad.

This chapter is not about doom and gloom, and it's not here to scare you nor make you think twice about surfing around and sharing videos on YouTube. Essentially, this chapter is about YouTube's community guidelines. It's about showing you the rules, how others might break those rules, and what you can do to avoid any unpleasant situations on the Tube.

So, no — we're not here to scare you. Instead, we're hoping that you'll find this chapter valuable because it shines a light on the areas of YouTube that can be misused by not-so-friendly Tubers. We're here to accentuate the positive to help you eliminate any negative YouTube experiences.

Understanding the YouTube Community Guidelines

YouTube is a place where millions of people can share their personal videos with millions of other people. Take a moment to think about some of the really objectionable things that people could videotape and upload to YouTube. Where to begin?

Sex. C'mon. Tell the truth. That's the first thing that popped into your head, right? No? Well, it's the first thing that popped into *our* heads.

Sex is usually the first thing to come to mind when you think about objectionable video content on YouTube, but sex is not the only issue that the YouTube community needs to consider. Sharing videos brings up all kinds of wonderful, charming, heart-warming issues — violence, war, cruelty, racism, and hate speech, just to name a few.

Along with the brilliant idea of creating a video-sharing Web site, the founders of YouTube also needed to come up with a few more brilliant ideas for creating Community Guidelines — guidelines for a community in which all types of videos can be shared and all types of messages can be conveyed. When you really stop to think about it, developing a set of Community Guidelines in a video-sharing universe is quite an intellectual undertaking.

Illegal content: What's not allowed in your video

As a concept, YouTube is yet another giant step for free speech, but like in our society at large, free speech has its limits. You can't yell, "Fire!" in a crowded movie theater, and you can't post certain types of content on YouTube.

Before you upload your first video, read through YouTube's Community Guidelines. Of course, you'd never even think about uploading any of this kind of offensive stuff, but it does make for fascinating reading just to see which types of content are officially YouTube no-no's. Here's how you find them:

1. **Go to the YouTube Home page; then scroll to the bottom.**
2. **Click the Code of Conduct link.**

   This takes you to the YouTube Community Guidelines page, as shown in Figure 11-1.
3. **Read through the Community Guidelines.**

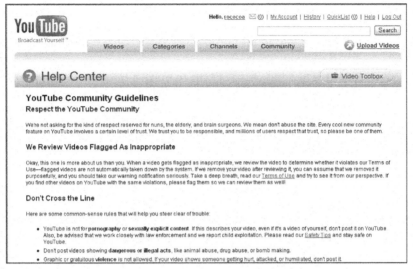

Figure 11-1:
The
YouTube
Community
Guidelines
page.

You can always go quickly to the Home page by clicking the red YouTube logo in the upper-left corner of any page.

You can also access the YouTube Community Guidelines page by clicking the Help menu at the top of the page.

In the 1970s, comedian George Carlin delivered a classic routine about "The Seven Words You Can't Say on Television." (We won't list them here, but it's worth noting that three of them — specifically, numbers 1, 2, and 7 — are now heard quite often on broadcast television. Things, as they say, do change.) The following is a list of seven things that your video *can't* contain if you want to post it on YouTube. This list is by no means complete, but it identifies all the really big and nasty gremlins that cannot be allowed to creep into the YouTube machinery.

- **Pornography:** We told you, didn't we? Sex! Sex! Sex! Don't make it X-rated. YouTube is not a site for pornographic nor sexually explicit videos. You might not be able to define what pornography is, but (as the saying goes), you know it when you see it. And nobody wants to see it on YouTube.

- **Nudity:** Your video of the big wave taking down your husband's bathing suit might be funny, but if we see too much information, it's not allowed on YouTube. And here's where it gets serious: Be very careful about uploading anything that might even suggest exploitation of children. Home videos of a toddler frolicking in the bathtub are exactly that — home videos. Don't upload them to YouTube.

- **Dangerous acts:** Here's an extreme example: Uploading a video of how to make a bomb would be a fine example of a violation of YouTube's Community Guidelines. How's that? Want more? Okay, avoid uploading any footage that suggests arson or other types of fun with fire. On the lighter side, a video of you jumping off of your three-story roof with a homemade parachute probably wouldn't fly, either (even though it might be very funny).

✓ **Illegal acts:** That video of how to make a bomb would fit into this category, too, as would a video of you robbing a house or vandalizing someone's car. Could anybody be so dumb as to upload such a video? Yes! Don't upload videos that show underage drinking or drunk driving, either, and don't upload a video of you throwing a big rock off of an overpass. Or even a little rock, for that matter. If it's illegal in the real world — or even questionably legal — don't upload it to YouTube.

Isn't this fun? Porn, nudity, bombs, arson, big rocks, and parachutes. And we still have three more categories to go!

✓ **Cruelty/violence:** Ah, yes, this one's a charmer. Don't even think of uploading a video that shows any sort of animal abuse. Or human abuse, either. If your video shows an animal or someone getting hurt or attacked — and that includes humiliation — don't upload it. Suffice to say that any type of beating or battery for the sheer fun of it is a non-starter.

✓ **Shock/gross-outs:** YouTube is not a shock site. Footage of dead bodies, car accidents with injured people, or the always-charming vomit videos are not welcome.

✓ **Hate videos:** This one's the real nasty one: Feel free to express an unpopular point of view, but don't stray into *hate speech* — words that use malicious stereotypes intended to attack or degrade a particular race, gender, sexual orientation, and so on. If your video shows you or someone else spouting off against this type of group or that type of person, the YouTube community will be quick to flag it, and YouTube will be quick to remove it.

Is YouTube really PG-13?

In the preceding section, we list seven things that your YouTube video can't contain: the seven deadly sins, if you will. If you're a parent, a sensitive person, or just somebody who's concerned with the overall pop-culture tone of our society, it probably pleases you to know that YouTube established its Community Guidelines policy to help keep the site within the bounds of reasonable good taste.

YouTube is very upfront and clear that it's not designed or meant for children younger than 13, and here's why: Every day, millions of people visit YouTube. They upload videos, they add to their blogs, they update their channels, they leave feedback on the videos they view, and they often communicate with other users. YouTube is — quite literally — a community of people: a *worldwide* community. And like any community, most people are good, some are not so good, and a few are really bad apples.

It's the bad apples you want to look out for, especially if you have kids or young teens who surf the site. But even adults, many adults, will find some content on YouTube objectionable. Or upsetting. Or shocking.

Drawing the line at 13-year-olds suggests that YouTube is PG-13. From an overall perspective, that is a fair assessment. If you're a parent, though, someone really should tell you this: Much YouTube content is distinctly R-rated, and nobody at YouTube is doing anything to stop that. YouTube is very much aware that some of its content goes beyond the bounds of what most would consider "good taste," but if it doesn't violate the Community Guidelines, YouTube simply provides a warning, as shown in Figure 11-2.

Figure 11-2:
YouTube
warns
you about
content that
many mem-
bers of the
community
have
flagged as
offensive.

Although YouTube has no way of verifying the age of anyone who registers an account, it will not allow you to do so if you state that you have not yet reached your teenage years. This means that any children who have registered with YouTube have had to supply false information about their age to do so. It also means that, if you're a parent, you really don't have a leg to stand on if you want to complain about something offensive that your 12-year-old saw on YouTube.

With this in mind, take another look at those seven no-no categories and see what the real deal is.

- ✔ **Pornography:** There's always the chance that somebody will upload something pornographic, but it will be removed quickly by the YouTube community. So this is the real deal; you won't see pornography on YouTube. However, you won't have any trouble finding X-rated language on YouTube, particularly in the comedy section. The title of comic Sarah Silverman's video "The Porn Song" pretty much speaks for itself. (It's very funny, too.) That's entertainment. Unfortunately, things get *much* uglier — and far less inspired — in the comments that users post for some videos. Yes, we're talking the F-word — and the B-word, the C-word, and the G-, K-, Q-, and Z-words, too. If you're a parent or someone who just doesn't care for obscenity, be aware that user comments on YouTube can get pretty rough.

✔ **Nudity:** In terms of full-frontal nudity, YouTube makes good on its policy, and you'd be hard pressed to find any. The key word here is *frontal* because — on the flip-side, so to speak — there's no shortage of bare butts on the Tube. Most of it falls into the comedy category — "mooning" and the like — and some of it is actually funny. There are also tons of videos of scantily clad male and female models cavorting about to an MTV-style soundtrack. Butts, briefs, and bras — that's the nudity deal with YouTube — but no full-frontal.

✔ **Dangerous acts:** Hah! This is one category where YouTube definitely looks the other way. If you're at all familiar with the *Jackass* TV show or films, you probably won't be surprised to hear that there are a lot of *Jackass*-type videos on the Tube. Generally, this means younger guys doing some crazy stunts — jumping off of roofs and bridges, setting off firecrackers and other explosions, driving cars on thin ice — all the types of things you don't want your kids trying at home.

However, none of these videos shows anybody getting killed or seriously injured. That would cross the line and YouTube would pull it.

✔ **Illegal acts:** On one hand, this is a pretty serious category, and YouTube is very up-front about the fact that it works closely with law enforcement to investigate any videos that show illegal acts being perpetrated. You won't see videos of shootings, muggings, or that type of thing. On the other hand, some videos (like "BIGGEST Bong Hit Ever!") suggest that YouTube isn't policing the site too thoroughly. This is the type of video that most parents of kids — even those older than 13 — wouldn't be too pleased to see on their home computers.

✔ **Cruelty/violence:** If you upload a video showing someone harming a defenseless animal, be prepared for an onslaught of condemnation from the large community of Tubers that avidly guards against cruelty to animals. You might even end up talking to your local police. Cruelty to human beings is another story. YouTube excludes videos of senseless violence, such as muggings or beatings. However, in the post-9/11 world, much of the news of the world is violent. If a violent video can arguably be called news, it will run on YouTube.

News/violence on YouTube has been a very controversial subject. American soldiers in Iraq have uploaded their own videos of fighting in Baghdad: That's war coverage not filtered through any journalist or news organization, and that's something new. Explicit footage of the 2005 bombings in Bali is also available for download, as are more videos of the 9/11 attacks on New York and Washington than you would ever care to watch.

YouTube was very much in the news in early 2007 when it broadcast the execution-by-hanging video of Saddam Hussein and the cockpit video of the friendly-fire bombing of a British military convoy in which a 25-year-old British soldier was killed. For years, the United States and United Kingdom had denied the existence of this video, and its worldwide broadcast was a landmark moment for YouTube.

In a proverbial nutshell, YouTube is very much a reflection of our society and our world, good and bad. If violence bothers you, beware that there are a lot of violent videos on the Tube.

✔ **Shock/gross-outs:** Whew! This category will lighten up this discussion. Some of the most fascinating videos on the Tube are shock videos: plane crashes, car crashes, and other types of spectacular accidents. You never see an actual person being seriously injured, but many of the videos — air show crashes, for example — show events in which people surely died. Now, while you're typing **air show crash** into the search field, make a note that showing *ambulance videos* — videos of seriously injured people — crosses the line, and YouTube will reject them. As for gross-outs and stomach-turners, there are *plenty* of them on the Tube. We're talking about nose picking, zit popping, and other examples of transcendent human behavior. If that's your thing, you'll find many kindred spirits and booger buddies on the Tube.

✔ **Hate videos:** This is perhaps the most offensive content on YouTube, and there's a lot of it. A video-sharing site is inherently at risk for becoming a place where hate and racism can rapidly propagate, and YouTube makes a legitimate effort to eradicate hate videos from the site. Unfortunately, there seems to be nothing that can be done or will be done about hate speech in comments and user feedback. Beware the dark side of the Tube, Luke.

Flagging a video as inappropriate

The two basic types of offensive content on YouTube are

✔ Content that some people would consider repellant or in bad taste

✔ Content that is a violation of the YouTube Community Guidelines

When surfing the Tube, you will run into content that you will find offensive. In most cases, the best thing to do about it — the only thing to do about it — is to move on. Change the channel. However, if you encounter a video that violates the YouTube policy regarding Community Guidelines, you can flag it as inappropriate. Here's how:

1. **Click the Flag as Inappropriate button — as shown in Figure 11-3 — beneath the video window.**

   This will take you to the This Video Is Inappropriate window, shown in Figure 11-4.

2. **Choose a reason from the pull-down list.**

3. **Click the Flag This Video button.**

Figure 11-3:
If you think it's just wrong, click the Flag as Inappropriate button.

Figure 11-4:
When you flag a video as inappropriate, you must give YouTube a reason why you think it is so.

When you flag a video as inappropriate, the video isn't automatically removed from the site. Instead, an alert is sent to YouTube's administration team. YouTube takes flagging very seriously and claims to work around the clock — 24 hours per day, seven days per week — processing flagged messages from the YouTube community. The YouTube administration team views the video; if it does indeed violate the Terms of Service, the team removes the video from the site.

Flagging a video is an anonymous act — sort of. The member who posted the video will not be informed that it was you who flagged the video. However, YouTube keeps track of all flagged videos — and all the users who have flagged videos. This is an important point because it allows YouTube's administration team to be on the lookout for rabid censors who see evil everywhere they look and have nothing better to do all day than flag videos. If you are a flagging addict, you might get an e-mail from YouTube requesting that you give the system a break.

What to do if your video is removed

YouTube removes a video from the site for one of two reasons:

- ✔ It violates YouTube's terms of use and Community Guidelines.
- ✔ It infringes on a copyright.

In this section, we discuss the first point. We discuss copyright issues later in this chapter.

If your video is removed by YouTube for violation of terms of use and Community Guidelines, it contains content that's specifically unacceptable in some way, shape, or form. In most cases, it will be a clear violation of one of YouTube's seven deadly sins. (See the earlier section, "Illegal content: What's not allowed in your video.")

When your video is removed, the YouTube police come to your house at night and interrogate your family to find out who in your house posted the video. Just kidding. No, what really happens is that you receive an e-mail from YouTube alerting you that your video was removed, giving you a brief reason why. Don't expect an elaborate explanation; this is pretty much a form letter, and the reason given will usually be chosen by YouTube from a preset list of violations.

Don't make the mistake of thinking that this action on YouTube's part is a result of some mindless computer program isolating your video and blindly removing it from the site. That's not the case. If your video is removed from YouTube, it is done so purposefully by a YouTube staffer for a specific reason. In other words, it's very unlikely that this is an accident.

So what do you do if your video is removed? You could do what we do whenever we're faced with any type of a personal challenge: Call Oprah. While you wait for her to call you back, the worst thing you can do is to upload it again to the site. That's an in-your-face move — a brazenly defiant act against the YouTube staff. Remember that these are real people, and you would be giving them a problem to deal with. This is not a situation you want to create.

The best response to take if your video is removed is to let it go, learn a lesson, and move on. Check out the YouTube Community Guidelines and Terms of Use pages to get a refresher on what goes and what doesn't go on the Tube. You can always re-edit your video to remove the offensive content, but it's usually best to leave the video on your computer and move on to other YouTube pursuits.

What to do if YouTube cancels your account

First of all, if YouTube actually goes so far as to cancel your account — wow! You must have done something that was in direct violation of the Community Guidelines or terms of use. That's not to say that you're automatically guilty or that it's impossible for YouTube to make a mistake, but chances are that You Messed Up.

If you upload pornography, that's a clear violation of YouTube's policies, and you'll probably get the boot, even for a single violation. Uploading videos that contain racist remarks or other types of hate speech and videos that show cruelty to animals will quickly put you on YouTube's hit list — and rightly so. **Remember:** You are a guest on YouTube. You don't have an inalienable right to post videos to the site; when you do so, you are bound by YouTube policies, whether you agree with them or not. In fact, when you register with YouTube, you specifically state that you do agree with YouTube policies, so you don't have a leg to stand on if you turn around and violate that which you have already agreed to.

If YouTube gives you the boot, that's pretty much it; you're outta there. Like in the movie *Witness,* you will be shunned by the YouTube community and never allowed to remarry. Your account will be wiped out — that includes all your account preferences, your playlists, and your list of friends and contacts. All the videos that you uploaded will no longer be available. And if you created and designed your own channel page, poof! That's gone, too.

What can you do about it? Not much. You will find that it's difficult to contact YouTube and quite unlikely that you'll get a response. Also, there's no official appeals process that you can access if you feel you've been treated unfairly. If that's truly the case — if you genuinely feel that you got the boot by mistake — send YouTube an e-mail. Scroll to the bottom of any page and click the Contact link.

If your account is cancelled legitimately, your best course of action is to clean the slate and make a fresh start. You can always register a new account with a new username. Remember that registering is an anonymous process; not even YouTube will know that you're the same guy they gave the boot to. However, you'll need an active e-mail address in order to register, and YouTube won't let you re-register with the same e-mail address. YouTube will recognize you and not let you back in.

Protecting yourself and your family

We said this before, and we'll say it again: By and large, YouTube is a good place with good people. However, it's also a large community and no less real just because it's a virtual online community. Like in any community, most people are good; they go to the site to have fun, not to do harm to anyone. You have no reason to be paranoid about interacting with the YouTube community, no reason to be afraid to upload a video of yourself, and no reason to lose sleep worrying that people can see you and your family in your videos on YouTube.

You do, however, have reason to be prudent, and that is what this chapter is about: being prudent. Playing it smart, playing it safe, and keeping the kids out of harm's way. In the following sections, we discuss options that you have to accentuate the positive, eliminate the negative, and maintain your anonymity on YouTube.

Keeping your identity secret

You are your username. For most of the YouTube community, that's all you are. Registering with YouTube is an anonymous procedure — you don't need to give your name, just your e-mail address. That information is kept private by YouTube, so really, all that other YouTube users know about you automatically is your username. Any other information gets divulged by you.

Keep your identity a secret. Let them call you Batman, not Bruce Wayne. YouTube is a community of millions of people, and you seldom truly know who it is that you are interacting with. That's why the best policy — the smartest policy — is to use the Tube within the shelter of your anonymous username.

The following is a list of things to consider when using YouTube anonymously:

✔ **Don't use your full name as your username.** Be johniscool rather than johnsmith. That might seem obvious, but it's not always the case. That's because many people use YouTube for exactly that reason: to get their name out there. If you're a comedian, chances are that you want your name on your videos. You want an agent. You want to get hired. It only makes sense. If you're not trying to get famous on YouTube, though, don't post your full name anywhere.

✔ **Don't reveal too much in your videos.** If, for some reason, your video contains footage of the outside of your house, avoid showing your full address. In other words, if we see the number 24 on the door and then in a later frame see you and your husband walking the dog past a street sign that reads *Princeton*, we have a pretty good idea of where you live. For the same reason, avoid showing the license plate on your car.

✔ **Be careful with kids and the family videos.** One of the greatest things about YouTube is that you can easily share videos with family and friends across the miles. For family videos, we recommend uploading them as *private videos* — ones that can be viewed only by people you designate. (See the section "Making your video private," later in this chapter.)

✔ **Don't reveal too much on your channel.** Customizing your channel on YouTube is a great way to introduce yourself to the YouTube community, creating a place where users can go to see all the videos that you uploaded and to learn more about you. However, make sure that they don't learn too much. Unless you're looking to get famous or want to be contacted by any random person on the Tube, don't post your full name or personal contact information. Remember that your channel is no more private than any other page on YouTube.

✔ **Think twice before giving out your personal e-mail address.** People often forget that YouTube is a chat site as well as a video-sharing site. You can message other users, and they can message you. But stay clear on this point: Any messages you send or receive are sent *through* YouTube. In other words, if someone watches one of your videos and sends you a message, he sent that message to your username. That's anonymous. He does not have your "real" e-mail address. You can swap messages anonymously — using just your username — with any other Tuber, so there's no real need for you to give your personal e-mail address to any other Tuber.

✔ **Consider carefully what you write in messages, comments, or feedback.** You probably aren't planning on getting into fights with people on the Tube, but you might be surprised at how easily things can get heated. Some Tubers leave some nasty comments, and you might be tempted to fire off a response. That's not a violation, but don't get so angry that you arrange a meeting place for a real-life fight. That might sound crazy, but believe it or not, it happens.

On the flip side, you might not be planning on falling in love on the Tube either, but you just might find yourself involved in a message exchange with some charming Tuber out there. Believe it or not, this happens, too. And what a coincidence — he lives in your city! He's rich, he's a brain surgeon, he looks like George Clooney, and he wants to meet you for a drink. Should you go? That's entirely up to you, but don't forget that this is a *total* stranger — and he just might not *really* be that handsome devil you see in his videos. Whatever you do, do not message that person your personal info. If you go out on a limb and actually do meet that person — this is not something that we are advising you to do, by the way — and sparks don't fly, you probably won't want him to know how to get back in touch.

✓ **Don't tell anybody your password.** YouTube will *never* ask you to reveal your password for any reason. If you get a message from YouTube asking for your password, that message is not really from YouTube. You're being scammed by someone, somehow, some way.

✓ **Don't libel.** *Libel* is defamation by written or printed words, pictures, or in any form other than by spoken words. What this means for you on YouTube is that you should be careful of making accusations or allegations about other Tubers. Don't say that someone is a thief. Don't say that someone has a disease, that he's insane, that he's a murderer, or that he's cheating on his spouse. Will you get sued? It might not be likely, but it's not impossible.

✓ **Don't assume that YouTube knows who every user is.** When someone registers with YouTube, all that she supplies is an e-mail address. No name. No credit card. So don't make the mistake in thinking that YouTube has the 411 on every user or that every user can ultimately be held accountable for their behavior.

Communicating YouTube safety to teens

Many of the points in the preceding section might seem obvious — don't give out your phone number or other personal contact info, for example — but consider that those points won't be so obvious to kids and young teens. If you have young persons in your family and are concerned about them using YouTube, your greatest concerns should be focused less on what they see on the Tube and more on who they meet and who they talk to.

When parents learn that YouTube is not for children younger than 13, they assume that's because kids will see videos that are risqué or inappropriate. That might be a risk, but the real risk is that a child might be contacted by an adult or an older child and lured into a dangerous situation. Don't forget: As much as YouTube is a video sharing site, it is a chat site. People meet people on YouTube. This is *exactly* why no child younger than 13 should use YouTube without adult supervision.

If you're the parent of a teenager, *communicate* your concerns. If you just say, "I don't want you using YouTube when I'm not home," your teen probably thinks that you're worried about the videos that she'll see on the Tube — the "dirty" stuff. Explain that you're more concerned with her maintaining her anonymity. Most teens haven't even considered this: It's not the type of thing kids think about, and that's how they can be taken advantage of.

Be clear to your teen that she should never reveal who she is, where she lives, or how she can be contacted outside the Tube. Explain the concept of healthy skepticism. If she's befriended another Tuber because he seems nice in his videos, explain that the person in those videos might not *really* be him. And be *very* clear that she should *never* arrange to meet with anybody that she meets on the Tube — or anywhere online for that matter.

Reading the preceding may cause concern for any parent, but don't be frightened or paranoid about your kids and YouTube. Keep your young kids off the Tube. Keep your teens smart about the Tube and check in with them often. Just a bit of parental oversight and communication goes very far in keeping a responsible teenager safe on the Tube.

Making your video private

One of the smartest things that you can do to protect your privacy is to upload your videos as private videos. This is especially the case with your family videos. One of the truly great things about YouTube is that it provides families with the opportunity to easily share videos with other family members and friends. For these types of videos — especially those involving children — you should *always* choose to upload them as private videos. A video that you designate as private cannot be seen by the YouTube community at large — it won't even come up in a search. Only the people whom you invite are able to view the video.

When you upload a video, follow these easy steps to keep it private:

1. **On the second page of the video-upload procedure, select the Private radio button, as shown in Figure 11-5.**

2. **If you want to e-mail the video to either your Family contact list, your Friends contact list, or both, select the appropriate check boxes.**

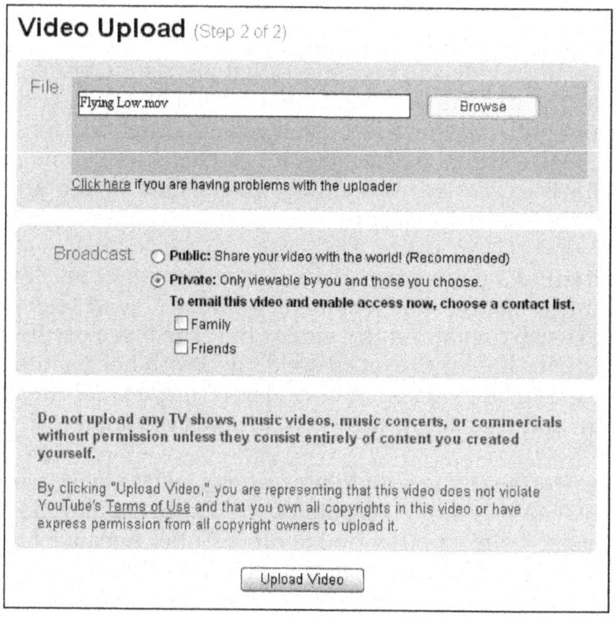

Figure 11-5:
Designate a
video as
private
during
upload.

If you don't designate a video as private at the time of upload and you want to change that, or if you don't designate which of your contact lists can view the video at the time of upload, you can always do either or both with the following steps:

a. After your video is uploaded, go to your account page and click My Uploaded Videos (`http://youTube.com/my_videos`).

b. Click the Edit Video Info button for the video that you want to make private.

This takes you to the Edit My Videos page, as shown in Figure 11-6.

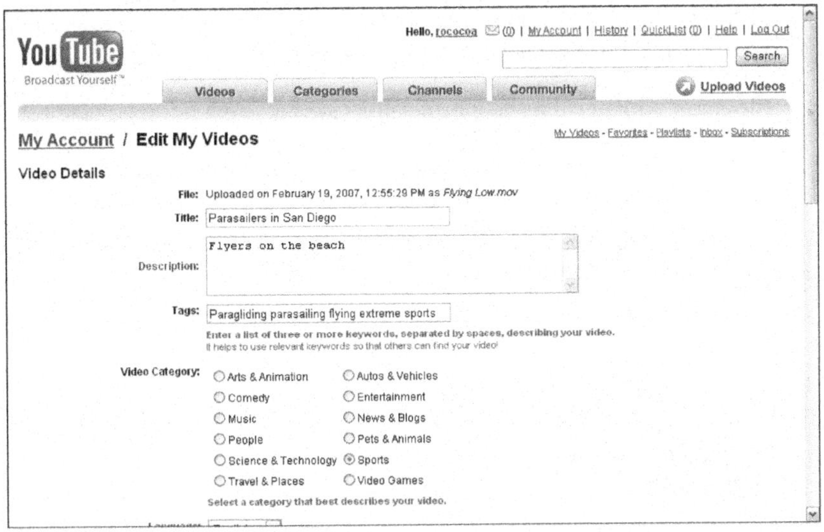

Figure 11-6:
The Edit
My Videos
page allows
you to
change the
parameters
of your
uploads.

3. **Scroll to the Broadcast section in the Sharing section and then click Private.**

4. **Choose the contact list that you want to be enabled to view the video: Family, Friends, or both.**

Your Broadcast section should resemble Figure 11-7.

Figure 11-7:
You can
make an
already
uploaded
video
private.

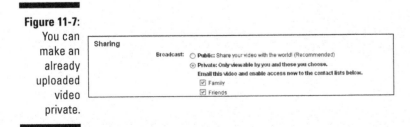

5. **Click the Update Video Info button.**

When you click the Update Video Info button, the contacts that you chose — and only those contacts — will receive a message in their YouTube accounts directing them to your video.

Blocking another user from contacting you

Another powerful feature that YouTube offers for protecting your privacy is the ability to block other users from contacting you. If someone contacts you and you think that he's rude or gives you the creeps, or you basically just don't like him, feel free to block him. You don't need any specific reason to do so; the fact that you want to is reason enough.

Blocking another user is simple. Just follow these steps:

1. **When you receive a message from someone that you want to block, click that person's username to go to their channel.**

2. **After you're on their channel, go to the Connect With section, as shown in Figure 11-8.**

3. **Click the Block User link.**

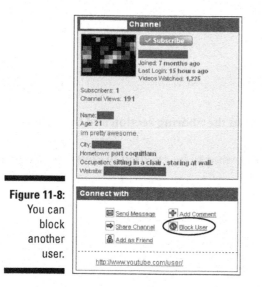

Figure 11-8:
You can block another user.

Avoiding Problems with Copyright Infringement

You don't need to be a lawyer to understand YouTube's policy on copyright infringement, but even so we're not going to go too far into the legalese of it all. Instead, we use this section to give you the basic rundown of what does and doesn't qualify as copyright infringement, what types of legally protected content you shouldn't include in your videos, and what to do if you're accused of copyright infringement.

The official word: The YouTube policy on copyright infringement

On the heels of YouTube's almost-instant rise to success came serious questions about copyright infringement. A very large percentage of the video clips on YouTube are copyright protected and were uploaded without the consent or written permission of the owners.

When YouTube was purchased by Google, those serious questions about copyright infringement became much *more* serious. Suddenly, YouTube was the child of a parent company with very deep pockets. Also, Google is a publicly traded company. If YouTube were to be faced with an onslaught of legal challenges, would that have a negative effect on the Google stock price?

YouTube maintains that it complies with copyright laws. Indeed, if a clip is uploaded in violation of YouTube's copyright policy, and if the owner of the copyright notifies YouTube, YouTube will immediately remove the clip from the site.

This is not theory; it happens every day. On the morning after the 2007 Golden Globe Awards broadcast, quite a few clips appeared on YouTube of former *American Idol* contestant Jennifer Hudson accepting her award for the film *Dreamgirls*. That's exactly the type of pop-culture occurrence that people flock to YouTube for. By mid-afternoon, all those clips were removed. The legal owners of the copyright to that broadcast contacted YouTube; and as a result, the clips were removed. The owners were well within their legal rights to take that action.

The YouTube-stated policy on copyright infringement breaks down to the following components:

- ✔ YouTube respects the rights of copyright holders and publishers.

- ✔ YouTube requires that all users confirm that they own the copyright or have permission from the copyright holder to upload content.

- ✔ YouTube is in compliance with the Digital Millennium Copyright Act (DMCA).

- ✔ YouTube will promptly remove any infringing content when properly notified.

- ✔ YouTube will permanently terminate the accounts of users who repeatedly violate YouTube copyright infringement policy.

Copyright tips part 1: The hard line

The best way to ensure that your video is not in violation of YouTube copyright infringement policy is to upload video content that is only of your creation. For example, if you shoot a video of your family at the Thanksgiving dinner table, that content would be purely your creation, and it wouldn't be possible that it violates someone else's copyright information. Right?

Well, if you want to play devil's advocate, make sure that the TV isn't on in the background when you're videotaping the Thanksgiving feast. That TV program is copyrighted. Even if you *can't see* the TV, being able to hear it could be considered a violation as well.

These are extreme examples and not in any way the reality of copyright infringement on YouTube. The basic rule is to not upload a video that flagrantly displays content that clearly belongs to someone else.

The following is a list of tips that you can follow to stay clear of copyright infringement problems:

- ✔ **Originality:** Be sure that all the content in your video is your own. This includes any music that you might overlay to accompany the video.

- ✔ **TV shows:** Any TV show that has been broadcast at any time is copyright protected. This includes old shows and new shows. This includes all types of TV shows: comedies, dramas, sports, classic TV, cartoons, and news shows. This also includes any type of television broadcast: network, cable, pay-per-view, and on-demand TV.

- ✔ **TV commercials:** All TV commercials are copyright protected.

- ✔ **Music:** Although most (old) classical music is in the public domain, consider all professionally produced music from the last five decades to be copyright protected. That means all types of music: rock, pop, disco, roots, rap — even Yanni and Kenny G. If your wedding video has the song "Hell's Bells" playing in the background, that copyright belongs to AC/DC and its record company.

✔ **Music videos:** Music videos, such as those that you will find on MTV or VH1, are all copyright-protected.

✔ **Live music recording:** You can't upload videos of concert performances. No, the fact that you shot the video yourself doesn't make the content yours.

✔ **Movies and trailers:** Movies and movie trailers are copyright protected. You're not supposed to upload even one scene.

The length of the video clip or the amount of content that is in violation doesn't matter. Even if it's just one second of your video, it's a violation.

It doesn't matter where the content comes from. In other words, if you find a clip of a trailer for the next *Superman* movie on some random Web site somewhere, that doesn't make it okay to upload it to YouTube.

✔ **Gain:** The fact that you're not selling the content for any personal monetary gain does not in any way relieve you of copyright laws.

✔ **Credit:** The fact that you give credit to the owner of the content doesn't mean that it's okay to upload copyrighted material.

Whew! That's a pretty strict list, don't you think? If you're saying, "Wait a minute, I've seen that kind of content all over YouTube, and it never gets taken down," read on.

Copyright tips part 2: The real deal

If you love old TV shows, you'll love YouTube. Type in **Bionic Woman,** for example, and you can choose from an abundance of clips of the classic 1970s TV show. Is Broadway your thing? Search for **Sondheim,** and you can watch Patty Lupone singing in the recent revival of *Sweeney Todd.* Are you a sports fan? Check out great moments from almost any broadcast event that you can think of. And if you like movies and movie stars, Tubers have uploaded all kinds of great montages of memorable movie moments. The Meryl Streep tributes alone can keep you watching for hours.

And all of it is copyright protected. And none of it is being taken down.

Along with its library of classic movies and vintage television broadcasts, YouTube is also a current events phenomenon — a place where you go for an instant replay of broadcast event. If something blips on the pop culture radar screen — "Did you see Matt Damon do his killer impersonation of Matthew McConaughey on *Letterman* last night?" — a clip will be on YouTube.

Make no mistake: YouTube is very much aware that this content is up there in violation of its own copyright-infringement policy. YouTube is also very much aware that it's exactly this type of content that users love, and it's exactly this type of content that has made YouTube so successful.

The real deal on YouTube's copyright infringement policy can be found in the following sentence from its online statement:

> *We comply with the Digital Millennium Copyright Act (DMCA) and promptly remove content when properly notified.*

The key phrase here is *when properly notified.* That's the loophole that allows YouTube to be YouTube. Of course, YouTube knows that all this copyrighted content is on the site, but so long as the owner of the copyright doesn't object by properly notifying YouTube, YouTube won't take it down.

This brings up all kinds of issues.

A lot of wink-wink is going on here, and it's not only YouTube that's doing it. For example, you can be certain that ABC Television is aware that YouTube contains dozens of clips from *The View,* particularly from the days when Rosie O'Donnell was a co-host and controversy lightning rod. At any time, ABC could demand that those clips be removed, and — *poof* — they'd be gone. But on the day we checked, those clips were still up there — because ABC recognizes YouTube for what it is: great publicity. It's in ABC's interest to promote *The View* and generate as much publicity and word of mouth as possible. ABC is very much aware that YouTube gets *way more* hits than the ABC Web site does and recognizes that, in reality, YouTube is doing a great service for ABC.

This can cut both ways though. Comic Artie Lange commented recently on *The Howard Stern Show* that he was not pleased that clips of his standup act were being broadcast on YouTube. The big difference here is that Lange is not ABC Television. Lange makes his living because people *pay* to see his act, either live or on the DVD that he has produced and released. People are downloading content off of his DVD and uploading it to YouTube. Although it could be argued that he's getting extra promotion and publicity on YouTube, you can be sure that Lange would rather have you pay for the DVD rather than get your yuks for free on the Tube — and who can blame him?

Another thing happening here is that many major broadcast entities are *partnering* with YouTube. Don't be surprised to see lots of CBS TV programming on YouTube: CBS is a major partner that (wisely, it seems) sees the advantage of strutting its stuff on YouTube. YouTube's partner list also includes such players as ABC, NBC, Capitol Records, Showtime, and Sony Pictures Classics, just to name a few. So, in a nutshell, this means that while it's against YouTube policy for you to upload clips from *The View,* your clips won't be removed because ABC won't report them to YouTube, and ABC is a partner of YouTube, and ABC itself is posting those *same* clips on YouTube. Whew! Gets pretty twisted, doesn't it?

One more point needs to be made: YouTube is *not* lying in any way about what it states in its copyright infringement policy:

✔ YouTube *does* respect the rights of copyright holders and publishers. This is true in both word and deed.

✔ YouTube *does* require that all users confirm that they own the copyright or have permission from the copyright holder to upload content. Make no mistake: Whenever you upload a video, you must confirm that your video is in compliance with YouTube's copyright infringement policy. In other words, you are stating that your video does not contain content that belongs to someone else. If you're lying, you really are breaking the law.

✔ YouTube *will* promptly remove any infringing content when properly notified. Not only is this true, it happens every day.

✔ YouTube *will* permanently terminate the accounts of users who violate YouTube copyright infringement policy repeatedly. There's no wink-wink going on here. If you continuously upload copyrighted material even after being told to not do so, YouTube will give you the boot.

Does all this mean that you should ignore YouTube policy and feel free to upload copyrighted content at will. No. Will users continue to do so? Yes. The bottom-line truth about all of this is that the Internet as a whole and YouTube as an entity are so revolutionary and so unprecedented that nobody really knows where this is heading — and everybody is figuring it out as they go.

Is the fact that somebody — not ABC — uploaded clips of *Ugly Betty* a good thing or a bad thing for ABC? Who knows? It seems like good publicity, but copyright laws exist for a reason, so who's to say? YouTube's rapidly growing Partners list of major broadcast entities in a variety of categories — music, TV, movies, and so on — suggests that the powers that be seem to think that working together might be a smarter plan than fighting over who owns what.

One thing is for certain: All that copyrighted content has a lot to do with what makes YouTube so great and so fun and so exciting. So while the big wigs figure it out, the rest of us can sit back and enjoy the show.

How to file a copyright infringement notification with YouTube

If you are the owner of copyrighted material and you feel that material has been uploaded to YouTube in violation of copyright laws and YouTube's copyright-infringement policy, you can file a copyright-infringement notification with YouTube. To do so, you must send YouTube written notification; you cannot use the YouTube Web site to alert YouTube of copyright infringement.

The YouTube Help Center lists the following elements that must be included in your written communication if you want to file notice of copyright infringement (in addition, YouTube also suggests that you consult your legal counsel and/or see Section 512(c)(3) of the Copyright Act to confirm these requirements):

✔ A physical or electronic signature of a person authorized to act on behalf of the owner of an exclusive right that is allegedly infringed.

✔ Identification of the copyrighted work claimed to have been infringed, or, if multiple copyrighted works at a single online site are covered by a single notification, a representative list of such works at that site.

✔ Identification of the material that is claimed to be infringing or to be the subject of infringing activity and that is to be removed or access to which is to be disabled, and information reasonably sufficient to permit the service provider to locate the material. **Providing URLs in the body of an e-mail is the best way to help us locate content quickly.**

✔ Information reasonably sufficient to permit the service provider to contact the complaining party, such as an address, telephone number, and, if available, an electronic mail address at which the complaining party may be contacted.

✔ A statement that the complaining party has a good faith belief that use of the material in the manner complained of is not authorized by the copyright owner, its agent, or the law.

✔ A statement that the information in the notification is accurate and, under penalty of perjury, that the complaining party is authorized to act on behalf of the owner of an exclusive right that is allegedly infringed.

Written communication can be in the form of a physical letter or an e-mail sent to YouTube's designated agent at the following address:

DMCA Complaints
YouTube, Inc.
1000 Cherry Ave.
Second Floor
San Bruno, CA 94066
Fax: 650-872-8513
E-mail: **copyright@youtube.com**

If you choose to report content as being a violation of copyright policy, be aware that doing so is a serious legal decision. In its Help Center, YouTube reminds you that under Section 512(f), any person who knowingly materially misrepresents that material or activity may be subject to liability.

Chapter 12

Bam!! Kicking It up a Notch

*Y*ouTube is like the proverbial onion. It's got layers — lots of layers. When you peel back one layer, you discover another, and another, and . . . you get the picture. As we write this book, YouTube is adding even more features. By the time you read this, YouTube no doubt will have added ten new features we couldn't dream of now. YouTube is changing all the time. In this chapter, we show you some more of the cool things you can currently do with YouTube.

Do you have a mobile phone with a video camera? Great. We show you how to upload your mobile phone videos directly to YouTube. Do you have a college e-mail address? If so, and your college is one of YouTube's elite, you can join your college's private channel. Do you have a Web site or a WordPress blog? You'll be happy to know you can embed a YouTube video in your Web page or blog. Last (but not least), we show you a few hacks for YouTube, such as downloading a YouTube video to your computer and playing it on your iPod. If this sounds like your cup of tea, read on, intrepid Tuber.

Uploading a Video from Your Mobile Phone

When you have a strong signal, mobile phones are wonderful things. But even when you don't have a strong signal, there are still some cool things you can do — especially if you have a tricked-out mobile phone with a built-in video camera and e-mail capabilities. For example, you can capture video of something interesting, like being caught in your city's most horrific traffic jam. Then when you're safely parked and a strong signal returns, you can upload your video to the Tube. That may sound far-fetched, but if you put a traffic jam on the Tube and e-mail the link of your YouTube "Crosstown Traffic Jam" video to the right city officials or your local news station, maybe something will get done. Before you can upload mobile phone video to the Tube, you have to do a few things online:

1. **Log in to the Tube.**

2. **Click the My Account link.**

   YouTube transports you to the My Account page.

3. **In the Account Settings section, click the Mobile Upload Settings link.**

   The My Account/Mobile Uploads Options page appears, as shown in Figure 12-1.

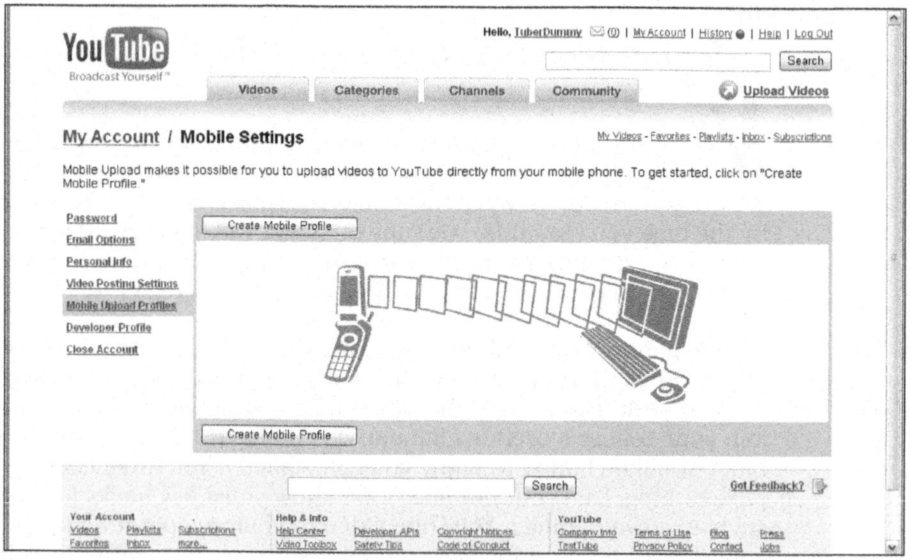

Figure 12-1: Create a mobile profile on a static Web page. Isn't that an oxymoron?

4. **Click the Create Mobile Profile button.**

   The page refreshes with default information, as shown in Figure 12-2.

5. **Accept the default Profile name, or enter one that suits you.**

   The default profile name is Mobile Profile 1, which albeit boring, is an apt description of what you'll do with this profile. However, it's your profile name, so get as wild and crazy as you like.

6. Accept the default Video Title, or enter one of your own.

This is seen on the Tube. The title will be appended by the filename of the uploaded video or the date (which is a choice that you make in the next step).

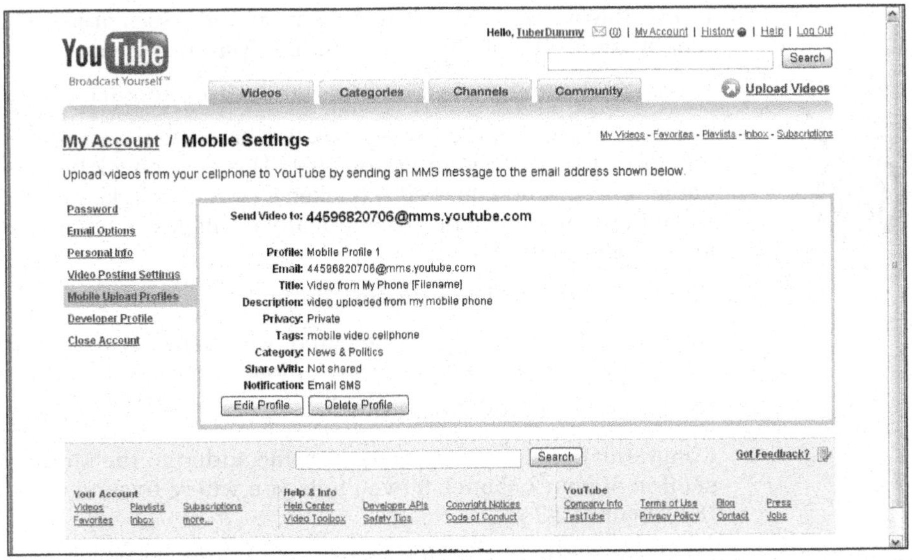

Figure 12-2:
Setting up a mobile profile that will end up being static on your channel.

7. Accept the default Filename option (Video From My Mobile Phone), or select the Date check box.

This option determines whether the video title is appended with the filename you specify, or the date you upload the video.

8. Accept the default description or enter one of your own.

If you're as creative as we think you are, we expect to see some very descriptive descriptions for videos uploaded from mobile phones.

9. In the Privacy section, select the Public or Private radio button.

This determines whether the whole world will see your video or just those on your Friends list.

10. Accept the default tags or enter those that pertain to the videos you capture with your mobile phone.

Tags direct Tubers to your videos. For a refresher course on tags, see Chapter 8. We suggest you leave in the default tags that identify the video as being captured by a mobile phone and then add tags that pertain to the specific videos you capture with your mobile phone.

If you capture different types of videos with your mobile phone, set up a profile for each type of video and remember to choose the right one when you upload.

11. **Choose an option from the Category drop-down menu.**

This determines the category in which your mobile phone videos appear.

12. **In the Share text field, enter the e-mail addresses of people with whom you'd like to share your mobile phone videos.**

Each e-mail address must be separated with a comma.

Click the Insert from Address Book link, and the page refreshes with the names of Tubers on your Friends list. There's a check box next to each name, which, when marked (checked), becomes linked to the profile. Then that person will be automatically notified when you add new videos using this profile.

13. **Choose the desired Notification options.**

By default, both options are selected, which means you'll be notified by e-mail and text message when the upload is successful.

14. **Click the Create Profile button.**

Congratulations! You have a new profile added to the Mobile Settings section of your channel. It even tells you where to send the video. (See Figure 12-3.)

After you create the profile, access your mobile phone's e-mail utility, and attach the video as a link. It will be uploaded to your YouTube channel.

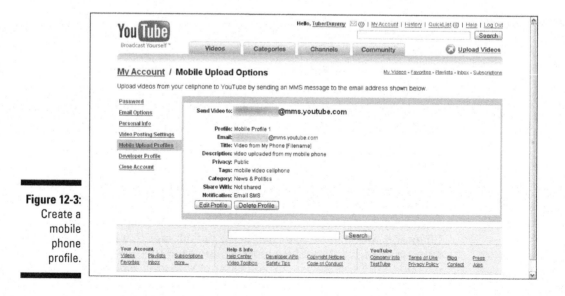

Figure 12-3:
Create a mobile phone profile.

Higher Education: Joining Your College's Private Tube

Are you a college student or alumnus? Do you have a valid college e-mail address? If the answer to both questions is yes, read on. You may be able to join your college's private YouTube. The caveat is that your alma mater must be on YouTube's college list. Joining your college on the Tube is sort of like having a super-secret handshake. The privileged get to go where other Tubers can't tread. To gain access to all this cool stuff, you've got to join your college by following these steps:

1. **Log in to the Tube.**

   Log in with your current username and password.

2. **Click Community and then click Groups.**

   The Community page of the YouTube site appears. (See Figure 12-4.)

Figure 12-4: YouTube, the virtual Woodstock of the 21st century.

3. **Choose Colleges from the Browse menu.**

   Hail, hail, the gang's all here on the Colleges page. (See Figure 12-5.)

   4. **Check whether your college is listed.**

      The YouTube Hall of Colleges does not list every college in the country.
      In fact, the list is fairly small. If your college isn't on the list, you're out of
      luck. After all, you can't join something that doesn't exist.

Figure 12-5:
The
YouTube hall
of brainiacs.

   5. **Click the Join Now button.**

      YouTube gives you another form to fill out. This is something you never
      had to do in school, right? Right.

   6. **Enter your e-mail address.**

      When you join your college, your user e-mail address is changed to your
      college e-mail address.

      If you want your other e-mail addresses associated with your current
      username, set up a new account with a different username and your
      college e-mail address. Remember that you can have multiple
      personalities . . . er, we mean identities, on the Tube.

   7. **Enter your college e-mail address. (See Figure 12-6.)**

   8. **Click the Send Email button.**

      YouTube sends a message to your college e-mail address. Click the link
      to confirm your account, and you can then hobnob with your alma
      mater on the Tube.

      If you don't get the message in a few minutes, check your spam folder.

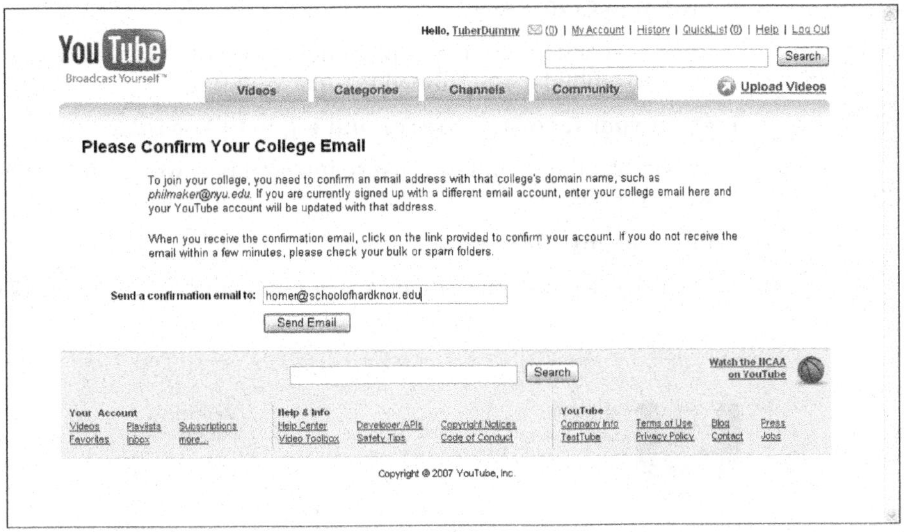

Figure 12-6:
Using a 2B
Eberhard
Faber,
please enter
your e-mail
address.

Embedding YouTube Video in Your Web Site

Video on a Web site is cool, but it also gobbles up a ton of bandwidth. If your Web site doesn't give you gobs of bandwidth but you want to display gobs of videos on your Web site, the answer is simple: Embed videos from YouTube in your Web site. YouTube takes care of the bandwidth problem, and you have video to show your site visitors. Sure, it's got the YouTube logo and player, but YouTube is cool, perhaps even considered *avante-garde* by some. Your site visitors will enjoy the video. You can embed a YouTube video in your Web site by using any HTML (Hypertext Markup Language) editor. In fact, if you're a card-carrying HTML geek who likes to do things the old-fashioned way, you can embed the code manually by using a word processor, such as the ubiquitous Notepad. In this section, we show you how to embed the video with Adobe Dreamweaver. Here's how:

1. **Launch Dreamweaver.**

2. **Create the Web page in which you want to embed the video.**

   Or, you may want to embed the video somewhere else — for instance, on your home page or services page.

3. **Position your cursor where you want the video to appear.**

   If you're a fastidious designer who has everything neatly tucked away in table cells, create another cell for the video.

4. **Switch to Code view.**

   Code is scary for some people. Luckily, you don't need to know a lick of code to embed a YouTube video in a Web page.

5. **Open your favorite browser and log in to YouTube.**

   It's simple. Enter the right username and password, and YouTube knows who you are.

6. **Click the My:Videos link.**

   YouTube displays the videos you've uploaded. (See Figure 12-7.)

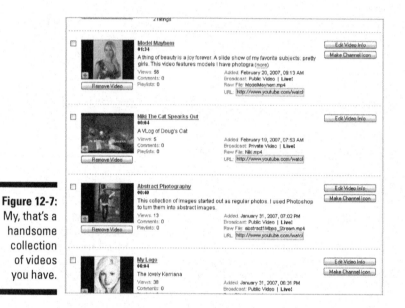

Figure 12-7:
My, that's a handsome collection of videos you have.

7. **Click the Edit Video Info button of the video you want to embed in your Web site.**

   The page refreshes, and you see everything about your video you need to know.

8. **Scroll to the Embed HTML section of the page. (See Figure 12-8.)**

9. **Select the code and press Ctrl+C (Windows) or ⌘+C (Mac).**

   The code is copied to your Clipboard.

10. **In Dreamweaver, press Ctrl+V (Windows) or ⌘+V (Mac).**

Figure 12-8:
The code
you need
is here,
dear reader.

Embed HTML: Put this video on your Web site! Copy and paste the code below to embed the video.

```
<object width="425" height="350"><param name="movie"
value="http://www.youtube.com/v/vGLI5svBV04"></param><embed
src="http://www.youtube.com/v/vGLI5svBV04" type="application/x-shockwave-flash" width="425"
height="350"></embed></object>
```

[Update Video Info]   [Reset]

The code is pasted from the Clipboard to your Web page.
(See Figure 12-9.)

11. Choose File⇨Save.

You have to save the page before you can preview it.

12. Press F12.

Dreamweaver previews the page in your default browser.

13. Play the video.

You see exactly what your site visitors will see. (See Figure 12-10.)

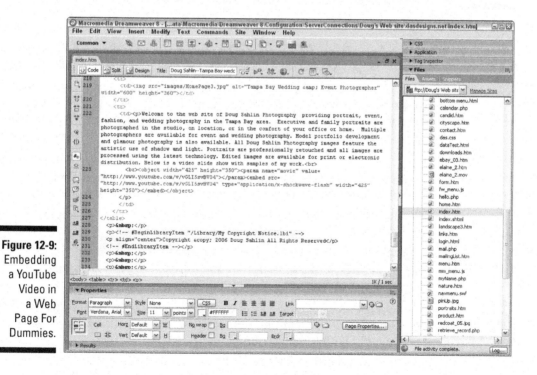

Figure 12-9:
Embedding
a YouTube
Video in
a Web
Page For
Dummies.

Figure 12-10:
From
YouTube in
your site,
your video.

Auto-Starting a Web Site YouTube Video

If you have a message to tell the visitors to your Web site, and you have a video of that message on YouTube, you can proudly display it on your home page. However, your visitors must click the Video Play button to view it. If they don't, your wonderful video message is lost. With a little bit of code wizardry, you can have the video embedded in your Web start as soon as it loads. Here's how:

1. **Launch your favorite HTML editing application and then open the Web page in which you want to embed a YouTube video.**

   We like Dreamweaver. But if you're an Adobe GoLive or Microsoft FrontPage person, have at it.

2. **Position your cursor where you want the video to appear.**

   It helps to keep your page neat and tidy if you create a table cell in which you want the video to appear.

   If you'd like to read more about Web design, consider purchasing *Building Web Sites All-in-One Desk Reference For Dummies*, by Doug Sahlin and Claudia Snell (Wiley).

3. **Open your favorite Web browser and log in to the Tube.**

If you're bored with Internet Explorer, try logging in with Firefox or Opera. As they say, variety is the spice of life. If you have multiple accounts on the Tube, log in with the username and password of the account that contains the desired video.

4. **Click the My:Videos link.**

   YouTube displays each video you've uploaded.

5. **Click the Edit Video Info button of the video you want to embed in your Web site.**

   The page refreshes and you see everything about your video you need to know.

6. **Scroll to the Embed HTML section of the page.**

   It's way down at the bottom. (See Figure 12-11.)

7. **Select the code and press Ctrl+C (Windows) or ⌘+C (Mac).**

   The code is copied to your Clipboard. Ain't keyboard shortcuts awesome?

Figure 12-11:
Oh, no!
More code!

Embed HTML: Put this video on your Web site! Copy and paste the code below to embed the video.

```
<object width="425" height="350"><param name="movie"
value="http://www.youtube.com/v/vGLI5svBV04"><param><embed
src="http://www.youtube.com/v/vGLI5svBV04" type="application/x-shockwave-flash" width="425"
height="350"></embed></object>
```

Update Video Info   Reset

8. **In your HTML editor, press Ctrl+V (Windows) or ⌘+V (Mac).**

   The code is pasted from the Clipboard to your Web page.

9. **Enter the following code after the URL of the video in the Value and Embed Source section of the code: &autoplay=1.**

   Listing 12-1 shows a sample of code that auto-starts a YouTube video.

Listing 12-1: Code to Auto-start a YouTube Video

```
<object width="425" height="350"><param name="movie"
          value="http://www.youtube.com/v/vGLI5svBV04&autoplay=1"></param><e
          mbed src="http://www.youtube.com/v/vGLI5svBV04&autoplay=1"
          type="application/x-shockwave-flash" width="425"
          height="350"></embed></object>
```

10. **Switch to Design view and preview your Web page.**

    Figure 12-12 shows a YouTube video that auto-started in a Web page.

Figure 12-12:
The video
plays itself.
Amazing.

Creating a Video HTML E-Mail

Microsoft Outlook and Internet Explorer work hand-in-hand. From Internet Explorer, you can send a Web page through the use of Outlook's e-mail functionality. However, Outlook has security, which prevents you from sending something that's potentially harmful to someone else. ActiveX controls are on Outlook's security hit list, and YouTube videos are Flash, which is powered by ActiveX. Thus, you can't easily send YouTube videos this way. You can however, change your Outlook security options. As long as you don't try to e-mail Web pages that have ActiveX controls that may muck up your or your recipient's computer, you can e-mail pages that have ActiveX content like YouTube videos. The following sections show you how.

Changing Outlook security settings

The security settings for the Internet Zone determine whether you can or cannot send or receive e-mail with ActiveX content. Flash ActiveX controls are recognized as not being a security threat. However, if your security settings are set to High, you won't be able to send or receive any ActiveX content. Follow these steps to restore the default settings, which permit sending and receiving of ActiveX content:

1. **Launch Microsoft Outlook.**

2. **Choose Tools⇨Options.**

   This opens the Options dialog box.

3. **Click the Security tab.**

4. **From the Zone drop-down menu, choose Internet. (See Figure 12-13.)**

Figure 12-13:
Change
Outlook
Internet
settings.

5. **Click the Zone Settings button.**

   A warning dialog box appears telling you that you're about to change security settings.

6. **Click OK.**

   The Security dialog box appears. (See Figure 12-14.)

7. **Click the Default Level button.**

   Your Outlook Security settings are changed to Medium, which allows signed ActiveX controls to be downloaded.

8. **Click OK to exit the Security dialog box, and then click OK to exit the Options dialog box.**

   Your Internet Zone settings are reset to Medium.

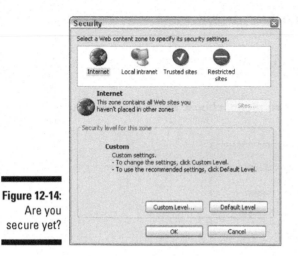

Figure 12-14:
Are you
secure yet?

Sending a YouTube video page via e-mail

If your Outlook Internet Zone security settings are configured to Medium (see the preceding section), you can send and receive e-mails of HTML pages with signed ActiveX controls. *Signed Active-X controls* are those approved by the chief security mucky-mucks at Microsoft and are deemed not harmful to computers. Of course, your recipients will need similar e-mail settings. If you're an instructor or businessperson sending material to clients who know and trust you, they shouldn't have any problem with changing their Internet security settings. To send a YouTube Video page via e-mail, follow these steps:

1. **Launch Internet Explorer.**

2. **Navigate to the desired Web page.**

    Figure 12-15 shows a Web page near and dear to our hearts with an embedded YouTube video.

3. **Choose File⇨Send⇨Page by E-Mail.**

    Outlook opens an e-mail window with the Web page.

4. **Enter the e-mail address of the desired recipient(s).**

5. **Click Send.**

    Outlook sends the message. Figure 12-16 shows an e-mail with an embedded HTML page, complete with YouTube video. Now how cool is that?

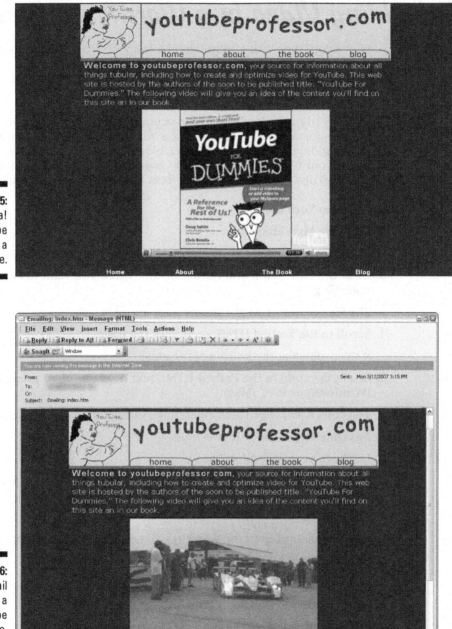

Figure 12-15:
Look, Ma!
A YouTube
video in a
Web page.

Figure 12-16:
An e-mail
with a
YouTube
video.

Embedding Video in a WordPress Blog

If you have your own Web site and you have a WordPress blog, you can easily embed a YouTube video in a blog post. And, hey! Video blogging is the coolest thing since, well, YouTube. So if you have a WordPress blog on your Web site, jump on the bandwagon.

Here is a way to post a YouTube video in your blog that gives you more control over the posts in which you embed a YouTube video. For example, in addition to adding a YouTube video to a blog post, you can add images, links, and format your text. You can't do this when you post a video from the Tube. To add a YouTube video to your WordPress blog, follow these steps:

1. **Log in to YouTube.**

2. **Click the My:Videos link.**

   The My Account/Videos page is displayed in your browser window.

3. **Click the Edit Video Info button for the video you want to embed in your blog.**

   The My Account/Edit My Videos page appears.

4. **Scroll to the Embed HTML section of the page.**

   It's way down at the bottom of the page.

5. **Select the code in the Embed HTML text field and then press Ctrl+C (Windows) or ⌘+C (Mac).**

   The code is copied to your operating system Clipboard.

6. **Navigate to your WordPress blog.**

7. **Log in to your WordPress blog.**

   Log in with the username and password you use to post entries to your blog.

8. **Click Login.**

   You're transported to the WordPress Dashboard for your blog.

9. **Click Write.**

   The Write section of the Dashboard appears.

10. **Enter a title for your blog post.**

11. **Enter the desired text in the body field.**

12. **Press Ctrl+V (Windows) or ⌘+V (Mac).**

    The code is added to your blog post. (See Figure 12-17.)

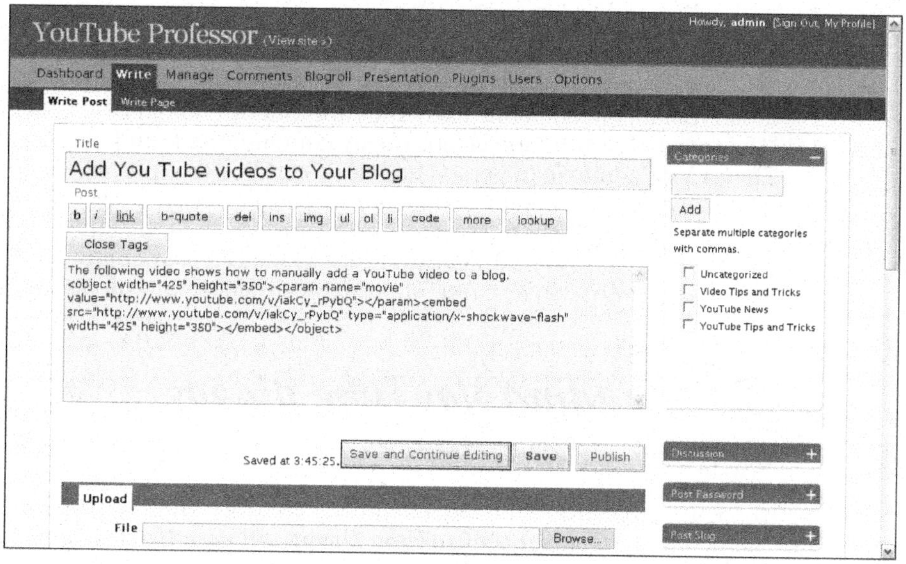

Figure 12-17:
They're
gonna put
my movie
in a blog.

13. **Click the Publish button.**

   Your post is added to the blog.

14. **Click View Site.**

   The YouTube video appears on your blog. (See Figure 12-18.)

Figure 12-18:
A-video
blogging we
shall go . . . .

Hacking YouTube

It had to happen. Someone liked YouTube videos enough to ask the question: "How can I play YouTube videos on my computer without being on the Tube?" Then a VidPodaholic (a person hopelessly addicted to playing video on an iPod) who was also a Tubeaholic wondered whether he could play YouTube videos on his iPod. Eventually both questions were answered. In the following sections, we show you how to download YouTube videos to your computer. We also show you how to convert YouTube videos into files you can play on your iPod.

Downloading YouTube videos to your computer

You can embed YouTube videos in your Web site and blog, but you can't right-click (or Control-click for you Macintosh users) a YouTube video and then download it to your computer. You can, however, use a third-party source to download YouTube videos to your desktop. In fact, you can use several Web sites to download YouTube videos to your desktop. We've tried quite a few. The one we're covering in this section is deemed Dummy-proof. If you surf the Net with Internet Explorer or Firefox, you can easily download a YouTube video by following these steps:

1. **Log into the Tube.**

    It's simple. Point your browser to YouTube, enter your username, password, and then click Login.

2. **Find a video you want to download to your computer.**

3. **While the video is playing, select the URL.**

    It's conveniently located in the URL field to the right of the video player.

4. **Press Ctrl+C (Windows) or ⌘+C (Mac).**

    This copies the URL to your Clipboard.

5. **Open another browser window.**

6. **Navigate to** `http://javimoya.com/blog/youtube_en.php`**.**

    This is the Web site for Video Downloader 2.0. (See Figure 12-19.)

7. **Position your cursor in the text field and then press Ctrl+V (Windows) or ⌘+V (Macintosh).**

    This pastes the URL for the YouTube video in the text field.

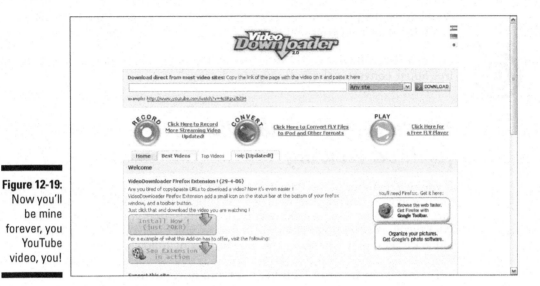

Figure 12-19:
Now you'll
be mine
forever, you
YouTube
video, you!

8. **Click the down arrow to the right of the text field, and then choose YouTube from the drop-down menu.**

9. **Click the Download button.**

   In the Download section, you see a circular Loading icon, which appears while the video is being prepared for download to your computer.

10. **Click Download Link in the Download section.**

    This downloads the video to your desktop with the default name: get_video.

11. **Change the filename of the downloaded video followed by the .flv extension.**

    The default name of the downloaded file is get_video. Give the file a name that makes sense to you. For example, if you download a video of your favorite comedian, you might call the video mrCool.flv.

Of course, after you download the video, you'll want to play it. To play the downloaded video, you'll need a player that can decode *FLV files. They don't happen to grow on trees, but you can download them for free from several sources, including Applian technologies:

```
http://applian.com/flvplayer/?src=VideoDownloadPlay
```

Scroll down the page and click the Play button to download the *EXE file to setup the player on your computer.

You can also convert the *FLV file into a different video format by using the free Super converter that we cover in Chapter 7.

Converting YouTube videos for iPod viewing

If you're a member of the throng that owns video iPods, you'll be happy to know you can convert your favorite YouTube video into an iPod-friendly format. In this section, we show you a free utility that you can download to your desktop. After you install the software, you can convert a YouTube video for iPod play whenever the urge strikes by following these steps:

1. **Open your favorite Web browser and navigate to**

   `www.benjaminstrahs.com/itube.php`

   From here, you can download the Ares Tube 2.09 application, which converts YouTube videos into iPod format. The free software is Windows. If you own a Macintosh computer, you can purchase a similar application for $4.99 at

   `http://djodjodesign.free.fr/podtube.html`

2. **Click Download Now.**

   The installer for the application is downloaded to your desktop.

3. **Double-click the installer file and follow the prompts to install the software.**

   We performed a virus scan on the *EXE file and found it to be squeaky clean. One of the install options is to use the installer's Web site as your home page. We did not choose that option, though, because we prefer to specify our own home page. We did, however, opt to install a desktop icon.

4. **Launch the application.**

   The interface is ridiculously simple. In fact, it looks like a mini Web browser. (See Figure 12-20.)

5. **Log into the Tube.**

   Use your favorite Web browser to navigate to YouTube; enter your username and password, and then click Log In.

6. **Find a video that you want to play on your iPod.**

7. **While the video is playing, select the URL.**

It's a text field located in the URL field to the right of the video player.

8. **Select the text and then press Ctrl+C.**

You may wonder why we didn't include the Macintosh shortcut. This application is Windows only, remember?

9. **Click inside the Ares Tube address bar.**

The default address is selected.

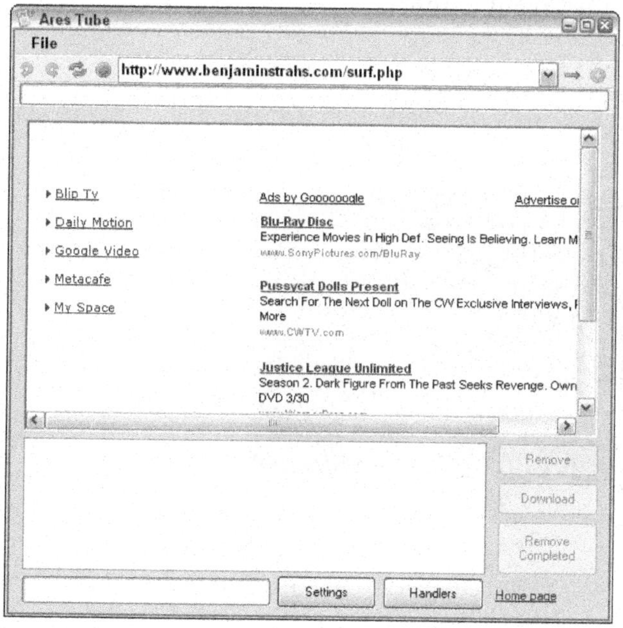

Figure 12-20:
Ares Tube is
not exactly
an arresting
interface.

10. **Press Ctrl+V.**

The URL is pasted into the application.

11. **Click the Go button.**

It's the button that looks like a right-facing arrow. After you click the button, the interface refreshes to the YouTube page from which the video can be played.

12. **Click the Add To The Download List button.**

It's a circular button with a plus sign (+) inside. After you click the button, the URL is added to the download list. (See Figure 12-21.)

If desired, you can add additional videos to the download list by repeating Steps 6–12.

13. **Click the Settings button.**

The Options dialog box appears. (See Figure 12-22.) The default settings are perfect for the iPod. We suggest you leave them as-is.

14. **Click OK.**

15. **Click the Download button.**

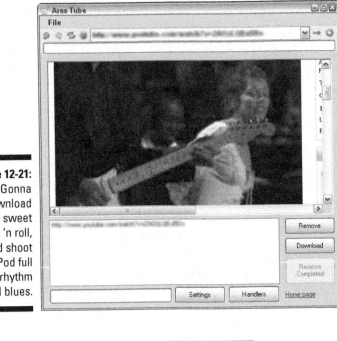

Figure 12-21:
Gonna download some sweet rock 'n roll, and shoot my iPod full of rhythm and blues.

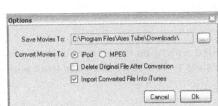

Figure 12-22:
Configure settings for the download.

Ares Tube begins the process of downloading the file and converting it. This may take a while. A progress bar at the bottom of the interface shows you the status of the download and conversion. This might be a good time to answer the call of nature or pause for a soft drink, especially if it's a long video. After Ares Tube finishes its handiwork, iTunes launches, and you can watch the video. (See Figure 12-23.)

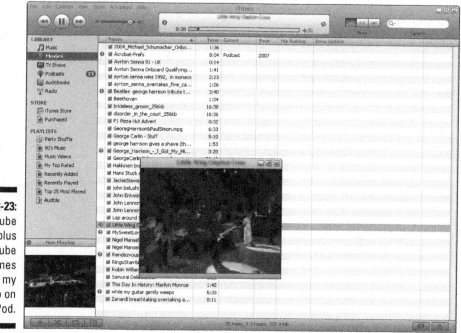

Figure 12-23:
Ares Tube
plus
YouTube
plus iTunes
equals my
video on
my iPod.

Part V
The Part of Tens

The 5th Wave   By Rich Tennant

"These are the parts of our life that aren't on YouTube."

In this part . . .

The beauty of this part is the math; it all adds up. Here you find two chapters, each with ten parts, which adds up to 20 tidbits of information you can use while surfing the Tube.

Chapter 13

Ten Tips for YouTube Videographers

*Y*ouTube is all about video. Some of the video on the Tube is very good, some of it is very bad, and some of it is just plain mediocre. If you shoot your own video and you want to stand out above the crowd, you can easily do so by following the sage advice that we present in Chapters 7 and 8. In this chapter, you'll find ten tips that apply to anyone who records their own video. We show you information on how to choose and master your equipment, how to create a makeshift studio, how to record video while driving, and much more.

Choosing a Camcorder

If you're going to record quality video, start with equipment that will capture quality video. We're not saying you have to get the latest and greatest, all-singing, all-dancing, high-definition camcorder with minty-fresh aftertaste. Just get the best equipment you can afford, especially if you're creating video to promote yourself or a product. The following list shows some features and specifications that will help you to choose the best possible camcorder for your needs, which in turn will give you the best possible video to present on the Tube.

✔ **Sensor type:** Camcorders have two types of sensors: CCD (Charge Coupled Device) sensors, and CMOS (Complementary Metal Oxide Semiconductor) sensors. Both offer excellent image quality. However, the CMOS sensor offers better performance in bright light and a slightly longer battery life.

✔ **Sensor size and number of sensors:** The size and number of sensors determine the quality of the image. Inexpensive camcorders offer a single ⅙" sensor, whereas top of the line camcorders offer three ⅓" sensors (one for the red color spectrum, one for the green color spectrum, and one for the blue color spectrum).

Single-sensor camcorders offer an image resolution beginning at 680,000 pixels, which equates to approximately 340,000 pixels when capturing video in 4:3 mode, or 450,000 pixels when capturing video in 16:9 mode. Three sensor camcorders offer an image resolution of 1,120,000 pixels per sensor, which equates to 1,070,000 pixels per sensor. Camcorders with higher resolution yield better-quality video.

✔ **USB:** Choose a camcorder that has a USB (Universal Serial Bus) port, which enables you to connect the camcorder to your computer and capture video.

✔ **Image stabilization:** Many camcorders feature image stabilization, which compensates for operator movement. Choose a model with this option if you record video with your camcorder handheld.

✔ **Zoom:** Camcorders have optical zoom and digital zoom. Optical zoom is a good thing; digital zoom is not. *Digital zoom* uses the highest optical zoom, crops the image to conform to the specified digital zoom, and then enlarges the image to fill the frame. This means the camcorder is redrawing pixels, which inevitably leads to image degradation.

If the ability to zoom in on a scene is important, get a camcorder with the highest optical zoom that is within your budget.

✔ **Camcorder monitor:** Camcorders often feature LCD (liquid crystal display) monitors, which enable you to preview the video you've just recorded. The LCD monitor is also used to access menu controls. If you wear glasses or have problems reading small print, get a camcorder with an LCD monitor that is large enough to comfortably read the menu choices.

✔ **Remote controls:** Most camcorders come with remote controls that enable you to start recording, zoom in, stop recording, and so on.

✔ **Other useful features:** Look for manual focus, manual exposure, manual zoom, manual white balance, and the ability to connect an external microphone to the camcorder.

✔ **Recording format:** MiniDV is currently the most popular recording media format. The tapes are small, compact, and affordable.

✔ **Broadcast format:** The two most common broadcast-quality video formats are NTSC (used in North America) and PAL (used in Europe). Make sure the camcorder you choose is the proper format.

Camcorder specs are one thing, but the proof is in the pudding. We suggest that you research your purchase by perusing the Web sites of major camcorder manufacturers. When you have a list of candidates, visit your local retailer to see which camcorder works best for you. Make sure that you can comfortably handle the camcorder and that the controls are easy to locate and use. The zoom control is especially important. Some camcorder zoom controls are very sensitive. In other words, when you use the control, the camcorder zooms in or out on the subject too quickly, which results in an amateurish video.

Before you go to your retailer to purchase a camcorder, check out online reviews of camcorders at a site like www.camcorderinfo.com.

Mastering Your Recording Equipment

After you choose a camcorder, the next step is to master the device. No, we're not suggesting you crack open the box, pop in a cassette, and record a video of your cat rummaging through your wastebasket for a new toy. Read the manual first. When we're learning how to use a new device, we prefer to have it by our side. When we read a section about features such as the camcorder menu controls, we find the controls on the camcorder and use them according to the instructions in the manual. This double-pronged approach reduces the learning curve when learning how to use a new device.

After you're familiar with the camcorder controls, the next step is to pop a tape in the camcorder and record something. Familiarize yourself with the position of the Record and Zoom buttons so you can find them easily without having to look away from the viewfinder. We suggest recording a 60-minute cassette to become familiar with the camcorder. If you're satisfied with the results of your first tape, you're ready to record the stuff you'll edit and upload to the Tube.

Steadying the Camcorder with a Tripod

Image stabilization is a wonderful thing, if your camcorder is so equipped. *Image stabilization* compensates for operator movement and as the name implies, stabilizes the image. If your camcorder doesn't have image stabilization, you'll have to be rock steady as you hold the camera to record video. However, even the most svelte camcorder with image stabilization can feel like a 50-pound bag of cement after several hours of recording.

You can solve this problem by mounting your camcorder on a tripod. Use the tripod controls to pan the camcorder from side to side. You can also use tripod controls to adjust the height and the angle from which the camcorder records. If equipped, use the camcorder remote to start recording, zoom in and out, and so on. A tripod is indispensable if you're recording an interview. If you've watched a video where the frame has bobbed up and down in rhythm with the camcorder operator's breathing, you know what we're talking about. If you use a camcorder with image stabilization, disable this feature when using a tripod. Your battery will last longer as a result.

If you don't have a tripod, position the camcorder on a level surface like a tabletop. Make sure that the surface isn't visible in the frame and then start recording.

Creating a Makeshift Studio

If you need to create videos of a person on a plain backdrop with professional lighting — a *talking-head* video — you don't have to break the budget and rent studio time. With a few household items and three clamp-on reflector lights, you can quickly create a makeshift studio in a large room of your house as follows:

1. **Clear the furniture from an area that has a blank wall for a backdrop.**

   In lieu of a blank wall, suspend a large white sheet from the ceiling. Spray Downy Wrinkle Release (www.downy.com/en_US/products/ wrinklereleaser.jsp) on the sheet to remove the wrinkles.

2. **Position your subject in front of the backdrop.**

   To alleviate harsh shadows, position your subject a few feet in front of the backdrop.

3. **Position one light in front of and higher than your subject. The light should also be on a slight angle.**

   You can clamp the light on a light stand or a ladder.

4. **Position a second light so that it illuminates the backdrop.**

   Position the light above the backdrop and far enough away so that it floods the backdrop with light.

5. **Position a third light to the side of the subject.**

   This light fills the shadow side of the subject's face. Your lighting setup should resemble Figure 13-1.

You can use household lights in the reflectors. However, they may cast harsh shadows, and the color temperature will throw your white balance off. An alternative is to purchase photo flood lamps from your local camera store. They vary in strength from 250 watts to 650 watts. If you decide to go this route, make sure you're not overloading the household circuits or the circuitry of the reflector lamp.

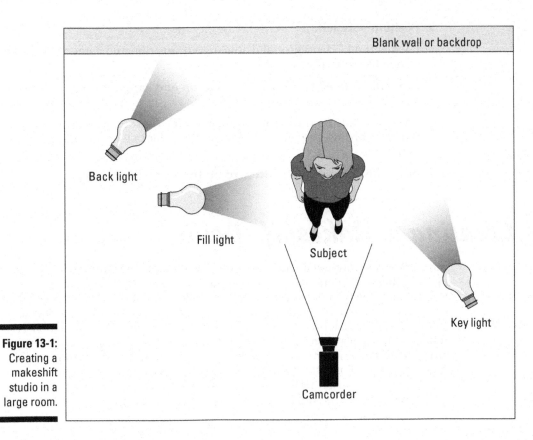

Figure 13-1:
Creating a makeshift studio in a large room.

Recording Yourself

If you don't have someone to operate your camcorder and record a video of you, do it yourself. All you need is a tripod and a camcorder with a remote. You can easily record yourself by following these steps:

1. **Mount your camcorder on a tripod and point it toward the area of the room in which you'll be sitting or standing.**

2. **Open the LCD monitor and position it so that it faces the area of the room in which you'll be sitting or standing.**

3. **Aim the camcorder.**

   You don't have to be perfect. Just make sure the camcorder is level and pointed in the right direction. You'll be able to see yourself in the LCD monitor and adjust your position, or use the remote control to zoom in or out.

4. **Start the camcorder in VTR mode.**

   This is the mode with which you can record video.

5. **Position yourself.**

   Look at the LCD monitor and adjust your position and camcorder zoom as needed so that you're in frame.

6. **Press the remote control Record button and capture your 15 minutes of fame.**

   After you start recording, move the remote control out of the frame. When recording, remember to look at the camera lens and not the LCD monitor.

7. **Press the remote control Record button to stop recording.**

Creating a Makeshift Dolly

Have you ever watched a video recorded by someone while they were walking? It's almost bad enough to give you motion sickness. The scene is bobbing up and down as the person makes each step. Professional videographers use a device called a *Steadycam,* which has counterweights and gimbals to steady the camcorder as the operator walks. These, however, are expensive, retailing for several hundred dollars or more. To create a makeshift dolly, mount your camcorder on a tripod and then secure it inside a shopping cart. Aim the camcorder at the subject you want to track and then push the cart. Just make sure you get permission to use the cart, choosing a cart with well-lubricated wheels that don't squeak.

Recording Video from a Car

If you want to capture video of city streets or scenic countryside while driving, you can easily do so. All you need is a lightweight tripod, two bungee cords, and a camcorder with a remote control. To set up a studio on wheels, follow these steps:

1. **Mount the tripod in the passenger seat.**

2. **Use the seat belt and shoulder harness to secure the tripod.**

3. **Connect the bungee cords to the bottom of the tripod, and hook them underneath the seat.**

4. **Mount the camcorder on the tripod.**

5. **Use the LCD monitor to aim the camcorder between the windshield supports.**

   Figure 13-2 shows a camcorder mounted on a tripod in the passenger seat of a car.

Figure 13-2:
A studio on wheels.

6. **Press the remote control Record button to record while you're driving.**

7. **When you're finished, press the remote control Record button to stop recording.**

Don't record while driving in heavy traffic. If you absolutely have to capture a scene while driving in heavy traffic, position an assistant in the back seat and give him the remote control. Tell your assistant when you want to record and keep your hands on the wheel and your eyes on the road.

Creating a Documentary-Style Video

Newspaper reporters and musicians create professional-quality recordings with handheld recorders. These devices are ideal when interviewing people. When you combine a high-quality, portable recording device with a good digital camera, you've got everything you need to create a documentary-style video.

M-Audio makes a device called MicroTrack 24/96, which is a professional-quality, two-track recorder (see Figure 13-3). The device uses CompactFlash cards as the recording media. The device has a built in lithium ion battery that has a life expectancy of up to eight hours when recording with the supplied microphone. When you see something you want to comment about, capture a picture of it with your digital camera, and then record your commentary. You can compile the still shots and audio into a video documentary using the slideshow and audio techniques presented in Chapter 8.

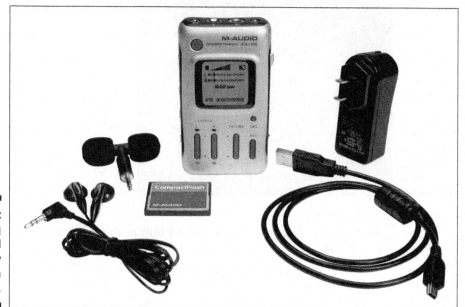

Figure 13-3:
Capturing professional quality audio on the run.

Capture Video with the Highest Quality

The only way to ensure that your YouTube videos are top-notch is to start with top-notch video. If you have a good camcorder capable of recording broadcast quality video, you'll end up with video you can capture to your computer and then edit. To ensure the highest quality, here are a couple of things to consider:

- ✔ **Set your camcorder to SP (Standard Play).** If you switch to LP (Long Play), you'll be able to record 30 additional minutes on a 60-minute cassette, but the quality will not be as good.

- ✔ **Use the highest-quality setting available when you capture video to your computer.** If you use Windows Movie Maker to capture video, the proper setting is Digital Device Format (DV-AVI). Don't use any option that compresses the video into a format other than AVI when capturing video.

Multi-Purposing Your Video

After you edit a video to pixel perfection, you're ready to render it for upload on YouTube. If, however, your video will serve multiple tasks, you can render it for other sources, such as a CD or a podcast. Each destination requires different settings. You can render the video in as many formats as needed from most video-editing applications. Alternatively, you can use video-compression software to accomplish this task.

As of this writing, the hottest ticket when it comes to compression software is Sorenson Squeeze. You import a file that you've rendered from your video-editing application, and then choose the desired compression settings to optimize the video for the intended device. The beauty of an application like Sorenson Squeeze Compression Suite (`www.sorensonmedia.com/products/?pageID=1#ppc3`) is that you can choose multiple compression settings, and the application renders the required files. Figure 13-4 shows the Sorenson Squeeze interface with a video that will be rendered with three compression settings. As soon as the Squeeze It button is clicked, the application begins rendering and outputs three files.

Figure 13-4:
Rendering
multiple
versions
of a video.

In case you don't have an application like Sorenson Squeeze, here are some suggested settings:

- ✓ **Streaming video for the Web:** Render as a Windows Media Video (*.wmv) file with dimensions of 320 x 240 and a combined data rate (video and audio) of 256 Kbps.

- ✓ **High-quality video for the Web:** Render as a QuickTime movie (*.mov), with dimension of 640 x 480, and a combined data rate of 384 Kbps. These are setting typically used with a video screen capture that is being used for instructional purposes.

- ✓ **YouTube:** Render as an MPEG4 movie (*.mp4) with dimensions of 320 x 240 and a combined data rate of 384 Kbps, or 512 Kbps.

  If you have a normal YouTube account, you'll have to keep the file size less than 10MB.

- ✓ **Podcast:** Render as an MPEG4 movie (*.mp4) with dimensions of 640 x 480 (high quality for viewing in iTunes), or 320 x 240 (for viewing on an iPod or similar device), with a combined data rate of 901 Kbps. The file may take a while to download, but these settings are ideal for computer viewing or for viewing on an iPod.

Your video-editing or video-compression application may have the option to render the file using either CBR (Constant Bit Rate) or VBR (Variable Bit Rate). If you choose CBR, you specify the data rate, which stays constant during playback. If you choose VBR, you specify the minimum and maximum allowable data rate. The application renders frames with lots of information (such as an object with multiple colors) using the maximum data rate, and frames with little information (such as a text on a black background) using the minimum data rate. All other frames are rendered with a data rate in between the maximum and minimum. VBR results in smaller file sizes. Your application may also have the option to render with two (or more) passes, which results in a better-quality video.

Chapter 14

Ten Things Not to Include in Your Videos

*W*hen it comes to YouTube's terms of use and Community Guidelines, here's our advice: Enjoy them! Yes, that does sound strange, because when you think of rules, you think of constraints — and constraints are a bummer.

That's a valid perspective, but another way to approach YouTube's rules is to find them intriguing. Think of them this way: They're YouTube's official word on what's right and what's wrong, and it's interesting to read just where YouTube draws the line on hot-button topics like copyright infringement, nudity, and pornography (not to mention shock, hate, and gross-outs).

YouTube is now a major player in the Internet world. As the child of a powerful parent company — Google — the eyes of literally the entire world are on YouTube. Just imagine all the meetings, all the lawyers, and all the editing and heated debates that you just know went down when YouTube had to put its rules and regulations in writing. That's what we mean by intriguing.

So here they are: The ten big no-nos. Many of them are things that YouTube says can't go in your video; others are things that we suggest you don't include not because they're against the rules, but just because they're against common sense.

After you've read through these, go up and check out YouTube's full Community Guidelines and terms of use policy. And enjoy!

10. Copyrighted Music

If you're playing by the rules, your video can't contain any music that you purchased. In other words, if you edited your video of your family's trip to the Jersey shore to include a few Beach Boys tunes, you're in violation of YouTube's copyright policy. Bummer, eh? Will your video be taken down? Probably not. The owner of the copyright would need to find your video and alert YouTube to take it down, and that probably won't happen. Nevertheless, your video is not supposed to include copyrighted tunes.

Concert footage is a bigger no-no, specifically because any footage you shoot at a concert is — by definition — obtained illegally. If you upload concert video footage, not only are you violating YouTube policy, but you're more-than-implying that you violated the concert venue's policy as well.

9. Nudity

We're taking it for granted that you already know not to upload pornography to the Tube. We're guessing that you already know that the Paris Hilton sex tape is not to be found there. We're figuring that you'll never confuse YouTube with "blue" tube.

Porno is no-no. The same goes for nudity. And though nudity and pornography are not the same things, they are both *verboten* on the Tube.

Make no mistake: You'll find *plenty* of risqué videos on YouTube, but if there's nudity to be had, it's not easy to find, and it's usually removed pretty quickly. So don't upload videos that contain nudity.

We're not only talking about sexy *ooh-la-la* nudity; we're talking streaking, mooning, the big wave taking down the wife's bikini top, or completely innocent footage of the kids running naked out of the bathtub — especially the kids. Remember, when it comes to YouTube, no nudes are good news.

8. Your Personal Identification

If you're shooting video around your house, avoid including footage that gives away too much info about who you are and where you live. You might not want to include a shot of your license plate, for example, or your mailbox that shows your complete address. Don't announce your phone number, either.

If you're doing business on YouTube, the whole point might be contrary to all of the above. Namely, you want people to know how to find you: You want them to contact you. In that case, consider a business phone, if you don't already have one; you might not want your kids picking up the phone to chat with any random Tuber who calls your private residence. For the same reason, post a business address or P.O. Box rather than your home address. Remember, there really are *millions* of people surfing the Tube.

One last thing: Don't be paranoid. If your home address or your car's license plate actually does sneak in to your video, it's probably unlikely that another Tuber will track you down and stop by for a visit. So don't be paranoid, but do avoid personal information in your video.

7. Your Big Thumb

When it comes to shooting video, most of us are amateurs. This is okay, but please try not to post a video that is so amateurish that it's just plain lame and no fun to watch. If you shot your video with your thumb in front of the lens, puh-*leeze* don't upload it to YouTube. Why not reshoot it the right way instead? Same goes for your two big feet: if you forget to turn off the camera, nobody wants to watch footage of your camera pointing down at the floor and showing off your grass-stained, size 12 Nikes.

Blurry videos, grainy videos, unsteady videos that jump and jerk all over the place . . . they're not a lot of fun to watch. With today's technology, relatively inexpensive video cameras all shoot good-quality video, so read your User's Manual and get good at operating your equipment.

The same goes for editing. Nobody's expecting you to take your YouTube video to a professional editing suite, but investigate the video-editing software that you already have on your computer. If you bought your computer in the last couple of years, whether Mac or PC, it almost certainly came with software that you can use to edit your videos and create a presentation that the rest of us will find just as interesting and fun to watch as you do.

6. Copyrighted Video

YouTube is just filled with great video of old TV programs, specials, and concerts as well as fun footage of old movies, new movies, movie stars, and celebrity tribute videos — and all of them are in violation of YouTube's copyright infringement policy.

Now we know you weren't born yesterday, and we know that you know that the DVDs you purchase and the programs you record on your TV are all copyright protected. So if you're playing by the rules, you're not supposed to upload even the shortest of snippets to the Tube.

This one's a bummer because some of the best features of YouTube are the recaps of Letterman and Leno — and Rosie on *The View* is always good for a few heated confrontations. And where else are you going to find clips from *The Bionic Woman,* the 1972 Academy Awards, and Dolly Parton on *Hee-Haw?*

If it's against the rules, why, you ask, is all that copyrighted video so readily available on YouTube? Basically, YouTube doesn't remove copyrighted content unless the owner of that content orders YouTube to remove it. In many cases, the owner is actually happy for the free publicity, so a sort of don't-ask-don't-tell situation develops around a lot of video clips that are — *technically* — forbidden.

The bottom line on uploading copyrighted video goes something like this: "Don't upload copyrighted video. It's against YouTube's rules." (But if you upload the *Wonder Woman* episode when she takes Steve Trevor back to Paradise Island and Cloris Leachman plays her mother and Debra Winger plays her little sister Drusilla, we'd love to see it, and we promise not to tell.)

5. Your Spleen

No, we're not talking about videos of body parts (although those are also a no-go: see #9). We're talking about *venting* your spleen. YouTube is certainly a supporter of free speech, and it openly defends a person's right to express unpopular views. As you surf the site, you'll find that YouTube does not have a censorious nature because it doesn't even discriminate against the lousy low-quality videos that make it up to the site.

But there is a line, and YouTube draws that line at hate speech or any type of video footage that is demeaning to or expresses malicious stereotypes about a person or persons based on their gender, sexual orientation, race, religion, or nationality.

4. Your Worst Enemy

If you've got a secret video of your ex-wife picking her nose, or if you captured some footage of your annoying neighbor's husband kissing the mailman, don't think of YouTube as the place to stick it to them.

YouTube is not a venue for people to embarrass their friends or get even with their enemies. Don't upload a video that says your business partner is a crook and cheats on his taxes, and don't include a soundtrack of your ex-husband yelling and swearing on your answering machine.

Libel is the defamation of another person by written words or by pictures — and that includes video. Libel is also a crime, and if someone wants to make your life difficult, a libel charge could do the trick.

"That's crazy," you say. "Who would ever even think to use YouTube that way?" You might be surprised at how slippery the slope can be. If you purchase a comedy DVD from someone on YouTube and it never arrives, you might be very tempted to post a message on that user's channel page warning other users to avoid him, that he's not to be trusted, that he's a thief. Oops.

Or, say you stumble on a video from some creepy Joe spouting off all kinds of bad things about women. You might be tempted to post a video response calling him an idiot — or worse.

Bottom line: Be sure that the video you upload or the text that you enter on the Tube can't be construed as defamatory, misrepresentation, or maliciously damaging. But you would never do that. Would you?

3. The Scene of Your Last Crime

Videos of drug use, arson, and drunk driving — as charming as they may be — are against YouTube's Community Guidelines. Videos of vandalism will get flagged in a heartbeat and might get you a visit from the cops. Bullying and intimidation are also on the short list, and don't even think of uploading anything that even resembles cruelty to animals. Here's a good rule: If it's illegal in the real world, video of it is not allowed on YouTube.

2. Your Death-Defying Acts

Now don't get us wrong: We love the whole *Jackass* thing, the crazy stunts, the wrestling with anacondas, Steve-O with a fishhook through his cheek, the limousine full of stinging bees and unsuspecting passengers, and Johnny Knoxville getting gored by a very angry bull. That's entertainment! But remember that that's Hollywood and those guys are all . . . um . . . professionals. Yeah, that's it. Professionals.

When it comes to amateur jackasses who want to upload video of their brushes with death, YouTube says, "Son, you're no Johnny Knoxville."

Videos that show dangerous acts, stunts, or any other demonstrations in which someone can go from brave to grave aren't going to get played on YouTube. Think of it this way: Nobody wants to see a nine-year-old "parachute" off of a roof with an umbrella because he "saw it on YouTube."

You've heard the phrase "Don't try this at home"? Don't try it on YouTube, either.

1. Roadkill

If you like getting grossed out, my-oh-my does YouTube have some videos for you. Don't take our word for it — just do a search on the word *zit*. All kinds of videos will pop up — if you get our drift. Better yet, try *booger,* and you'll have plenty of choices to pick from.

YouTube has an admirable tolerance for all the benign gross-outs that human beings — especially teenaged human beings — can produce, but there definitely comes a point when a little too much is a little too much.

YouTube is not a shock site, and it doesn't show disturbing or violent images of death, dismemberment, or other types of shock video. It's an interesting line, actually, because YouTube will show war footage and other types of violent "news" footage. YouTube also shows plane crashes, car crashes — all kinds of crashes, actually — and even though you know somebody got hurt and even killed, you don't actually see it.

That's the YouTube death deal, folks: Crashes, yes; gashes, no.

Index

BUSINESS, CAREERS & PERSONAL FINANCE

0-7645-9847-3   0-7645-2431-3

Also available:
- Business Plans Kit For Dummies
  0-7645-9794-9
- Economics For Dummies
  0-7645-5726-2
- Grant Writing For Dummies
  0-7645-8416-2
- Home Buying For Dummies
  0-7645-5331-3
- Managing For Dummies
  0-7645-1771-6
- Marketing For Dummies
  0-7645-5600-2

- Personal Finance For Dummies
  0-7645-2590-5*
- Resumes For Dummies
  0-7645-5471-9
- Selling For Dummies
  0-7645-5363-1
- Six Sigma For Dummies
  0-7645-6798-5
- Small Business Kit For Dummies
  0-7645-5984-2
- Starting an eBay Business For Dummies
  0-7645-6924-4
- Your Dream Career For Dummies
  0-7645-9795-7

HOME & BUSINESS COMPUTER BASICS

0-470-05432-8   0-471-75421-8

Also available:
- Cleaning Windows Vista For Dummies
  0-471-78293-9
- Excel 2007 For Dummies
  0-470-03737-7
- Mac OS X Tiger For Dummies
  0-7645-7675-5
- MacBook For Dummies
  0-470-04859-X
- Macs For Dummies
  0-470-04849-2
- Office 2007 For Dummies
  0-470-00923-3

- Outlook 2007 For Dummies
  0-470-03830-6
- PCs For Dummies
  0-7645-8958-X
- Salesforce.com For Dummies
  0-470-04893-X
- Upgrading & Fixing Laptops For Dummies
  0-7645-8959-8
- Word 2007 For Dummies
  0-470-03658-3
- Quicken 2007 For Dummies
  0-470-04600-7

FOOD, HOME, GARDEN, HOBBIES, MUSIC & PETS

0-7645-8404-9   0-7645-9904-6

Also available:
- Candy Making For Dummies
  0-7645-9734-5
- Card Games For Dummies
  0-7645-9910-0
- Crocheting For Dummies
  0-7645-4151-X
- Dog Training For Dummies
  0-7645-8418-9
- Healthy Carb Cookbook For Dummies
  0-7645-8476-6
- Home Maintenance For Dummies
  0-7645-5215-5

- Horses For Dummies
  0-7645-9797-3
- Jewelry Making & Beading For Dummies
  0-7645-2571-9
- Orchids For Dummies
  0-7645-6759-4
- Puppies For Dummies
  0-7645-5255-4
- Rock Guitar For Dummies
  0-7645-5356-9
- Sewing For Dummies
  0-7645-6847-7
- Singing For Dummies
  0-7645-2475-5

INTERNET & DIGITAL MEDIA

0-470-04529-9   0-470-04894-8

Also available:
- Blogging For Dummies
  0-471-77084-1
- Digital Photography For Dummies
  0-7645-9802-3
- Digital Photography All-in-One Desk Reference For Dummies
  0-470-03743-1
- Digital SLR Cameras and Photography For Dummies
  0-7645-9803-1
- eBay Business All-in-One Desk Reference For Dummies
  0-7645-8438-3
- HDTV For Dummies
  0-470-09673-X

- Home Entertainment PCs For Dummies
  0-470-05523-5
- MySpace For Dummies
  0-470-09529-6
- Search Engine Optimization For Dummies
  0-471-97998-8
- Skype For Dummies
  0-470-04891-3
- The Internet For Dummies
  0-7645-8996-2
- Wiring Your Digital Home For Dummies
  0-471-91830-X

* Separate Canadian edition also available
† Separate U.K. edition also available

Available wherever books are sold. For more information or to order direct: U.S. customers visit www.dummies.com or call 1-877-762-2974.
U.K. customers visit www.wileyeurope.com or call 0800 243407. Canadian customers visit www.wiley.ca or call 1-800-567-4797.

SPORTS, FITNESS, PARENTING, RELIGION & SPIRITUALITY

0-471-76871-5   0-7645-7841-3

Also available:

- Catholicism For Dummies
  0-7645-5391-7
- Exercise Balls For Dummies
  0-7645-5623-1
- Fitness For Dummies
  0-7645-7851-0
- Football For Dummies
  0-7645-3936-1
- Judaism For Dummies
  0-7645-5299-6
- Potty Training For Dummies
  0-7645-5417-4
- Buddhism For Dummies
  0-7645-5359-3

- Pregnancy For Dummies
  0-7645-4483-7 †
- Ten Minute Tone-Ups For Dummies
  0-7645-7207-5
- NASCAR For Dummies
  0-7645-7681-X
- Religion For Dummies
  0-7645-5264-3
- Soccer For Dummies
  0-7645-5229-5
- Women in the Bible For Dummies
  0-7645-8475-8

TRAVEL

0-7645-7749-2   0-7645-6945-7

Also available:

- Alaska For Dummies
  0-7645-7746-8
- Cruise Vacations For Dummies
  0-7645-6941-4
- England For Dummies
  0-7645-4276-1
- Europe For Dummies
  0-7645-7529-5
- Germany For Dummies
  0-7645-7823-5
- Hawaii For Dummies
  0-7645-7402-7

- Italy For Dummies
  0-7645-7386-1
- Las Vegas For Dummies
  0-7645-7382-9
- London For Dummies
  0-7645-4277-X
- Paris For Dummies
  0-7645-7630-5
- RV Vacations For Dummies
  0-7645-4442-X
- Walt Disney World & Orlando
  For Dummies
  0-7645-9660-8

GRAPHICS, DESIGN & WEB DEVELOPMENT

0-7645-8815-X   0-7645-9571-7

Also available:

- 3D Game Animation For Dummies
  0-7645-8789-7
- AutoCAD 2006 For Dummies
  0-7645-8925-3
- Building a Web Site For Dummies
  0-7645-7144-3
- Creating Web Pages For Dummies
  0-470-08030-2
- Creating Web Pages All-in-One Desk
  Reference For Dummies
  0-7645-4345-8
- Dreamweaver 8 For Dummies
  0-7645-9649-7

- InDesign CS2 For Dummies
  0-7645-9572-5
- Macromedia Flash 8 For Dummies
  0-7645-9691-8
- Photoshop CS2 and Digital
  Photography For Dummies
  0-7645-9580-6
- Photoshop Elements 4 For Dummies
  0-471-77483-9
- Syndicating Web Sites with RSS Feeds
  For Dummies
  0-7645-8848-6
- Yahoo! SiteBuilder For Dummies
  0-7645-9800-7

NETWORKING, SECURITY, PROGRAMMING & DATABASES

0-7645-7728-X   0-471-74940-0

Also available:

- Access 2007 For Dummies
  0-470-04612-0
- ASP.NET 2 For Dummies
  0-7645-7907-X
- C# 2005 For Dummies
  0-7645-9704-3
- Hacking For Dummies
  0-470-05235-X
- Hacking Wireless Networks
  For Dummies
  0-7645-9730-2
- Java For Dummies
  0-470-08716-1

- Microsoft SQL Server 2005 For Dummies
  0-7645-7755-7
- Networking All-in-One Desk Reference
  For Dummies
  0-7645-9939-9
- Preventing Identity Theft For Dummies
  0-7645-7336-5
- Telecom For Dummies
  0-471-77085-X
- Visual Studio 2005 All-in-One Desk
  Reference For Dummies
  0-7645-9775-2
- XML For Dummies
  0-7645-8845-1